PUSHED TO THE EDGE

Inclusion and behaviour support
in schools

Val Gillies

First published in Great Britain in 2016 by

Policy Press
University of Bristol
1-9 Old Park Hill
Bristol
BS2 8BB
UK
t: +44 (0)117 954 5940
pp-info@bristol.ac.uk
www.policypress.co.uk

North America office:
Policy Press
c/o The University of Chicago Press
1427 East 60th Street
Chicago, IL 60637, USA
t: +1 773 702 7700
f: +1 773-702-9756
sales@press.uchicago.edu
www.press.uchicago.edu

© Policy Press 2016

British Library Cataloguing in Publication Data
A catalogue record for this book is available from the British Library

Library of Congress Cataloging-in-Publication Data
A catalog record for this book has been requested

ISBN 978 1 44731 746 3 hardcover
ISBN 978 1 44731 747 0 paperback
ISBN 978-1-4473-1751-7 ePub
ISBN 978-1-4473-1750-0 Mobi

The right of Val Gillies to be identified as author of this work has been asserted by her in accordance with the Copyright, Designs and Patents Act 1988.

Cover design by Qube Design Associates, Bristol
Front cover image: Istock
Printed and bound in Great Britain by CPI Group (UK) Ltd, Croydon, CR0 4YY
Policy Press uses environmentally responsible print partners

Contents

Acknowledgements

I owe a debt of thanks to many people who made this book possible. I am especially grateful to Yvonne Robinson who played an integral part in the research. I very much wish we had been able to write this book together. I am also very grateful to the Economic and Social Research Council who funded the research and the follow on project. My heartfelt thanks also go to all the young people, school staff and parents who participated in the study. I enjoyed the support of too many people to mention in writing this book but am particularly appreciative of the conversations I had with Steve Benson, Kathryn Ecclestone, Christy Kulz. Also Ros Edwards and other members of the Women's Workshop. Many thanks also to Dorrett Boswell, Carlton Cameron, Paulette Douglas, Sarah Lemay, Ginny Morrow, and Rachel Thomson for all their generous advice and help during the research process.

ONE

Disciplining pupils: from exclusion to 'inclusion'

Prevailing discourses of excellence and equity demand that schools raise standards while also narrowing attainment gaps. This relentless pressure produces a troublesome underclass of pupils within mainstream schooling. Deemed to be 'at risk of exclusion' by nature of their lack of conformity and academic progress, such pupils are now regularly consigned to internal, 'behaviour support units' (BSUs). These are usually self-contained centres located on school premises and administered by 'inclusion managers'. Crucially they enable the removal of demanding pupils from mainstream classrooms for extended periods without recourse to official exclusion channels. This book examines how such segregation mechanisms operate in practice to manage the internal contradictions and tensions inherent in neoliberal market-led education reforms.

Despite tacit acknowledgment that variants of these units now exist in most British secondary schools (MacBeath et al, 2006) there is a remarkable gap in knowledge and literature about their workings, to the extent that internal school exclusion currently operates almost entirely outside of any public scrutiny. There are no statistics collected confirming the number of schools employing separate units and hence no objective monitoring of referrals. There is no independent analysis of how many pupils are placed in such units, or how long they stay there for and no collation of characteristics like ethnicity, socio-economic background or special educational needs status. This book offers a much needed insight into the politics and practices of internal school exclusion, as highlighted through the experiences of the young people attending the units. Drawing on uniquely situated ethnographic research in three London-based behaviour support units, it shines a spotlight on to the institutional and interpersonal dynamics characterising internal school exclusion.

Based on intensive research with pupils, their teachers and parents, this book will detail how and why particular young people are pushed to the edge, and in many cases over the edge of school. At a more fundamental level it will explore how this de facto exclusion is enacted and normalised. School exclusion is accepted to map onto and exacerbate ingrained patterns of disadvantage and discrimination. For example, it is widely known that African-Caribbean boys are most likely to face exclusion. Yet it is that very perception of risk that has become double edged, translating into a need for intervention. It is on this basis that onsite segregation in behaviour support units comes to assume the mantle of a progressive alternative to exclusion. If internal exclusion is discussed at all it is usually to highlight a school's commitment to meeting the needs of its more challenging pupils. However, as the following chapters will outline, a BSU referral may result in a drastic distancing from formal education, with some pupils languishing in units for years, barely able to read or write.

The subtle but effective shift toward routine segregation of those classified as 'at risk' of school exclusion is widely known in education circles, but is little discussed. The practice escapes the scrutiny it deserves largely because the language of 'benevolent humanism' (Tomlinson, 2012) acts as a very effective camouflage. BSU pupils are represented as having particular needs, recognised and subsequently met, within the bounds of the school. Somewhat paradoxically then, internal exclusion has come to embody a core commitment to inclusive education. From this perspective pupils are regarded as being set apart to enjoy special help rather than being ghettoised. This masks the extent to which a framework of 'inclusion, with its roots in a radical agenda for social and structural change, has seamlessly morphed into a psychological deficit model' (Gillies, 2011).

More specifically, inclusion retains its progressive claim to social and political transformation but has come to rest on a very particular understanding as compensating for the personal effects of disadvantage. As a result, exclusion has been re-framed as a state of mind while inclusion is approached as an active remedial process through which deficits and dysfunctions are corrected (Gillies, 2011). The aim of this book is to challenge this individualised orthodoxy by illuminating hidden institutional practices and revealing the complex and socially connected reality behind acting out in the classroom. This socially situated approach exposes the paucity of personal deficit models and reasserts the need for an explicitly political understanding of the ways in which progressive sounding values of social investment and moral necessity operate within contemporary neoliberal regimes to delegitimise and problematise poor and/or minority ethnic children and families.

In this first introductory chapter the political context shaping and containing the intensification of internal school exclusion will be outlined in relation to a 'politics of disposability' (Giroux, 2014). From this perspective the emergence of the 'behaviour support unit' in Britain can be understood through reference to broader global political trends, with internal exclusion operating as part of a neoliberal government of social insecurity (Wacquant, 2009). In particular I show how the turn towards routine segregation of troublesome pupils becomes an inevitable cost of the implementation of a neoliberal 'standards agenda', which prioritises attainment scores, exam results and school league tables. Social inequities are maximised and amplified in the context of this ruthless emphasis on narrow performance indicators, with practices of marginalisation, rationalised through reference to concerns over 'school readiness' and 'character'.

The rise of the behaviour support unit

Since the 1980s the core justification for education reforms in the UK and beyond has been the maximisation of economic development and efficiency. As Stephen Ball (2008) notes, the social and economic purposes of education were folded into a single driving force of economic competitiveness, drowning out alternative visions of education as a social good. Efforts focused on standardising and measuring teaching and learning, both within and across nation states. Contained within this market-based ethos children came to assume key significance as human capital requiring effective investment to secure their futures as productive citizens in the global economy. The introduction of national testing and school league tables was designed to facilitate this economic centric model by exposing failing institutions and increasing performance standards. The most immediately noticeable effect, however, was a huge rise in rates of school exclusion as institutions sought to ensure poorly attaining students did not drag their indicators down.

Permanent exclusion rates in the UK reached a peak in the mid-1990s and then fell back dramatically when the New Labour government incorporated national exclusion targets in institutional measures of performance. The Education Secretary at the time, David Blunkett, addressed pressure on schools and accusations that 'exclusions had been banned' through a tough talking pledge to deal with disruptive classrooms and truants. This authoritarian sounding approach was reported in the *Times Education Supplement* under the headline 'School "sin bins" to combat exclusions'.

> Disruptive pupils will be removed to 'sin bins' in their school
> as part of a £500 million campaign to reduce exclusions

and truancy. In his speech to conference, David Blunkett, the Education Secretary, said he would be providing extra money to provide practical help to counter classroom disruption. …Schools will be able to set up special units on site to deal with disruptive pupils and pupils who are excluded will be taught the full timetable. (Rafferty and Barnard, 1998)

By the time the initiative was introduced the rhetoric had softened considerably. Funding was made available under the Excellence in Cities programme and was used to set up 1,000 'Learning Support Units', with criteria for referral extended to include shy, withdrawn and anxious pupils, as well as those deemed to be disruptive. This coincided with New Labour's appropriation of, and broadening out of, a critical discourse of 'inclusion' to encompass a communitarian focus on morality and personal responsibility. Through the late 1990s and into the next century poverty and disadvantage were primarily addressed in terms of social exclusion through a focus on disconnection from mainstream values and aspirations (Levitas, 1998; Fairclough, 2000). This condition was seen as best tackled through helping or coercing the excluded back into the ranks of the included either by increasing opportunities, or by altering their motivation and ability. 'Inclusion' became a shorthand term for describing policies orientated towards re-attaching the afflicted through modification of their lifestyle and conduct (Gillies, 2005).

In the context of education policy the inclusion agenda shifted away from debates about special educational needs to a considerably wider ranging concept of 'barriers to learning'. Identified barriers spanned a range of characteristics including disaffection, ethnicity and cultural issues, unstable family circumstances and even 'being from a community which has a disregard for education' (Hayward, 2006: 2). This newly dominant conceptualisation of inclusion channelled the social investment model characterising the neoliberal infused politics of the time. Children were re-envisioned in terms of 'human capital' as constituting a set of resources (skills, talents, qualifications, dispositions etc.), which can be converted into economic value for the good of the wider nation and the individual concerned. Child development was identified as a key mediator and risk factor for poverty and inequality, with policy and practice shifting ever further away from concerns with economic disadvantage, discrimination, social recognition and material security. Instead, emphasis was placed on supporting children to become 'entrepreneurs of the self' (Foucault, 2008: 226) in order to transcend their 'barriers to learning'. In the process children's best interests become seamlessly elided with the best interests of neoliberal regimes.

As Beverley Skeggs (2011) notes, value has come to eclipse values in public discourse, hampering abilities to see beyond the logic of capital to recognise alternative and more meaningful modes of existence. The conflation of inclusion with human capital acquisition has reduced the socially transformative potential of education to a matter of individualised venture, speculation and investment. More specifically, there is no acknowledgement of the differential access to resources that facilitate, limit, and in many cases, prohibit the attachment of sanctioned value to the self. A fiction is maintained that deliverance into the ranks of the included requires only personal change; for the excluded to become more like the enterprising white middle-class achievers. Thus, rather than challenging the systematic devaluation of marginalised pupils, contemporary approaches to inclusion compound the injury by pathologising their differences as psychological flaws. The formal introduction of the 'learning support unit' represented a combining of this logic with a more reactionary instinct to tackle bad behaviour. It was claimed that for their own good and the good of the school, difficult pupils must be temporarily excluded from the mainstream classroom in order for them to be made includable. As such, the preoccupation with modifying behaviour becomes re-framed in terms of 'learning'.

Given the serious implications for those referred for 'inclusion', there has been remarkably little written on the subject since LSUs began to proliferate at the end of the century. In 2002 'good practice guidelines' were issued by the Department for Education and Skills, on the basis of findings from self-report questionnaires and interviews with school practitioners. Couched in the language of inclusion the guidance provides an impressive list of benefits flowing from LSUs, ranging from raised attainment to general improvement in school behaviour. There is, however, little information given as to how these benefits were reliably assessed and ascertained.

More robust research was published by Ofsted in 2003 as part of an evaluation of the Excellence in Cities initiative, offering a slightly more mixed picture. Ofsted (2003) highlighted a lack of suitable educational provision in a quarter of units, and cautioned against viewing them as a panacea. The predominant finding from both reports was the high value accorded to them within participating schools. School staff viewed them very positively and they appeared to be popular with the pupils who attended them. Interestingly, the main focus for dissent was their name. Hardly any of the schools stuck with the terminology of learning support unit, preferring a range of alternative euphemisms (as is discussed in Chapter 2).

Reflecting their popularity, it seems that many schools took the decision to continue allocating resources to their units once the Excellence in Cities funding ran out, while a large number of schools outside of the initiative went on to found their own. This is despite the removal of exclusion targets in 2001. Although the trail goes cold in terms of published literature, an indeterminable but very sizable number of schools operate some kind of behaviour support unit within (or close to) their premises. In the current context of an accelerated expansion of free schools and academies operating outside of local authority control, the prevalence and nature of internal exclusion becomes even harder to evaluate. Research reveals that academy schools are considerably more likely to exclude pupils (Maddern, 2010; Kultz, 2015) suggesting the more punitive among them may be less inclined to resort to segregation as a discipline policy. Nevertheless, some evidence points to the extensive use of BSUs in the independent state sector. For example, Mossbourne Academy in Hackney, East London, a school highly acclaimed for discipline and attainment standards, houses a 'learning support unit' in a portakabin behind the main building, Reflecting the authoritarian ethos of the school, the referred pupils work in silent isolation (Kultz, forthcoming).

It is not hard to see the appeal of the BSU system to school staff. The units liberate classroom teachers from difficult and demanding pupils, allowing them to focus attention on those more likely to raise the school's position in the league tables. They also mark a useful disciplinary boundary, keeping less troublesome pupils in line while simultaneously fulfilling school inclusion policies. Most powerfully, they remove the troubling and troublesome from sight and mind without leaving any enduring administrative trace. And this absence extends beyond schools themselves to encompass broader policy and practice arenas. Searches of media, policy and academic literature return next to no mention of segregation within schools as an issue, suggesting the practice has become normalised into invisibility.

However, it seems concerns may bubble under the surface only rarely finding a public outlet. In May 2014, Nigel Utton[1], the former head teacher of what was Bromstone Primary School in Kent, vented his anger at the poor treatment of children with special educational needs. Speaking at an event bringing together policy makers and practitioners, Utton is reported as lambasting the way schools were segregating pupils to improve their standing in league tables, claiming that, "Schools, particularly academies, are setting up annexes where you put children you don't know what to do with".[2] Liberated by the fact he had already resigned his post, Utton did not pull any punches in sharing his concerns. His interjection represented a brief rupture in the prevailing silence on the ethics of internal exclusion units, which was then very quickly resumed.

The lack of critical debate concerning the nature and moral justification of segregation units in British schools highlights the power of discursive and regulatory frameworks rather than any simple lack of concern for marginalised pupils' welfare. The BSUs featured in this book were (for the most part) staffed by sensitive, caring and well-meaning education practitioners, but their efforts to do the best for the referred pupils were contextualised and curtailed by a largely uncritical centring of a personalised inclusion agenda, as well as the often blatant marginalisation of units from the mainstream schools. The units operated as places where obvious injustice could be made to disappear from public view, a fate BSU staff often fought hard against. However, their power to challenge mainstream school practices was very limited. Indeed, success in advocating for vulnerable pupils could undermine job security. Drastic restructuring and redundancies of behaviour support practitioners occurred in all three schools with few of those participating in the research staying in their post long enough to see its conclusion.

A British school to prison pipeline?

Therapeutic and emotional pedagogies have risen to ascendancy in numerous countries, delivered in school programmes in Finland, Sweden, Australia and beyond (Ecclestone and Brunila, forthcoming). But the prolific spread of behaviour support units seems to be a largely British phenomenon. At first glance BSUs appear to mark a strong contrast from the authoritarian neoliberal ethos so evident in US school discipline policies. As Arran Kupchik (2009) outlines, schools in America are characterised by centrally enforced 'zero-tolerance policies' requiring the automatic expulsion of any student caught violating a rule. Such policies are backed up with a range of enforcement measures including CCTV cameras, drug sniffer dogs, strip-searching and physical restraint. Many schools employ law enforcement officers as part of their staff, requiring them to patrol corridors and deal with disruption and misconduct. The result has been increasing suspension and/or criminalisation of students (often very young children[3]) for minor misdemeanours, setting them on a path toward later incarceration. Many US children have gained police records for trivial behavioural infringements, which have carried strict probation conditions (zero lateness or grade attainment). Violation of these conditions can land the offender back in the juvenile justice system (Krueger, 2014).

This disciplinary approach has been widely termed the 'school to prison pipeline', by virtue of its gravity-like funnelling into the juvenile and criminal justice systems, with the impact being felt in particular by minority ethnic (mostly African-American) students (Tsai, 2013). In some US jurisdictions, suspended or expelled students lose their entitlement to education, while in other states they are sent to 'disciplinary alternative schools'. The numbers of these across America has been growing in response to the draconian school discipline regime, with demand outstripping supply (Vanderhaar et al, 2013). Disciplinary alternative schools are often privately run, operating outside of the school system and the regulatory framework that determines adequate educational services (Glassett Farrelly, 2013).

This harsh punitive regime appears at odds with the imperative of inclusion and ethos of support characterising the British school discipline interventions (Kupchik et al, 2014). But there are many disturbing parallels hidden beneath the more progressive rhetoric. For example, in Britain, schools can and do pursue similar 'zero-tolerance' policies, but from within a framework of inclusion, commonly utilising behaviour support units to clear mainstream classrooms of miscreants. Indeed, Ofsted, England's school inspectorate has explicitly encouraged the use of 'zero-tolerance' and 'non-negotiable' behaviour codes in struggling schools[4], meaning that pupils who fall foul of the rules may be consigned to a BSU, often ironically, to spend time learning tolerance and negotiation skills.

Discipline enforcement measures resembling the US model are also employed in British schools. In contrast to the American-centric appeal to public safety and homeland security, a progressive sounding language of early intervention is stressed. In 2002 the UK government published a 'Youth Crime Action Plan' urging schools to develop partnerships with their neighbourhood police. The Safer Schools Partnership (SSP) saw police stationed in schools across the country, ostensibly to reduce bullying, truancy and prevent vulnerable young people being drawn into crime. SSPs were also presented as improving community police relations, illustrated by policy literature peppered with pictures of friendly smiling 'bobbies' helping school children[5]. The real and distinctly less benign impact of SSPs is outlined in the following chapters of this book, which details how police now work closely with teachers, resulting in the criminalisation of mundane misdemeanours.

The UK has also made extensive use of CCTV in schools, with a 2012 freedom of information request revealing that one in ten have placed cameras in toilets and changing rooms[6]. And more extreme measures were contained in the 2014 Anti-Social Behaviour, Crime and Policing Act, which equipped head teachers themselves with the power to issue a 'Crime Prevention Injunction' (CPI). A CPI is a civil order, which if breached can result in electronic tagging, curfews, and even a three-month prison sentence for those over 14. Introduced explicitly to tackle bullying, the injunction is again justified through a soft, liberal sounding appeal to early intervention and support to achieve individual change. According to proponents of the legislation the injunction is designed not to instantly criminalise children, but to provide for positive interventions to change behaviour[7]. It is also worth noting that despite the different rhetoric and policy discourses, formal school exclusion rates are broadly the same on both sides of the Atlantic (Kupchik et al, 2014).

A small-scale study by the Communities Empowerment Network lays bare some of the arbitrary and punitive decisions behind many contemporary school exclusions, revealing how a blaming, intolerant culture drives discriminatory outcomes (Kultz, 2015). The report highlights numerous disturbing examples and also notes an increasing tendency for infant schools to exclude reception age children for alleged sexual assault. As in the US, evidence suggests that children experiencing educational marginalisation are considerably more likely to end up in prison, with this trajectory compounded by risk management focused practices and early entry to criminal justice systems (McAra and McVie, 2012). Yet such explicit criminalisation of children continues to be discussed in the progressive sounding policy lexicon of 'early intervention', stressing support and prevention. This disguises the ruthless authoritarianism revealed in a freedom of information disclosure that 400 children had tasers drawn on them by police in England and Wales in 2013 alone. The brutal and abusive regime child prisoners find themselves subject to is also well documented (Willow, 2015), with 65 teenagers and young adults dying in custody in the four years up to 2015.[8]

Back to the future: building character

In the context of virtual silence about the mistreatment of children by institutions, publicly expressed concern in Britain tends to focus instead on perceived familial neglect and cultural deprivation. There has been no shortage of hand wringing about child poverty, inequality and low levels of social mobility, with a durable model of personal deficit customarily placing such evils at the door of parents (or, more accurately, mothers). As I show in Chapter 6, troublesome behaviour in the classroom is habitually presented as evidence of poor parenting, regardless of the circumstances. Cycle of deprivation narratives are now deeply ingrained in British social policy and in popular common sense ensuring that even in situations of severe hardship it is the child and mother who are identified as requiring modification. Disadvantage becomes personalised and constructed as a problem that must be corrected for a meritocratic order to flourish.

There is, of course, a very long history to the personal deficit model, reflecting deeply held convictions among the privileged that deprivation is distinct, self-perpetuating and disconnected from mainstream society (Jordan, 1974; Townsend, 1979; Welshman, 2006). The language used to describe and categorise socially and economically marginalised people has shifted and evolved over the centuries, reflecting the different preoccupations of the day, along with in-vogue, prescribed policy solutions. Inclusion as a broad policy ethos emerged in response to the appropriation of exclusion as a discourse, and in particular Tony Blair's conception of 'deeply excluded' children as needing to be 'saved'[9]. This mirrored and reinforced a therapeutic turn towards emotional pedagogies as a way of safeguarding children's acquisition of human capital. By the middle of the last decade the nationwide schools initiative SEAL (Social and Emotional Aspects of Learning) was operating at primary and secondary level with the aim of providing 'a whole-curriculum framework and resource for teaching social, emotional and behavioural skills to all pupils' (DfES, 2005; Gillies, 2011).

As will be detailed in the following chapters of this book, the parameters of SEAL profoundly shaped the experience of the young people referred to the behaviour support units. Activities within the units were delivered via an emotionally styled curriculum designed to address the perceived emotional antecedents of disruptive conduct rather than the behaviour in question. This emphasis on underlying psychological or developmental causes operated through the marking out of a particular behaviour or incident as a personal pathology, with little space separating pupils' actions from who they were at an integral level. This therapeutic framework of inclusion also made entitlement to classroom education contingent on having the right kind of self. Echoing the dominant policy discourse of 'school readiness', school staff participating in the research commonly positioned BSU attendees as lacking the prerequisite emotional and social skills for classroom learning. As I will show, the value attached to SEAL inspired assessments of personal competence and 'readiness for learning' inevitably positioned and defined pupils against racialised, classed and gendered ideals, producing discriminatory patterns of 'inclusion' as well as exclusion.

While a change of government in 2010 saw the demise of SEAL as a centrally promoted initiative, its frameworks and ethos remain embedded in schools, facilitating the introduction of new but similarly orientated programmes. Most noticeably, there has been a hardening of what were previously termed 'soft skills', articulated through a remasculinising discourse of character and resilience (Burman, 2014). As Kathryn Ecclestone (2012) has demonstrated, the therapeutic ethos characterising SEAL has been central to the resurgence of a traditional lexicon of character as enabling personal capacities. Following the launch of a 'Character and Resilience Manifesto' in 2014, the Conservative education minister, Nicky Morgan, launched a government scheme to support schools in positioning England as a '"global leader" in teaching character, resilience and "grit" to pupils'. Unlike the previous incarnation of SEAL, the appeal of character education spans across the party political spectrum enthusing right wing Conservatives as well as the liberal left (including the Green Party). For example, in a discussion about the importance of parenting, *The Guardian* journalist and Young Foundation Associate Yvonne Roberts claimed:

> The public schools recognised the answer long ago. They invest heavily in character education and life skills. They encourage self-discipline and grit; and develop in pupils a sense of agency and the ability to communicate, empathise and collaborate with others (in politics, see the Eton-Westminster coalition in action).[10]

Tristram Hunt, a Labour shadow education minister and the privately educated son of 'Baron Hunt of Chesterton' has similarly called for state schools to embed character education and resilience in their curriculum, claiming:

> Research clearly shows that vulnerable and disadvantaged young people are far more likely to deal with the consequences of failure and setbacks in a negative way.[11]

Hunt does not specify the research he is referring to, but the tautology inherent in his statement betrays a fundamental lack of understanding of disadvantaged young people's lives. As I will demonstrate throughout this book, the BSU attendees participating in my research were above all else distinguished by their resilience and resourcefulness. Most had little choice to be anything other than resilient, given the experiences of poverty, insecurity and vulnerability they and their families were coping with on a daily basis. The very real 'grit' and courage sustaining these struggles highlights the perverse travesty inherent in elevating elite temperaments, as well as the political agenda at stake. The valorisation of 'character' is unavoidably historically located, conjuring up a nostalgic stiff upper lip 'golden age' populated by Downton Abbey style heroes who know their place and love their country.

The revival and re-popularisation of an old discourse of character may have shifted markedly from its original incarnation, but threads from the past stubbornly remain, most obviously in the spirit of empire that is invoked. As Peter Cain's (2007) work demonstrates, the Victorian elite was preoccupied by 'character' as the basis of Britain's greatness and leadership across the world. Empire was viewed as the embodiment of British 'character', which, as Seumas Milne reminds us, consisted of 'avowedly racist despotism built on ethnic cleansing, enslavement, continual wars and savage repression, land theft and merciless exploitation'[12]. When references to character are made today the silent precursor 'British' hangs in the air, implicating and marginalising those who might be seen as anything other. Indeed, Tristram Hunt has quite explicitly framed his discussion of character education in terms of helping children to develop a 'British spirit' in the context of increased global competition[13].

Such contemporary appropriations of character rely on a slippery, inchoate vision of purposeful determination, self-direction and restraint; virtues most often projected onto white public school boys (as evidenced by Roberts' comments above). Structural power and privilege become naturalised and personalised in the process, presented as achievable for all who can 'cut the mustard'. More specifically the rehabilitation of 'character' marks the acceleration of a neoliberal moralism operationalised through a discourse of personal responsibility and self-optimisation. While traditional understanding of character conveyed notions of moral virtue, contemporary invocations denote psychological competence and wellbeing (Ecclestone, 2012). Drawing on a conceptual framework of positive psychology, onus is placed on individuals to develop the appropriate capabilities to overcome life barriers (including structural constraints).

In other words, morality is no longer assumed to inhere in any trait, capability, skill or personality, but rather in the very act of transferring value to the self. The experience of poverty and disadvantage come to be taken as evidence of a failure to learn 'character' (or inculcate it in children), which equates to personal failure in its own right. This morally infused logic has driven a hardening of judgemental attitudes towards the poorest in British society and a general acceptance of extreme levels of inequality (Dorey, 2010). In policy terms it manifests in the rise of the authoritarian neoliberal state and its efforts to manage, disenfranchise and even disappear those displaying insufficient self-reliance and personal plasticity. Contemporary education policy, school practices and more specifically, 'inclusion', as realised in the rise of the behaviour support unit, can all be viewed through this lens of statecraft.

Punishing the poor

With the repositioning of education as an economic policy, characteristic market based reforms have unfolded alongside the emergence of a distinctly punitive ethos (Wacquant, 2009). As part of a shift away from postwar ethics of universal provision and social security entitlement, a new model of the 'enabling state' has prevailed. Government support has become conditional and directional, provided with the aim of initiating and encouraging self-sufficiency and personal optimisation. Reflecting this instrumentalist ethic, state education became firmly harnessed to the needs of late capitalism, with schools positioned as in the business of manufacturing those willing and able to meet the needs of a flexible labour market. An increasingly marginalised population is the by-product of this approach, with their plight recognised only in terms of potential disorder and resistance (Wacquant, 2009). The erosion of established social protections in the context of free market fundamentalism has seen a normalisation of obscene levels of inequality, and a lurch toward chronic precarity for a growing number of those at the bottom of society (Standing, 2011).

Loic Wacquant (2009) has argued that this escalating social insecurity is being governed though swingeing authoritarianism, as evidenced by increasingly strict law enforcement policies and dramatic rises in incarceration rates across neoliberal reformist states[14]. He documents how a paternalist regime of poverty management operates through deterrence, surveillance, stigma and graduated sanctions. Rather than the state acknowledging an obligation to the poor and dispossessed, the poor and dispossessed are now generally depicted as having a responsibility to society (Barrie, 2013). Those falling short are reviled, made abject and expunged to the margins of society, often out of public sight and mind (Bauman, 2003; Tyler, 2013). This has played out across a number of dimensions including the shaming and persecution of those dependent on welfare benefits (Crossley and Slater, 2014) and the development of 'hostile architecture' (anti-homeless spikes, sloping seats at bus stops etc.) designed to drive the poor and destitute out of public spaces[15].

Moreover, the insufficiently market compliant are rooted out early with schools playing a key role in sorting, regulating and containing emerging surplus populations. Henry Giroux (2014) conveys this more eloquently in terms of a new 'politics of disposability':

> What has emerged in this new historical conjuncture is an intensification of the practice of disposability in which more and more individuals and groups are now considered excess, consigned to zones of abandonment, surveillance and incarceration.

As will be outlined, behaviour support units can be viewed as a manifestation of these politics of disposability, particularly in relation to the referral of boys. For all the talk of inclusion, building emotional skills and cementing a foundation for learning, the reality is more likely to amount to long-term segregation and confinement, leading in many cases to formal exclusion.

Again, Wacquant's (2009) reading of contemporary socio-political forces offers insight into the appropriation of exclusion as inclusion in education policy. Drawing on Pierre Bourdieu's conceptualisation of the 'bureaucratic field' and the contradictory struggles inherent in state bureaucratic mechanisms, Wacquant (2010) elaborates on the distinction between the 'Left and the Right hand of state'. The former represents softer welfare directed policies, while the latter is concerned with masculinised enforcement of reforms. Wacquant interprets the increasing jurisdictions of behavioural regulation, the criminal justice services and prisons as a slant toward the Right hand of the state. He describes this in terms of a remasculinisation of the state, characterised by 'transition from the kindly "nanny state" of the Fordist-Keynesian era to the strict "daddy state" of neoliberalism' (p 201). The result is choreography of Left and Right hands of the state working to achieve a 'double regulation of the poor'. Inclusion becomes a form of exclusion.

Yet as I will demonstrate, the conflicting struggles constituting the 'bureaucratic field' remain very alive in the field of education. The socially supportive Left hand may now focus on personal change to deliver 'inclusion', while the more dominant Right ruthlessly enforces the standards agenda through reference to zero tolerance, but this is an uneasy alliance within schools. The policy makers driving forward market-orientated reforms (the 'higher state nobility' in Bourdieu's [1999] words) coerce, convince and compel but never entirely subjugate the education practitioners charged with executing the model. Behaviour support units may help relieve the contradictory demands placed on schools but they are sites of contestation and high tension, manifested in open conflict, institutional restructuring, redundancies and resignations.

Insights from Wacquant and Bourdieu can be placed alongside a more Foucauldian reading of 'inclusion' as an apparatus of disciplinary power seeking to shape its subjects through surveillance, diagnosis and rote learning of appropriate thoughts and feelings. Performativity and subjectification operate as key analytical lenses in this book, but they run far short of explaining the blatant futility attached to so many of the everyday emotional pedagogies comprising the BSU curriculums.

Although the ideology of inclusion enthused and inspired the work of the education professionals, it was in effect impossible for many of the unruly minds and bodies inhabiting the BSUs to ever become 'includable' in the unforgiving environment of the mainstream school. Wacquant's work allows the proliferation of BSUs to be viewed as part of a broader segregation and management of marginality through territorial fixation and stigmatisation. Operating in practice as 'sin bins', BSUs contain those branded as the refuse of the school, while discourses of inclusion offer the moral and moralising spectacle of redemptive opportunity.

As Diane Reay (2013) notes, social mobility shapes dominant contemporary narratives of justice, obscuring the insidious, structurally ingrained processes that render its realisation little more than a fairy tale. Policy solutions that focus on securing better educational opportunities for disadvantaged children present knowledge and learning as neutral practices. Access, ability and application are assumed to translate into educational success with no acknowledgement of the 'cultural arbitrary' that drives the reproduction of privilege (Bourdieu and Passeron, 1977). Schools and other institutions act as agents of cultural enforcement with elite social groups imposing an unquestioned status on the principles, beliefs and values that best suit them. Working-class children are likely to experience conflict between their situated cultural knowledge and the sanctioned, white, middle-class knowledge they encounter in the classroom. However, they are socialised to view their own struggles and the success of their middle-class peers as evidence of their own inferior ability versus their classmates' superior potential. With educational progress presented in terms of hard work and natural intelligence, social and economic inequalities are transformed into a hierarchy of academic achievement (Bourdieu and Passeron, 1977).

The myth of social mobility presents middle-class style achievement as accessible to all who aspire and try hard enough (Reay, 2013). Yet the obvious reality is that there could be no mobility without some children existing as markers of failure or ordinariness. It is not difficult to imagine the howls of outrage and the formidable mobilisation of resources that would follow from even a moderate increase in downward social mobility among the middle classes. The fact that year-on-year improvements in exam results in the UK have generally been met with consternation about declining standards rather than celebration, provides some clue as to what is at stake. It is this imperative of distinction that lies at the very heart of the education system (Bourdieu and Passeron, 1977) requiring middle-class entitlement to be established in relation to working-class inferiority.

Dominant social groups and institutions elevate arbitrary cultural characteristics (white skin, particular accents and vocabulary, deportment, appreciation of specific forms of literature, etc) then work to inculcate them as inherently superior, overwriting and obscuring lived experiences of inequality. Pierre Bourdieu and Jean Claude Passeron (1977) describe this imposition of an arbitrary cultural framework as an act of 'symbolic violence'. Rhetorical frameworks and significations comprising the contemporary education system work to buffer and reinforce relations of oppression and exploitation by 'hiding them under the cloak of nature, benevolence and meritocracy' (Wacquant, 1993). The concept of symbolic violence is core to the analysis of behaviour support units presented in this book, and is drawn on to reveal how 'inclusion' operates as a particularly effective cloaking device.

The shifting agenda of social inclusion in schools is a key thread running through each chapter of this book. I trace how contemporary 'inclusion' practices can be understood as part of a cultural preoccupation with therapeutic development, resulting in enormous significance attributed to psychologised conceptions of personal deficit as a means of understanding and addressing long-standing social issues and problems (Furedi, 2004; Ecclestone and Hays, 2008; Illouz, 2008). As I will outline, educational initiatives increasingly centre on developing the emotional and social skills of 'at risk' young people while overlooking the institutional and structural context framing the behaviour. The effect has been a conflation of troublesome with troubled, encapsulated within a simplistic and depoliticised discourse of early intervention

Research, aims and ethics

The detailed ethnography underpinning this book was conducted in three mainstream urban secondary schools with pupils attending behaviour support units.[16] Participatory observation was undertaken within the units alongside weekly group work sessions with selected pupils over the course of each term. In-depth interviews were also conducted with pupils, their parents and teachers. A total of 73 pupils aged between 12 and 15 participated over the course of the research. Further details about the ethnographic process and methods pursued are provided in Chapter 2. Lack of any broader research on BSUs makes it impossible to judge how typical the units featured in this book are in comparison with the national picture.

While each school was different in its approach and procedures, all were positioned by what Diane Reay (2007) has termed the middle-class imaginaries of demonisation. Marked out by their deprived catchment areas and their high numbers of working-class and minority ethnic intakes, the schools were publically labelled as underperforming.

Some of the particularities of the BSUs described in these pages will relate to social geographies and the pressures faced by struggling schools, but it would be surprising given the climate of competition and the lack of monitoring if similar injustices were not occurring across the country. It is this uncontended invisibility that this book seeks to challenge by bringing the murky issue of internal school exclusion into the light. There has been no public discussion of the ethics of segregation in schools partly because so little is known about its extent and nature. Wildly misleading school policies and the 'cloak' of apparently benevolent inclusion have conspired to keep the issue under the radar. The everyday practices and assumptions underpinning ghettoisation as a disciplinary strategy are subject to critical scrutiny here with the explicit aim of breaking a prevailing silence on the issue.

The purpose of this book is also to convey the real human stories behind educational marginalisation and to highlight the mechanisms through which poor and minority ethnic pupils and their families are positioned as inferior and 'unincludable'. Much of the book is taken up with the lives and experiences of those who found themselves referred to the units. In foregrounding these narratives I draw attention to the blunt operation of systems of power and the acts of symbolic violence wrought against pupils in the name of inclusion. I deliberately avoid the more agentic sounding epithet 'student' in order to emphasise the heavily disciplined reality of being a school pupil. Nevertheless, the stories presented here are of resistance, subversion and resilience. The BSU pupils and their families were a far cry from passive victims but their ability to challenge injustice and claim entitlement to education was commonly countered with righteous opposition and uncompromising denial from the schools. By unpacking these experiences and prioritising the perspectives of pupils, I highlight how the politics of disposability operate through the largely well-meaning words and actions of school staff.

As Elizabeth Murphy and Robert Dingwall (2001) note the ethnics and the politics of ethnography are inextricably intertwined. The values motivating the research inevitably shape conduct in the field and the interpretation of ethically sensitive judgement calls. Professional codes of ethics may provide guiding principles but are by necessity confined to broad and blunt categories of practice (confidentiality, informed consent, non-maleficence, etc). Meanwhile, ethnographers are left to navigate the everyday dilemmas that characterise fieldwork and writing up. The controversy surrounding Alice Goffman's (2014) acclaimed study of young black men in West Philadelphia, illustrates the highly contingent and contextual nature of ethnography, as well as the discomfort this arouses in many. Goffman was accused of 'going native' and participating in a conspiracy to commit murder while immersed in her fieldwork (see for example, Lubet 2015). The accuracy of Goffman's portrayals were also questioned as part of a wider backlash that subjected ethical dimensions of ethnographic methods to critical scrutiny.

But as many have pointed out, the unpredictability, risks and judgement calls that characterise the real world demands of ethnography are at the centre of its value in generating unique grounded perspectives. Ethnographic knowledge is dependent on emotional relations that defy the most detailed methodological planning. Writing in response to the Goffman controversy the anthropologist Paul Stoller (2015) articulates this particularly well.

> In ethnography the personal and the professional are never separate, meaning that good ethnography is not likely to consist of bloodless prose. Put another away, doing ethnography, like living life, involves love and hate, fidelity and betrayal, and courage and fear... Like all scientific endeavors, ethnography involves a set of interpretations, the contours of which are shaped by personal disposition,

theoretical and methodological training and the inter-
subjective dynamics of the ethnographic setting, which
consists of an ever-changing matrix of social relations and
events that taxes our cultural desire to transform social chaos
into some semblance of social order.

In this book I attempt to foreground and detail the social relations that
produced my account of in-school inclusion units. The text is threaded
through with dilemmas, troubling stories and uneasy knowledge about
the unjust, dangerous or unhappy nature of certain pupils' lives. Where
possible, I attempt to give an honest account of how these challenges
were negotiated in a context where lack of resources, services or
solutions severely constrained responses. Judgements were also framed
by the need to respect trust and maintain confidentiality. The three
schools participating have been allocated fictional names and care has
been taken to protect their anonymity. Similarly, all of the pupils, school
staff and parents are referred to by pseudonyms. The pupils themselves
enthusiastically chose many of these.

Structure of the book

As I have outlined, the tone and content of this book reflects the affect-
laden nature of the research and difficulties inherent in documenting
experiences of injustice. In the next chapter I will consider in more
depth how research relationships with pupils and teachers were
established and sustained in the context of emotionally fraught
institutions. More specifically, I provide a full and frank account of how
the ethnographic research project informing the book was designed and
put into practice. The chapter constitutes a highly reflexive description
of negotiating access into the schools, managing institutional dynamics
and establishing positive, trusting relationships with BSU pupils.
This detailed exploration draws inspiration from Shane Blackman's
(2007) concept of 'hidden ethnography' which seeks to draw out
the significance of powerful research encounters normally hidden by
more formal accounts of the research process (Cooke and Kothari,
2001). As Blackman argues, it is crucial to consider the complex
entanglements between the researcher and the researched to obtain a
fuller understanding of how academic knowledge is constructed. As
I will outline in Chapter 2, the dynamics constituting the research in
the BSUs provided vital insights in its own right.

Chapter 3 then moves on to centre on the young people attending
the units and explore the particular challenges they faced. These

encompassed a range of stresses and hardships including poverty, poor housing, family illness, bereavement and other traumas. As I will show, these difficult circumstances were often associated with escape from ordeals like domestic violence or migration from a war-torn country. In addition, I describe how the school catchment areas were blighted by violent crime, with spates of gang violence and teenage stabbings directly involving the research participants. This chapter will examine how the BSU pupils managed these challenges and how in the process they came to be seen as exhibiting problematic behaviour by school staff. It demonstrates how a contemporary inclusion agenda de-contextualises social and economic struggles, reducing concepts of risk to individual needs and personal problems. The routine construction of unit attendees 'at risk' was drawn on to warrant their segregation and intensive monitoring.

Following on from this focus on the lives of BSU pupils, Chapter 4 examines how a distinctly gendered discourse of risk orders the understandings and experiences of challenging young people. It details how a therapeutically inflected curriculum pursued through the Social and Emotional Aspects of Learning (SEAL) programme conceptualised and targeted troublesome behaviour in terms of personal deficit or sickness. For young men, narratives of psychological disorder or damage were commonly drawn on to position them as potentially dangerous. This is explored through a particular focus on anger, its expression and interpretation in the classroom and its perceived link to gang activity. For young women, constructions of developmental immaturity and 'neediness' tended to shape their school encounters. Analysis presented in this chapter highlights how the theme of vulnerability is drawn on to trivialise the acting out of girls and normalise socially located difficulties.

Chapter 5 explores how the psychologisation of challenging behaviour relies on a construction of inadequate parenting. Home life was cited by teachers to make sense of conflict in the classroom and was viewed as an influence to be countered and compensated for through an active process of 'inclusion'. Accusations of bad parenting are traced back to specific examples to emphasise the gap between institutional assumptions about family life and everyday lived experience. Attention is drawn to the often invisible labour parents undertook to address their children's problems and the way particular challenges (poverty, insecurity, homelessness, ill health etc.) shaped and limited family school engagement. This chapter also emphasises the central importance of family to the young people attending the units. No other theme in the research aroused as much passion or pride among pupils. The contradictions and often volatile tensions associated with the invocation of family in a classroom setting and the problematic place that home occupies in the current inclusion agenda are brought into focus.

Chapter 6 looks specifically at how a prevailing rhetoric of inclusion and diversity masks and further ingrains patterns of discrimination and inequality. It will be argued that efforts to make students 'includable' within a broadly unchanged framework compound existing social divisions and inequalities. Unprocessed racialised narratives informing inclusion policies, procedures and referrals are drawn out to show how they result in a disproportionate problematisation of black boys. Also highlighted is the extent to which behaviour support interventions sought to compensate for the psychological effects of class disadvantage, with therapeutic ideals readily translating into a narrative of personal and family deficit. Building on the previous chapter, it will be argued that schools are increasingly positioning themselves as arbiters of the values and identities children need to develop appropriately, with little recognition of the cultural subjugation this encompasses.

The focus in Chapter 7 is on how experiences of educational marginalisation frame and inform young people's understandings of their opportunities and prospects, and how administered 'inclusion' can foreclose a sense of possibility. In the context of financial turbulence and austerity there has been growing anxiety over the high numbers of young people not in education, employment or training (NEETs). Chapter 7 examines how this concern shaped activities in the BSUs and how attendees' hopes, fears and anticipated strategies for constructing a liveable future could be in tension with institutional practices. In particular, the central importance young people accorded to a highly idealised concept of education as a virtuous, but largely unattainable pathway is explored and contrasted with Paul Willis's classic 1977 study, *Learning to Labour*. It is argued that the contemporary drive to diagnose and segregate troublesome pupils has replaced the struggle for symbolic and physical space characterising Willis's study with a more basic struggle to claim any entitlement at all to educational space.

A final short chapter, Chapter 8, draws together all the proceeding themes and tracks back to the broader political context framing the rise of in-school exclusion units. The main findings of the research are reviewed and related to the increasingly brutal and exclusionary practices that characterise policy making in late capitalist societies. I conclude the book with a discussion of how the orthodoxies of 'inclusion' must be challenged through a more sophisticated and radical engagement with social dynamics, power relations and education as an enfranchising resource.

13 Judith Burns (2014) 'Schools must build British spirit says Labour', *BBC News Online*, BBC online http://www.bbc.co.uk/news/education-30345282

14 England and Wales has the highest per capita prison population in Western Europe.

15 See Ben Quinn (2014) 'Anti-homeless spikes are part of a wider phenomenon of "hostile architecture"', *The Guardian*, http://www.theguardian.com/artanddesign/2014/jun/13/anti-homeless-spikes-hostile-architecture

16 The project Disruptive Behaviour in the Classroom: Exploring the Social Subjectivity of Disaffection was funded by the Economic and Social Research Council under grant number RES-061-23-0073.

TWO

An ethnography of 'inclusion': reflecting on the research process

This chapter aims to locate and situate the study informing the book. It seeks to highlight the importance of setting the research aims in their context and exploring the ethnographic fieldwork as a fluid, contingent and fragile process. The groundwork, missteps, realisations, accomplishments and disasters were formative in producing this account of internal school exclusion. Instead of polishing them out of the final version, I draw on them as a research resource here and show how they informed the interpretive process.

The motivation for conducting the study in the first place was formed somewhere in the middle of a hyperbolic policy cycle problematizing youth disorder and antisocial behaviour. Anxieties about 'hoodies' and 'feral youths'[1] were crystallising into a moral panic at the beginning of the new millennium, echoing centuries old concerns over youth disorder, delinquency and societal contagion. By 2006, the then Prime Minister, Tony Blair, and his New Labour government were launching a 'Respect Action Plan', pledging to 'eradicate the scourge of antisocial behaviour and restore respect to the communities of Britain'[2]. Some areas of the UK were also pursuing a 'naming and shaming' policy, distributing leaflets or displaying posters carrying the images of alleged miscreant youths. Despite failing crime rates, marginalised children and young people were being problematised and targeted at an alarming rate, finding themselves issued with curfews, banned from public spaces and subject to civil orders limiting movements, behaviour and even in some cases the types of clothing they could wear.

References to disadvantaged young people were also increasingly articulated through the hate filled discourse of the 'chav' as an ignorant vulgar, loutish, lowlife (Tyler, 2008; Jones, 2010). In the context of this fear-filled antipathy a new electronic device was marketed with the explicit intention of dispersing and driving away young people from 'trouble spots'. Widely reported at the time, the gadget was said to send out ultra-high pitched frequencies which can only be heard by those under the age of 20. Endorsed by the police and local authorities, the device was described in *The Telegraph* as 'sweet revenge', producing a sound 'so distressing it forces them to clutch their ears in discomfort'[3].

Emotionally infused discussion of youth disorder also encompassed lurid case studies of extreme and violent youth transgression, often set alongside reports that children's wellbeing was in crisis. For example, alarming media coverage of a so-called epidemic of 'happy slapping'[4] (where young people slap strangers and film the attack on their mobile phones) featured in conjunction with angst-ridden stories decrying the 'toxic' quality of contemporary children's lives. For instance, a campaign to 'halt the death of childhood' and highlight the 'intolerable burdens placed on the shoulders of our young people' was launched by *The Telegraph*, ironically in the same year it gleefully advocated use of the high-pitched frequency device.[5] As I watched these affect laden debates play out I was struck by the complete absence of the voices of the young people positioned within them.

Discipline in the classroom was a particularly hot topic when I began to write my first research proposal. Riding on the rhetoric of youth disrespect as a growing problem, the government had turned its attention to schools. Rates of permanent school exclusions were still climbing and a variety of measures were being introduced in an attempt to strengthen behaviour support in schools. My first attempt at procuring funding for research centred on experiences of school exclusion, I had planned to access young people through pupil referral units. Serendipitously, as it turned out, this proposal failed to secure funding. However, while scouring the policy literature I stumbled across references to learning support units (LSUs) as a mechanism for improving discipline. Unable to find any information on how LSUs actually functioned, I trawled my own personal network and consulted all the teachers and school counsellors I could access. Questions about learning support units were generally met with blank faces, but everyone I spoke to mentioned the established places within their schools where 'at risk' pupils might be referred. These often had unique and quite striking names, the 'Road to Redemption Centre' being among the most memorable. This more strategic focus on 'at risk' pupils attending LSUs won me Economic and Social Research Council (ESRC) funding[6] to pursue an ethnographic project over the course of three years (subsequently expanded to five years with maternity leave and follow-on funding).

Minding the gap: moving from theory to practice

Initiating any substantial research project is always a daunting prospect. Ethnography is by its very nature unpredictable. Embedded locations and real world demands are difficult to plan for and require considerable flexibility and sensitivity. While I had previous experience of researching with teenagers, I had limited familiarity with secondary education settings and even less knowledge of behaviour support initiatives. Similarly, Yvonne Robinson, the researcher recruited to work alongside me, was well qualified, but not in the area of education or youth. Taking the methodological plan outlined in the research proposal as a starting point, we did what most academics do when faced with a challenge – we read extensively.

There is a vast literature on creative methods with children and young people and on the practice of researching in the classroom more specifically. We dutifully parsed every key text we could find and also convened an advisory group of highly experienced academics and practitioners to help guide us through the research. After lengthy consideration and consultation we arrived at four key principles to guide our practice:

• Explain the research clearly and carefully to gain pupils' informed consent.
• Involve them in setting ground rules and planning sessions.
• Avoid panicking and shifting between lots of activities in group sessions. Hold your nerve and persevere.
• Ensure group activities are strategically targeted towards answering research questions.

Motivated by a desire to conduct methodologically sound and ethically responsible research, and emboldened by theoretical knowledge, our attention was turned to identifying suitable schools.

In choosing the first school to approach I relied heavily on the advice of an education professional with a borough-wide knowledge of secondary education. Halingbrooke School was identified as research friendly and a good fit for the ethnography. Located in a deprived catchment area, Hailingbrooke had received a good rating in its most recent Ofsted report. However, it also had a notoriously troubled history and continued to accept large numbers of pupils previously excluded from other institutions onto the school roll. As a way in I contacted the Pastoral Support Manager, Paul Baker, in an effort to get him onside before approaching the head teacher. Paul was very amenable and agreed that we could come in to the school and meet with him. This felt like a very positive start, but belied the considerably more complex terrain to be navigated. We quickly came to realise that a clear distinction operated in the school between 'troubled' and 'troublesome' pupils, the former being referred to pastoral support, while the latter were sent to a separate unit to address behaviour. This split was more than organisational, with the two areas existing as opposing factions within the school. Bitter disputes raged over where pupils were to be directed, how resources were to be allocated and the philosophy behind this division.

During our first visit to the school we established from Paul that challenging behaviour was managed through a tiered system comprising four different interventions. Tier one was the referral room, where pupils committing mild incursions were sent to cool off. This was a classroom in the main body of the school where pupils sat silently in rows doing their homework. Those visiting the referral room three or more times in a week were sent to the short-term unit for a week (tier two). This was located away from the main body of the school in a separate behaviour support block. Directly opposite the short-term inclusion unit was the behaviour support unit (tier three). To add to the complexity of this system, 'difficult' BSU pupils were commonly sent to an off-site provision (tier four) catering for 'at risk' pupils from across the borough. We quickly established that the BSU was the most appropriate location for our research, but this was outside of the remit of pastoral support and Paul was decidedly reluctant to let us go.

Paul talked at length about discipline structures within the school and made no attempt to hide his contempt for the manager of the BSU, Dave Stirling. He painted a vivid picture of a 'prickly', unprofessional man prone to tantrums. Dismissive of the practices pursued in the BSU, he outlined his own passionately held theory about the nature and cause of disruptive behaviour. According to Paul, it was the result of insecure family attachments producing emotionally damaged children. He backed his theory up with anecdotes featuring dead-eyed children committing mindlessly destructive acts. This was the first of many occasions we heard the narrative of psychological damage invoked to explain troublesome classroom behaviour.

Reluctantly, Paul took us across to the behaviour support block and we were ushered into the main classroom where a group activity was under way. Around eight pupils were sitting at desks arranged in a U shape with the BSU manager, Dave Stirling, standing in the middle, facilitating what looked like a kind of game. All were boys, and most were from minority ethnic groups. One was slumped on his desk, while another two were swinging back on their chairs. They all seemed very engaged in the game though, and took little notice of us. We sat awkwardly in the corner, watching as Paul tried and failed to get Dave Stirling's attention. The antipathy between two men was barely disguised, making for an excruciating first visit, as recorded in my field notes from the time:

> Paul started talking about the children and the staff (albeit in a low voice), which seemed a bit inappropriate given that we were in the same room. He said that Dave didn't really look like people's idea of a teacher because he was 'scruffy'. Dave has long hair and was wearing cotton trousers and a sweatshirt. Paul pointed to the other member of staff who was in a suit and said, "that's what a teacher looks like". Again we felt quite uncomfortable. I asked if any of the children had any particular developmental problems. He said that was the kind of question that would send Ben apeshit. He explained there is tension between the SEN centre and the BSU about who deals with what pupils. Eventually Paul approached Dave while he was still engaged in the group work. Dave seemed quite irritated and said something like, "well, I obviously can't see them now".

Eventually, Paul won a terse agreement that there could be a conversation after the lesson and then explained he was needed for lunch duty in the playground. We were left cringing in the corner waiting to speak to a visibly annoyed Dave. Our first conversation with him was difficult. He was initially suspicious and uncertain of our motives, but we appeared to stand up to the interrogation. He softened eventually and became quite enthusiastic about the research. Dave explained that he operated relatively independently from the main school and that there was no need to approach the head teacher; a formal letter explaining the research would suffice. Dave announced this quite proudly but with hindsight it underlined the extent to which the BSU was marginalised from everyday school business.

Scoping Hailingbrooke

We got agreement from Dave to conduct participant observation one day a week and run group activities with around six or seven pupils for one hour a week across each term (which in practice then became two hours). We then began a preliminary period of observation and discussion with BSU staff. Initially we focused on trying to get to grips with the complex referral systems in the school. Everyone we spoke to assured us that pupils were sent to the BSU for six weeks at a time and that regular meetings were held between key staff to discuss allocation and progress. It soon became obvious to us that this was an 'in principle' description which bore little resemblance to the reality.

Of the seven boys that were first assigned to us for the groupwork sessions almost all were long-term BSU stalwarts and several ended up staying for years (or until they were permanently excluded). We also found that decisions concerning referral, exclusion or even more rarely, reintegration, were commonly made without consultation with Dave Stirling. Our research during this period turned into a form of detective work aimed at uncovering how things really worked. As we were to discover, practices in the schools were flexible, inconsistent and often defied written procedures and practices (Gillies and Robinson, 2010).

Spending time observing everyday interactions was also a crucial way of acculturating us to the everyday routines and fault lines that would shape our experience of the school.

An initial concern that our presence might make pupils feel self-conscious quickly receded in the noisy and chaotic environment of the BSU. Arguments, fights and pupil/staff confrontations were common alongside other daily dramas. Teachers (often supply), mentors and classroom assistants came and went throughout the day. Pupils also regularly moved in and out of the unit to attend different interventions and appointments with professionals, with some being allowed to attend the odd lesson in the mainstream school. We had little sense that we were disturbing or unsettling normal classroom routines. In particular, these early observations helped us gain a better feel for the ebb and flow of BSU life and the dynamics shaping the enforcement of discipline. What was considered acceptable and unacceptable behaviour varied from pupil to pupil, from situation to situation and depended heavily on whoever was in charge. We came to admire the patience and commitment the staff members demonstrated, but also noticed the subtle and sensitive strategies they used to avoid futile or inflammatory confrontation.

Staff picked their battles. For example, chewing gum, eating sweets and swearing were not openly tolerated. Offending pupils were often challenged, sent out of the classroom or made to apologise. But equally there could be pretence that these misdeeds had not been seen or heard, for a variety of reasons. Some pupils (particularly those diagnosed with ADHD) were impulsive and found it difficult to control their behaviour. Twelve-year-old Peter was a compulsive gum chewer and frequently yelled 'fuck' at the top of his voice. While he was certainly not given free rein in the classroom he was a persistent offender and got away with far more than other pupils did, as another entry from my field diary demonstrates:

About 12 boys present, with some turning up towards the end. Boys were quite restless. Dave did a lot of shouting but again he caught their attention and they seemed quite engaged in the end (topic was water cycles – Dave told them it was key stage three or four stuff)… Peter was not allowed to participate in the lesson and was told to work on making a [paper maché] model. He seemed quite hyper – swearing a lot e.g. shit and bollocks. Shouted several times to Dave "this is getting on my tits". At one point Dave emptied [wallpaper] paste into a bowl for him and told him not to touch it until he'd got some water. Peter immediately stuck his finger in and said, "it's do the opposite day!".

Dave calmly ignored this provocation and went off to get the water. Peter had been taking the stimulant drug Ritalin for years in an attempt to control his behaviour. A side effect of the medication was lack of appetite and stunted growth, meaning he was tiny for his age. He often had the dosage altered, which resulted in considerable variations in his behaviour and mood. Some days he came into school over-medicated, looking pale, subdued and miserable, but most of the time he was exuberant, boisterous and mischievous. There was very little point in trying to force Peter to obey rules. In other cases staff would recognise that particular pupils were having a bad day (or week) and greater leeway would be given. Swearing and shouting at staff might also be overlooked in the context of an escalating argument, and sometimes bad behaviour would be dealt with by gently steering a pupil into the back office and attempting to reason with them.

Interactions between staff and students operated on a subtle and seemingly intuitive level, with Dave Stirling demonstrating impressive skills in managing often large groups of highly challenging pupils. Having been a teacher for over 26 years and specialising in behaviour for seven of them, Dave appeared to have developed an almost instinctive knack for keeping even the most distracted pupils interested, engaged and under control. By comparison, many other staff members were less successful in handling such a volatile atmosphere. As a result, lessons were often chaotic, punctuated by frequent flare-ups, resentments, defiance and, at times, aggressive behaviour. We observed these dynamics as active participants. It would not have been possible to have sat passively watching on the sidelines, even if we had wanted to. The pupils engaged us in conversations, joked with us and on several occasions we found ourselves having to break up fights.

On our first day in the unit, a smiling, heavyset black boy with his hair in corn rows sidled up to us while we were talking to a teaching assistant (TA). We later came to know him as 12-year-old Jamal. He extended a hand to greet me, said, "Hello Miss", and asked who we were. Before I could launch into my prepared explanation the teaching assistant introduced us as, "teachers who had come to see what went on in the BSU". The boy wandered off and I was left feeling perturbed that he had been misled. I emphasised again to the TA that we were researchers not teachers, but this clarification was waved away with the explanation that we must pretend to be teachers to gain the authority we needed. At the time I was quite appalled by this suggestion and determined to set the record straight. But despite our best efforts to patiently and carefully explain our role, we found it meant little to pupils, who continued to refer to us as teachers. In fact, pupils tended to call mentors, classroom assistants and youth workers teachers, leading us to realise that professional distinctions were far more significant to us than to them.

From participant observation to groupwork

A key plank of our research methodology was regular groupwork sessions with cohorts of BSU pupils each term. This required thought and negotiation both in terms of the composition and the activities to be pursued. For the first group, Dave put forward the names of seven boys he felt would benefit from involvement, but was highly sensitive to any accusation that he might be covertly including or excluding particular groups of students. He handed us the list alongside a copy of the register so we could see there was no "funny business going on". He was however, adamant that we should not include girls at that point in time. We had noticed that girls were rarely seen in the unit and had been told they were more likely to be sent to group sessions run by pastoral support. Dave expressed his serious concern about gender relations in the school and the extent to which sexual bullying was rife. Recognising this was a sensitive area we took the list of seven boys and set about brainstorming activities to engage them over the course of the term.

In devising activities we wanted to be inventive, unconventional and imaginative in order to distinguish ourselves from standard classroom learning. We drew on art, drama and photography to come up with a range of ideas that we hoped would appeal to the pupils while also allowing us to collect valuable data. We nervously ran these past Dave and were in equal parts relieved and concerned that our apparently innovative ideas already formed a significant part of the SEAL (Social and Emotional Aspects of Learning) agenda pursued in the unit. We had not wanted to be controversial but were more than a bit dismayed to realise how conventional our ideas were. Dave explained that the group sessions were to be held in a small sports hall at the back of the BSU that was often used as a drama space. It had a high roof and small high windows, meaning we could include ball games in our repertoire of activities. We shifted our attention to planning the introductory session and spent considerable time designing an attractive, accessible leaflet that would clearly explain the research to the pupils.

At the first group session only four of the seven boys were present, two were absent, one had been temporarily excluded and one other arrived very late having been sent home to get his correct uniform. All four were 12 years old and from minority ethnic groups. Lindon was black African, Kai was Vietnamese, while Jamal was African-Caribbean. The latecomer Kari was also African-Caribbean. We sat on chairs in a circle, introduced ourselves and with our first guiding principle in mind earnestly handed round our leaflets in an effort to explain the research and gain explicit consent. But the pupils were bored, impatient and immediately suspicious of us. They seemed confused by our insistence that they had a choice to participate and eyed us mistrustfully. Jamal and Kai swung dangerously far back on their chairs while contorting their necks and Lindon looked as though he had chewed on a wasp. Our lovingly crafted leaflets were barely glanced at before they were chewed, made into paper airplanes, or discarded on the floor by their seats. A direct question about who was interested in taking part was met with shrugs and grunts. We took this to mean yes and continued on with the session feeling distinctly guilty about failure to secure unambiguous consent from them.

However, as we came to realise, this charade of 'gaining informed consent' was pursued more for our benefit than theirs. Quite reasonably, the pupils were not going to commit to something before they knew exactly what it was. Their consent was conditional and given on a minute-by-minute basis. They had no intention of taking part in activities if they did not want to and they were not slow to make this clear. We clung instead to the second of our guiding principles and focused on involving them in setting ground rules and planning sessions. We began by gently encouraging them to think through behaviour that should not be tolerated within the group. As we discovered, constructing guidelines was very far from a novel or liberating experience for them and there was much yawning and rolling of eyes in response. We pushed and coaxed until we had a standard list of forbidden antisocial behaviour, but it felt disingenuous and formulaic. In a later introductory session I went through the whole process not realising there was an almost identical set of guidelines drawn up by a previous class hanging behind me on a clipboard. While often perceived by teachers and researchers as a democratic opportunity, the pupils more often approached guideline setting as a test and resented the pretence.

The guidelines drawn up in that (and other) introductory session included no swearing, no shouting, no aggressive behaviour, no eating and no using phones. But these rules were either too vague or completely unenforceable and we found most were broken even before the first session was out. More to the point, we rapidly discovered the clear need for explicit researcher-imposed rules to prevent dangerous mayhem. As time went on we found ourselves having to ban chair throwing, physical fighting, mother-based insults and, after losing several pupils, the opening of the back door onto the playground. Repeat offenders were sent out of the session, but were given the option of returning the week after. We were relieved to find that while few went quietly almost all came back.

Our effort to engage the pupils in planning the sessions was considerably more successful, but not quite in the way we had anticipated. Participation was often enacted through vetoes of our carefully prepared activity suggestions. If we tried to abide by our third principle of holding our nerve and persevering, we could face disengagement, play fights, mass walkouts and even demands to opt out of the research entirely. By this point the demands of researching the topic area came into sharp focus. Exuberance and high levels of physical energy precluded activities that involved sustained periods of sitting down, particularly for those diagnosed with ADHD. Low literacy levels combined with a general lack of confidence around writing meant that anything that involved marker pens was risky. Even an introductory activity which required pupils to write their names triggered an excruciating display of self-consciousness. These constraints were compounded by an emotional volatility characterising life in the unit more generally. Arguments and laughter were loud and frequent, and one could morph into the other at lightning speed. Play fights often escalated into real fights and it could be difficult to tell the difference or recognise trigger points.

To maintain any semblance of control we needed to keep pupils engaged with the activity at hand. If we lost their attention events could quickly spiral out of control, as we learnt at our cost. For example, in one session we had been trialling the use of a video camera and allowing the pupils to film themselves playing a volleyball-based activity. Tiring of this, one pupil opened the back door and was followed en masse into the playground. An impromptu game of football was started but ended almost immediately when the ball was accidently kicked over a high fence. Oblivious to our pleas to return to the drama studio, Amari (just back from temporary exclusion) began a precarious climb to retrieve the ball. Kari, who was operating the video then turned it on to me to film my horrified reaction. Meanwhile Lindon and Kai began fighting and swearing loudly, drawing the attention of a passing teacher. This incident, unfolding at incredible speed, almost lost us our place within the school. The teacher complained vociferously and our presence had to be robustly defended by Dave Stirling. Impulsive behaviour like this also meant attendance at our sessions was sporadic, with large numbers of pupils receiving a temporary or permanent exclusion.

Finding research activities that pupils could and would take part in was initially difficult. Pupils were very keen to put forward ideas for the things they would like to do during the sessions, but these suggestions were not particularly well tailored towards collecting research data. Card games, volleyball, football and 'wink murder' provided limited opportunities to probe specific issues, meaning we struggled to enact our fourth and final guiding principle of strategically targeting activities towards answering research questions. Instead, though we learnt how to target data collection towards sessions. We sought to creatively weave questions and themes around the kinds of activities pupils enthusiastically nominated (Gillies and Robinson, 2010). We also began to recognise the opportunities that came with the challenges. Underdeveloped reading and writing skills often seemed to be compensated by an exuberant exhibitionism. Most taking part in the groups were performers, expressing themselves through a highly animated kinetic style. Our decision to introduce a video camera was part of an effort to capture and explore this more systematically, although in practice it provoked more acting up and arguments than it was ultimately worth.

Taking our cue from the pupils' love of football we procured large portable goal posts which we assembled before each session. This immediately became the focus for much theatrical play acting. Live commentaries, championship matches and goal celebrations were enacted with great enthusiasm, belying initial passionate rejections of any activities involving 'drama'. We decided to risk building on this by introducing some stealth improvisation techniques. Using the video camera and posing as 'Match of the Day' reporters we conducted interviews, asking questions that were analogous to school life. The idea for this came from discussions with a systemic family therapist who pointed out the parallels. Drawing on his infinitely superior knowledge of football, he helped us come up with a list of model questions which explored among other things 'fouls', 'red card incidents', fitting into the team, working with the manager and advice they might give to younger players coming up behind them[7]. The pupils recognised the analogy and enthusiastically played along.

But despite all our efforts to devise clever and subtle data collection techniques, the most important insights during the project came from simply spending time with the young people. By relaxing, and allowing pupils to set the agenda we learnt far more about their lives than attempting to follow through a methods centred approach. We were also surprised at just how quickly this allowed us to build good relationships. We began to see the best, alongside the worst of their behaviour, as this field diary excerpt describing a volleyball session indicates:

> They behaved really well, didn't shout at each other (very much) when they dropped the ball and were really kind to me when I made some silly moves and dropped the ball. Linden was particularly sweet, reassuring me that it didn't matter. Kai also made a particular effort to pass it to Yvonne because she hadn't had a turn for a while. At one point Yvonne fell over while reaching for the ball. They went into fits of exaggerated laughter and threw themselves against the door on top of each other. It made enough noise to make Sarah [teacher] and Dave look in through the window in the door.

Broadening the focus – Gravensdale School

Having carved out our place in Hailingbrooke and after working with two cohorts of young people across two terms we started to look for an additional base for our research. Again I consulted education professionals and pored over Ofsted reports. Gravensdale seemed like a good choice. It had previously been singled out for poor discipline and had a relatively new head teacher keen to address the issue and amenable to research. After an initial meeting with Kate Blackman, the head of the behaviour support department, she summoned us to meet the head teacher. The cultural difference between the two schools was evident right from the very first visit. Nestled among housing estates, it looked drab and poorly maintained. At Hailingbrooke, once you were let into the locked main entrance there was an expanse of space with a mezzanine level above. You then faced a courtyard filled with pupils coming and going. In contrast, at Gravensdale you stepped straight into a small waiting room. A member of staff would then have to accompany you into the school. From the waiting room you entered a network of corridors, which were often jammed at peak times.

Most noticeable was the absence of anything on the walls. Hailingbrooke was decorated with pupils' art work, photographs and posters promoting events, healthy eating, etc. The corridors at Gravensdale were largely bare, giving it a stark institutional feel. Mike Wickes, the relatively young, white head teacher, seemed supportive and encouraging of the research. He was particularly interested in finding out about the discipline policies at other schools and seemed half frustrated and half relieved that we remained firm in concealing the real identity of Hailingbrooke. Feeling that the meeting was going well I began talking about our experimental work with video cameras and how well received it was by the pupils. At this point I watched the colour drain from the head teacher's face. He and Kate, the behaviour support manager, exchanged a frozen stare until Kate gently explained how they had recently had to dismiss a classroom assistant caught surreptitiously filming for a television station exposé on poor classroom discipline. "No cameras then", I conceded. They nodded their heads firmly.

Given the pressures the school was under I was somewhat surprised that we were allowed into Gravensdale in the first place. The enthusiastic support of Kate was crucial, but we received outright hostility from some other members of staff including a teaching assistant who coldly ignored us, and an educational psychologist who was openly scathing about the aims of our research. Kate seemed oblivious to this opposition and set about drawing up a list of pupils for us to work with. Her detailed description of the behaviour support unit suggested that it operated various interventions including groups targeted at particular pupils (problem girls, those with anger issues, bullies, etc), a containment unit where pupils were removed entirely from the mainstream classroom for short periods and an off-site provision where those whose behaviour remained problematic were sent. Unlike Hailingbrooke, most pupils spent only part of their school day in the unit, usually attending their various groups. They also appeared to deal with a far larger number of pupils. My first meeting with Kate left me with a sense that the unit was managed with careful efficiency, as my field notes document:

Kate's office is quiet, long and bare and very cold. I got the impression she didn't spend much time there. She explained how the behaviour support system operated at Gravensdale. She is obviously very committed and keen to pursue good practice, but it's quite an elaborate and extensive system and she spoke at quite a speed. From what I can gather the unit is a "sin bin" (her words) where pupils are sent if their behaviour is bad. They would spend up to two days before being sent off-site to a kind of pre- PRU [Pupil Referral Units] provision. Most go back into the classroom. Apparently the children don't like being sent off-site even though they do some good work. It's seen as being a bit scary and a punishment... Kate frequently referred to written documents describing the system (she photocopied them for us). I got the sense that things are quite regimented and very well organised. The groups are age based. Maturity was a theme that Kate drew on often when discussing the pupils. She also talked about the 'cool group', anger management and the 'nerds' (anti-bullying).

As this excerpt demonstrates, Kate articulated a curious mixture of procedural regulation and unguarded musing. At a broad level she was very informal with a dry sense of humour and she was apparently much loved by the pupils attached to the unit. She had clearly built very close relationships with the young people she nominated to work with us, and spoke about them with great optimism and fondness. But we could not help but notice she had allocated us a predominantly white group in a context where most of the pupils consigned to the 'sin bin' were minority ethnic. Given the tenuous nature of our place in the school, I decided not to probe about the basis on which pupils had been selected, but instead resolved to ask for a more ethnically diverse group for the following term. In all, Kate had listed 10 young people and this group did at least contain equal numbers of girls. The list was largely assembled from attendees of the unit's various groupwork sessions, although most had spent time in the 'sin bin' and a large number had received fixed term exclusions.

Ten was an unwieldy number but we deduced from our previous experience that we would end up with far fewer participants than we started out with. In fact, six young people attended our first group session, located in the school dance studio. Most were 13 years old, although some had just turned 14. The boys, Luke, Alfie and Tom, did most of the talking while the girls, Amy, Charmaine and Sancha, sat rigidly in their chairs and barely spoke. It was a deeply uncomfortable hour. Luke quickly assumed a role as spokesman for the group and responded to our attempts to negotiate informed consent with mock sincerity. He was articulate, confident and brutally sarcastic, eliciting knowing sniggers and guffaws from the others. We hung in there, answered as many faintly ridiculous questions as we could ("Can we play hide and seek Miss?") and laughed along. By the end we seemed to have won Luke over, and by default, the rest of the group who shrugged and nodded when we asked if we would see them the week after.

While I grew to like Luke, his barbed humour could be cruel. Sessions often descended into verbal sparring among the boys. Worse still the boys regularly ganged up together to mock the girls, who remained largely silent during any group activities. When we spoke to the girls alone they complained of feeling intimidated and threatened by the boys. We ended up running parallel groups and pursuing more structured activities with the boys (based around football, volleyball and Jenga) and more talk-based activities with the girls. The gender dynamic only grew worse when the other young people joined the group. Bond (also 13) adopted a similar style to Luke, but embroidered it with a heavy dose of sexualisation. Lots of jokes went completely over our heads or were justified loudly with faux innocence. Keeping the girls separate from the boys made the sessions manageable but the girls could never properly relax, especially since the boys repeatedly tried to ambush their space. It was a disturbing insight into gender relations in the school and just the tip of the iceberg, as I outline in Chapters 4 and 5.

Unfortunately, Kate Blackman left the school the term after we began our research. She was replaced by Anita Jones, who was distinctly less enthusiastic about our presence. Anita was very polite but clearly had little time for us or any demands we might make on her tight schedule. Fortunately, one of the mentors (Tony) suggested we work with one of his regular groups, comprising six African-Caribbean boys and one white girl (all of them 15 years old). We were initially apprehensive about the unbalanced gender mix, but Tony reassured us that they were a tight knit group of friends and curiosity and desperation got the better of us. The first session we held with this group was unexpectedly successful. Four of the boys (Mica, Shane, Lloyd and Marcus) and the girl (Chireal) attended and expressed real enthusiasm about taking part in the research. It became clear that all had bitter resentments to articulate about the school and in particular the racism they felt victims of. Chireal was as vocal as the boys in describing injustices and claimed she was picked on simply for associating with black boys. All of the pupils were highly articulate and recounted deeply disturbing accounts of discrimination and harassment. It was very noticeable that the two black mentors, present at this introductory session, nodded in recognition throughout.

By this stage a somewhat perturbing picture of Gravensdale was beginning to emerge, suggesting quite overt racist practices were embedded within the culture of the institution. As I elaborate further in Chapter 5, racial and or ethnic taunting among pupils in the playground was shockingly rife. The 'N word' was used regularly by white pupils and a variety of creative names were used to describe all kinds of ethnic groups. Right from our first group sessions at the school we had been taken aback by how quickly discussions could descend into an ugly denouncement of 'immigrants' (sometimes by pupils who were themselves second generation immigrants). Our unease was compounded when we began to interview the parents of the second group and a wider range of school staff. There was much anger expressed about unchallenged and uninvestigated racism in the school. On discovering that Gravensdale was being monitored because it had previously excluded large numbers of African-Caribbean pupils I began to feel ethically conflicted. Did we have a responsibility to report what we were observing and what was being recounted to us? If so, to whom? I decided we should at least attempt to feed some of our concerns back to the head teacher.

I was under no illusion about the sensitivity of this conversation. I thought very carefully about how to frame it and decided to raise it at the end of a more general verbal progress report on the research. But as I walked into the head's office that morning I could tell that word of our concerns had already reached him. Mr Wickes and the new behaviour support manager, Anita, sat with their arms folded and it became obvious that they were expecting criticism. I began with an attempt to emphasise the positive aspects of the school, but this was angrily dismissed by Anita as something they already knew. In fact, Anita was strikingly provocative throughout, expressing scepticism about the very existence of special educational needs, claiming that in 98% of cases the mothers were to blame for misbehaviour, and calling the young people we worked with "idiots" and "time wasters". I took a deep breath and launched into a description of what we had observed about race relations in the school. This entry from my fieldwork diary summed up their response:

> I don't really know what I expected but I was a shocked at
> how they dealt with it. The head said he had investigated

lots of complaints about racism but they were all rubbish. He went on to list the numbers of ethnic minority staff he had. When I told them about our observations that racial abuse was widespread and generally tolerated among the pupils Anita butted in and said it was because it was such a multicultural area. When I said we hadn't seen anything similar in the other school, she said the borough was a very specific case (It really isn't). She said they call each other 'pakis' and 'niggers' in a friendly way.

That meeting took place after the end of the summer term, and in a context where the school had become a virtual building site. Much of it was boarded up and there was loud drilling and hammering throughout. It was to become unrecognisable, with an impressive modernist façade and a new reception area. More significantly, there was to be a restructuring of the behaviour support department to incorporate a fully self-contained unit, allowing 'temporary' segregation of difficult pupils. Numerous staff left or were made redundant during this period, including the two mentors we had worked closely with. Mr Wickes and Anita Jones remained.

Meedham Girls

Our troubling experience at Gravensdale and lack of confidence in our ability to continue researching there led to a search for another school. A chance meeting I had with a youth worker resulted in an introduction to a school counsellor at Meedham Girls. On the back of this we were invited to Meedham's behaviour support unit to pitch our research. The school was spread over two sites a short distance apart and located in a deprived catchment area. The site housing the BSU was set back among relatively quiet residential streets. The building was very old and poorly maintained. It was plastered with posters imploring pupils to reflect on their feelings, listen, recognise how their words might hurt others, eat healthily and above all 'stay calm'. We were accompanied through a maze of gloomy corridors out into a playground and into a large breeze block building. Inside it was comparatively bright, modern and comfortable. We sat drinking tea on big, soft chairs with the head of the unit, Jocelyn Reed, and the two BSU mentors (Jennifer and Zena) and Rita the classroom assistant. All were very enthusiastic about the research and keen for us to include the school in the study, so we arranged to conduct our first session soon after.

Again we were told that pupils were referred to the unit for six weeks at a time, although the staff did concede it was more often a bit longer. In practice, most spent about a term there before either being reintegrated back into the mainstream school or sent out to an off-site provision. Permanent exclusion was very rare. As in the other schools, a majority of the pupils referred to the units were minority ethnic, with only one white girl attending during the period of our research. At the end of each term there were 'graduation' parties for girls who had experienced successful 'placements'. This reflected the distinctly different atmosphere and routine at Meedham compared to the other co-ed schools. There were cushions and (unlit) scented candles, and activities that often involved knitting or embroidery. Jocelyn was a warm, charismatic black woman who was very popular with the pupils. She prided herself on her authoritative plain speaking and sometimes broke into patois as a way of keeping order. Her background was youth work rather than education but she had a strong pedagogic orientation and was adept at engaging and enthusing the pupils in educationally focused projects.

Rita, the classroom assistant had a very different style and she struggled to gain the respect and sometimes even the attention of the pupils. She was a middle-aged white women who had previously worked in special needs support. She was extremely boundaried in her work and invested in enforcing rules, procedures and protocol. She clearly found her job very stressful and these structures appeared to give her some sense of control and worth, although this rigidity did not particularly endear her to the unit pupils or staff. But Rita's stickler approach did seem to reflect a risk-averse, bureaucratic culture operating within the mainstream school. In preparation for each of our visits to the school a member of staff from the BSU was required to submit a form in advance to reception and we would then need to wait and be personally escorted by said staff member. On the occasions that the form was not submitted on time the receptionist became irascible, both with us and the staff.

The heightened sense of risk embodied within the school culture became very obvious when I arrived to conduct our first group session. Meedham was the only school to have asked explicitly to see our Criminal Records Bureau (CRB) check. The other two schools both asked if we had CRB checks, but no one actually bothered to inspect them. At Meedham we had been required to submit them in advance by Rita, which we willingly did. However, as my field notes demonstrate, this was the focus of a small drama when it became apparent there was a mistake on one of them. Yvonne had arrived earlier than I, intending to start some participatory observation. When I arrived an hour or so later I was escorted over by a tight-lipped Rita.

> On the way over to the centre she said there was a problem, but wouldn't be drawn on what it was. She said Yvonne would explain it to me. She was quite cryptic but with hindsight I think she was quite enjoying what she seemed to view as our embarrassment. As we went through the playground a girl ran past us. Rita called her back, but she kept running. Rita shouted louder saying she was going the wrong way. The girl huffed and puffed and swore under her breath ("Fucking …"), and I realised she was [going to be] one of our group members. When I got to the unit Rita took me and Yvonne into a small side room and left us there. It was as though Yvonne needed to confess something shameful. Yvonne explained that there was box on her CRB that was filled in 'not requested' rather than 'none recorded' (as it was on mine). Everything else on the form was fine. Rita had scrutinised the checks and discovered this herself. Yvonne had been taken to the deputy head who had hugely overreacted and told her she would have to be escorted off the premises. Apparently Yvonne was told that it would be a problem if she even brushed against a child on the way out because there could be an accusation. Rita had said this would not be necessary, as she would accompany her [back to the unit]. The upshot was that we would have to conduct the session with staff present.

While this was all unfolding, the four pupils assigned to our group (aged between 13 and 14) sat patiently waiting for us. I wondered what they made of Yvonne being ushered into a separate room, unable even to say hello. After some careful negotiation with Rita it was agreed that we would be able to conduct the session with her present, on the grounds that my CRB check was valid and I would take responsibility for Yvonne. We introduced ourselves to the girls (Chanelle, Charpaine, Natasha and Choima) with Rita sitting alongside us watching protectively. Despite the difficult beginning, the introductory session was successful in a way we had not previously experienced in the other schools. The girls listened carefully to what we had to say and even looked (albeit briefly) at our leaflets. Their consent was enthusiastically and unequivocally given and they were clearly delighted at the thought of taking part. During this discussion it emerged that all four of the girls had a strong interest in acting and performing. There were particularly animated discussions about the TV singing competition 'The X Factor', which was being screened at the time. This gave us plenty of scope to design activities drawing on improvisational drama techniques. We also adapted the 'Match of the Day' activity we used to great effect at Hailingbrooke, restructuring it around the format of the 'X Factor' and employing questions such as, 'What are your ambitions for the future?' and 'What's it like making it to boot camp?'.

Our sessions were a wildly popular and the numbers of girls turning up each week began to expand. Towards the end of term we ran a session that included almost all the girls in the unit. Particularly striking was the eagerness of the girls to discuss their interpretation of what needed to change in the school. During a brainstorming session on the words 'school' and 'teacher' they commandeered the session to list what was wrong with the school and how it could be improved. The suggestions were so articulate and well thought out that I asked whether they had done the exercise before. They assured us that they had not. Their main gripes centred on an overreliance on supply teachers, the bad design of the building and rude, disrespectful school staff. They talked about how depressed and undervalued the gloomy, badly maintained structure made them feel and described incidents where they had been misunderstood and maligned by teachers. There were some strong characters in the group with forceful opinions but altercations were rare and quickly resolved (in the sessions at least). Fourteen-year-old Chanelle was sharp tongued and adept at biting sarcasm, but used this to build alliances within the group, directing her scorn at those outside the unit. Choima (also 14) was something of a loner and often explicitly positioned herself differently from the others, but her eccentricity and dry humour was unintentionally endearing and she appeared to be generally very well liked. Although comedy was very much to the fore there was noticeably none of the weaponised humour and verbal grandstanding displayed by the other (male) groups.

Acting into context?

By the end of the first term at Meedham we had spent the best part of six terms at Hailingbrooke and two at Gravensdale. While we had interviewed mainstream teachers at all three of the schools and observed the reintegration of particular pupils back into mainstream lessons, we were left wondering what exactly constituted the ideal learner that young people were expected to approximate. Observations of classrooms often revealed the same kind of low-level disruption and rowdy behaviour we had become accustomed to in the BSUs. The the volatility and non-compliance that characterised Hailingbrooke BSU definitely set it apart from the mainstream school, but individual pupils within the unit could, and often did, behave in compliant, self-controlled ways. In fact, we had noted that many of the BSU lessons conducted by Dave Stirling rivalled any mainstream classroom for well-disciplined, enthusiastic participation. Following a suggestion made by our advisory group we decided to organise focus group interviews with 'well behaved' pupils, sampled on the recommendations of teachers.

Teachers generally seemed pleased to have the opportunity to pick their favourites and confidently predicted their opinions. At Hailingbrooke we asked a year head (Mr Phillips) to invite a group of generally well behaved mainstream pupils to share their experiences. He chose an ethnically mixed set of four girls and two boys, all of whom were achieving well academically. As my field notes document, Mr Phillips clearly expected them to echo his own sentiments about the pernicious influence of the ill-disciplined:

> He came back with six pupils and introduced me to them in the lobby. He said I was from South Bank University and that I was doing research on the importance of discipline in schools. He said I wanted to speak to the best-behaved pupils in the school and joked, "You were the best I could do". The pupils smiled and rolled their eyes. He then said, "You need to tell her what you have to put up with and how it affects you".

But in his absence the conversation was considerably more nuanced and multifaceted. All drew on examples of having been in trouble themselves at various points at the school, and while bad behaviour from other pupils was identified as annoying, it was also acknowledged as fun in some situations:

> "Sometimes when there's a cover teacher and everyone's mucking about; they might be throwing stuff like paper balls or pencil and papers and if everyone gets involved then everyone has fun."

The consensus was that what set them apart from those in the BSU was academic ability and their capacity to gauge what they could get away with. It was noticeable that they ate sweets throughout the focus session and swore regularly, judging correctly again that they would not get into trouble for it. Their knowledge of the BSU was sketchy and while they knew where the building was they had little sense of what it was like inside. However, they expressed scepticism about its function in addressing disruptive behaviour:

> "If you get sent three times or twice or something then it's long-term, so you're there for the rest of the year and it's different lessons and different teachers and the teachers aren't that good in inclusion. There are always cover teachers, so you don't really learn anything ... The kids who are coming out of inclusion, when they come back out they are kinda like behind, so they kinda just mess about more because they are behind everyone else, so they don't really concentrate and they kind of like ... they just come out worse really."

As the use of 'you' in the beginning of this quote suggests, there was little sense that those sent to 'inclusion' were essentially different, although they were seen as emerging with a distinct disadvantage.

Similar sentiments were expressed in the focus group we conducted at Gravensdale. Anita Jones had been vociferous about the disgust she predicted her chosen pupils would express towards the 'bad' ones, as I documented in my field notes:

> When I brought up the issue of peers, Anita cut me off and said, "I'll tell you what the good students think about the bad ones, they think annoying idiots and they just want rid of them". She talked quite enthusiastically about this and seemed to be very confident about knowing what students thought. She kept using the terms good and bad.

We arrived at Gravensdale after a gap of several months and were accompanied to meet the pupils by a school receptionist. We were taken to a tiny room not much bigger than a cupboard buried in the bowels of the institution, which once had been used as the medical room. It was particularly grim with very little light and old bandages strewn everywhere. The four chosen pupils sat on rickety chairs and looked nervous. There were two boys and two girls from year nine. All were white. Although they were clearly tense and edgy it did not take long for their bitter resentments about the school to emerge.

They raged about the petty and inconsistent rules and appeared to feel considerably less secure than those from Hailingbrooke that they would not end up in inclusion themselves. They were unequivocal that teachers were to blame for bad behaviour and each recounted stories of personal victimisation. While there was some contempt reserved for pupils acting up to promote a 'bad boy' reputation, there was real sympathy expressed towards those who had fallen foul of the rules.

> Nicola: But sometimes people get really annoyed with the teachers because they do say things that REALLY annoy them, like there was like a situation before with how people used to get certain types of jewellery taken off of them because apparently they were GANG RELATED when they wasn't ... people found it kinda horrible ... classed it as racism. You know Rosary Beads? They used to take 'em off of people, saying they were gang related! And then ... people say..., "You don't take off the headscarves off of Muslims and say they are gang related because it's not only English people and Christians and stuff that are involved in things like that..." You have to wear plain, black shoes ... fair enough and that. They take it a bit far really with everything in the school. "You are NOT allowed to wear this, you are NOT allowed to wear that, you are NOT allowed to do this and you are NOT allowed to do that!"

> Donna: And at school it's just the extent of the rules and how far they go... They think they are helping but they are just making children more like [utters frustration–aggression grunt].

> Val: What do you mean by that? Sorry?!

> Donna: Like, "Urgh what is the point of being in this school?" People don't want to be in the school because of the rules!

We were unsurprised to see the issue of race emerging once again in Gravensdale. It was raised again later on in the session by one of the boys who felt he had fallen victim to racist bullying from a black girl. He described his genuine bemusement when he got into trouble for racially abusing her. This sense of confusion about what was and what was not acceptable was shared among the group. One of the biggest resentments related to an edict that had recently been issued about the size of bags that could be carried in school (all had to conform to the exact size of regulation backpacks). The pupils were angry and perplexed by the apparent pointlessness of this as stipulation, but were also unsure how rigorously this would be implemented. There was real uncertainty about the exact nature of the rules, compounded by their shifting nature and the inconsistency of their enforcement.

> David: But if you think about it like sometimes the teachers take it too seriously ... if you swear ... "Oh you can never come back to school!"

> Val: So when does that happen then; does that mean that it's about luck then? You swore and you got detention but...?

> Donna: It's not exactly luck. That was quite a while back. As long as I've been in school ... the worse ... how hard the discipline has been taken like ... if you don't have your shirt tucked in or you have your tie wrong then you get your name in a notebook and if you get your name in a notebook three times then straight away you get an hour's detention.

> Mark: It depends what mood the teacher is in as well.

> David: Yeah if he's had like a class that's been bad he'll write your name down straight away but sometimes he will let you off with a warning but it mostly depends on what teacher it is...

> Nicola: It depends what teacher it is and if it's a strict teacher you can't get away with it and if it's a laid-back teacher then you're alright...

The focus group we conducted at Meedham was different in that the four 14-year-old black girls who participated did very clearly distinguish themselves from the 'bad types', although they too had been in trouble for talking in lessons and one had even experienced a temporary exclusion.

> "Miss, can I say something? We're talking but we're not BAD ... we would do well in our work but we're NOT

the type of students that will swear at teachers and behave
... we're not that type ... we're just the type that we're good
but what ... we're trying to say is ... good but we're not the
quiet people in class that just sit there and put our hands
on our lips and just do everything we're told. We do what
we're told but then we also ... there are limits that we pass,
we don't go over that extreme so basically that's what we're
saying and that's why Miss Jennings chose us because we're
on BOTH sides; we know how it is to be extremely good
and how it will be to be in trouble."

The deputy head teacher had chosen the girls and the session was
conducted in the BSU building (while the BSU girls were off on a trip
somewhere). Ironically perhaps, they were a difficult group to manage
as my field notes from the session demonstrate:

> Although they started off okay they weren't particularly
> well behaved and were quite rowdy, loud and rambling.
> There was a lot of whispering, mucking about, posturing
> and shared secret jokes. They made quite a lot of strong
> statements but I wasn't very sure how seriously they
> were taking things (and sometimes I suspected they were
> taking the piss). They often seemed to make statements
> off the top of their heads (they were making a lot of
> contradictory statements e.g. parents are to blame or not
> to blame). Interestingly, I found them harder to deal with
> than the 'challenging pupils' we'd been given to work with
> previously. On reflection this is because I was expecting
> something very different and we hadn't put the effort into
> building trust in the same way. They were quite mistrustful
> of us and obviously didn't believe we would not be reporting
> back to teachers. Miss Jennings [the deputy head] had told
> them not to mention any teachers' names (although they
> did). Apparently she had also said we would be asking about
> their boyfriends! Once we turned the tape off they were
> anxious to tell us how much they disliked Miss Jennings.

The focus groups were certainly enlightening but they did not confirm
our expectations that BSU pupils were 'othered' by their mainstream
peers. The physical isolation of the units and the contempt referred
pupils were held in by mainstream teachers had led us to assume
there would be a level of scapegoating and demonising of challenging

pupils by their classmates. Instead, we found a pervasive sense of shared vulnerability. Mainstream pupils seemed to regard themselves as being always just a drop in academic performance and three minor infringements away from referral. This begs the question of who exactly does end up in 'inclusion' and why.

Notes

[1] See for example, Duncan Gardham (2005) 'Feral street gang who killed for kicks', *The Telegraph*, http://www.telegraph.co.uk/news/uknews/1505524/Feral-street-gang-who-killed-for-kicks.html

[2] Tony Blair's Respect speech, 10 January, 2006, http://news.bbc.co.uk/1/hi/uk_politics/4600156.stm

[3] See Richard Alleyne (2006) 'Plagued by teenagers? You'll like the sound of this', *The Telegraph*, http://www.telegraph.co.uk/news/uknews/1510610/Plagued-by-teenagers-Youll-like-the-sound-of-this.html

[4] See for example, Mark Honigsbaum (2005) 'Concern over rise of happy slapping craze', *The Guardian*, http://www.theguardian.com/uk/2005/apr/26/ukcrime.mobilephones

[5] See for example, Ben Fenton (2006) 'Daily Telegraph campaign to halt the death of childhood', *The Telegraph*, http://www.telegraph.co.uk/news/yourview/1528718/Daily-Telegraph-campaign-to-halt-death-of-childhood.html

[6] The project, Disruptive Behaviour in the Classroom: Exploring the Social Subjectivity of Disaffection, was funded by the Economic and Social Research Council under grant number RES-061-23-0073.

[7] Thanks to Steve Benson.

THREE

Contextualising challenging behaviour

In this chapter I take a closer look at the practices and relationships constituting the behaviour support units (BSUs) and attempt to illuminate the workings of a place that appeared for the most part to remain out of sight and out of mind to those in the mainstream schools. I also explore the experiences of the young people who had been referred to a BSU and examine how they became constructed as 'unincludable' within a standard classroom. A key objective of this broader contextualisation is to move beyond the narrow realm of personal pathology to show how therapeutically orientated pedagogy can distort and produce particular classroom behaviours. Detailing the accounts, interpretations and histories of pupils confined to the BSUs foregrounds the relational dynamics shaping and informing the acting out of emotions, and highlights the impoverished conception of the 'social' characterising initiatives that claim to build social skill through reshaping personal capabilities.

Separate and different

While BSUs occupy highly visible territory within the schools, their routines, conventions and everyday dramas are played out well away from the mainstream gaze. While everyone in the school knows where they are situated, few are aware of what actually goes on inside them. Teachers rarely found cause to visit the units and readily drew on disparaging nicknames ('zoo', 'sin bin') to describe them. At Hailingbrooke, Dave Stirling successfully lobbied for timetabled slots on core curriculum subjects, insisting that mainstream teachers came into the units to deliver them. This was much resented and resisted by permanent staff members, who engineered for supply teachers to fulfil this role. This meant there was a high turnover of teachers in the units and little opportunity to build relationships. While some of the supply teachers were creative and engaging, most relied on worksheets and resignedly allowed chaos to reign.

Maths sessions on Thursday mornings were a particularly appalling spectacle characterised by despair and discomfort all round. The white, middle-aged supply teacher would arrive, sweating and puce, hand out the worksheets and then feebly attempt to police the uproar that ensued. The pupils reacted with frustration, anger and contempt, exclaiming loudly that they could not and would not do the sums. On more than one occasion the teacher allowed them to draw pictures instead. Dave was perturbed and embarrassed by the situation and was keen to assure us the issue of poor quality maths teaching was being addressed. But his dogged determination to push the needs of BSU pupils onto the agenda won him few friends in the mainstream school and highlighted the unit's virtual isolation in the institution.

This isolation had some upsides in that BSU managers (particularly at Hailingbrooke and Meedham) were accorded significant autonomy in the day-to-day running of the units, but this was more than offset by a general lack of support from and dialogue with the mainstream school. Even discussions around referrals, reintegration and permanent exclusions were relatively sparse, and often seemed to involve senior management informing the BSU heads of a decision rather than consulting with them. There was more integration at Gravensdale partly because there was less explicit segregation, but the marginalisation in terms of resources and support was similar.

Behaviour support was a contentious subject among school staff across the institutions, with many feeling that bad behaviour was pandered to in the units and that too many school resources were given over to lost causes. Yet the BSUs clearly served many important functions for teachers, not least in enabling the physical removal of challenging pupils. The symbolic containment of 'bad behaviour' to a particular part of the school and the construction of particular pupils as 'at risk' also facilitated a professionalised narrative in which mainstream pupils must first be 'ready to learn', or have developed 'learning power' (Ecclestone and Hayes, 2009). Internal exclusion could then be framed as a caring act instigated to better meet particular 'difficult' children's needs (Gillies and Robinson, 2013).

Still, tension around the purpose and justification of the BSUs bubbled under the surface and erupted with some force during our time at Hailingbrooke. Despite improving results and a good Ofsted report the school had been named and shamed as part of the then government's 'National Challenge' scheme. Hailingbrooke was publicly issued with three years' notice to improve GCSE results or face closure. We were not party to any of the internal meetings or discussions but by all accounts frustrations were vented and accusations flew with abandon. Some of the more powerful senior staff members argued for a new commitment to discipline claiming that the BSU was an unnecessary indulgence. A decision was made to immediately remove the 25 long-term BSU attendees, some of whom had never experienced a standard secondary classroom, and place them in mainstream lessons. The speed at which this was enacted allowed for no time to prepare the pupils, inform parents or even ourselves and so we arrived in the morning to discover an empty BSU. Dave Stirling was weary but unruffled. 'Give it a week', he said and he was absolutely right. All the BSU pupils were returned by the following week after large numbers of mainstream teachers threatened to walk out.

This incident very effectively highlights the binary terms of debate framing understandings of challenging behaviour within the schools. Strategies were conceived in terms of responsibilising measures (often putative) designed to build 'character', or were articulated through a more child-centred, therapeutic-based approach. While the latter dominated in the BSUs, many mainstream teachers emphasised the importance of helping pupils to build a framework of self-discipline. The short-term containment rooms operated by each school to deal with one-off misdeeds enforced strict obedience. Pupils sat in silent rows completing set work, usually rejoining their class after an hour or two. Experiments were also undertaken with military style discipline in the mainstream co-ed classrooms. Periodic 'zero tolerance' regimes were enforced, swelling the ranks of the BSUs, and in Hailingbrooke mainstream pupils were for a time expected to stand up each time a teacher entered the room.

The BSU managers and staff across the institutions were broadly scathing of such approaches and relied instead on a curriculum explicitly structured around SEAL (Social and Emotional Aspects of Learning), which they broadly welcomed as validating a more therapeutic approach. Concepts of social competency and emotional literacy were enthusiastically promoted as a more enlightened and effective response to problematic behaviour in the classroom. The specific activities relied on heavily individualised conceptions of self and other, pursued through a dedicated focus on 'social skills' and 'empathy' as core learning objectives. 'Circle time' was one of the most common activities, with pupils assembled in small groups to discuss and share their feelings. In this context, speaking thoughts out loud is virtually compulsory, opening up the interiority of pupils' lives to public scrutiny (Ecclestone and Hayes, 2009). Silence was viewed as problematic in itself and targeted as skill deficit or special need. As Kate Blackman, BSU manager at Gravensdale articulated, "It's the quiet ones that you have to watch out for".

Ostensibly, circle time was practised with the aim of building self-esteem, fostering empathy and listening skills. In practice, these group activities operated within considerably more normative boundaries, through the routine censoring of thoughts and feelings considered to be inappropriate. This often made for highly moralised encounters with only certain forms of emotional expression encouraged. The content of circle time was monitored carefully by the teachers. If boundaries were breached (as they frequently were) an opportunity was taken to expose the inappropriateness of a feeling or thought and an effort was made to inculcate a more suitable response.

Observations of circle time in the units revealed how skilled and practised staff members had become at policing them as group activities. Sometimes pupils expressed thoughts or shared experiences that went well beyond the SEAL preoccupation with bullying or arguing with friends. Discussions that bypassed requisite personal reflection to touch on accounts of crime, family troubles or the challenges of poverty were quickly closed down or diverted. While teachers well recognised the significance of these wider issues, they had no capacity to meaningfully address them, in circle time or beyond. Wayne, a relatively new learning mentor at Gravensdale BSU, described how the limitations of his role were quickly dawning on him in relation to a boy referred for aggressive behaviour.

> "You have to be honest, as much as you probably don't want to, you have to be honest and say, 'This is out of my remit', you know, or, there's one, I've got a mentee at the moment, and he's been here since year seven, and he came. He suffered three deaths in the space of a year, a year and a half, when he was in year seven, year six/year seven, and he hasn't had bereavement counselling, he watches reruns of the funeral on video… So he really holds on to the death. He really holds on to it. And he needs bereavement counselling, or he needed it two years ago. He's in year 10 now. To be honest with you, there's nothing I can do, as a mentor. He's just the way he is. Everyone's accepted it, and I think they're just letting him see his time out. 'Oh well, he's like that. He's got another year and then he's gone'."

If such pupils began to 'overshare' in circle time their presence could become untenable, as Kate Blackman described:

"You might realise, very quickly, that, 'This is not the appropriate support for you'.... and that's happened before, where, you know, some girl is talking so inappropriately about stuff, that, 'This is not the right place for you to be talking about, you know, sharing your, your home life here'."

More commonly this 'oversharing' drew on alternative moral frameworks, sometimes presenting teachers with challenging dilemmas. Seemingly intrinsic 'rights' and 'wrongs' could be flipped, leaving teachers flailing to uphold core principles, particularly when emotional responses were tied to powerful narratives of risk or justice. For example, teachers struggled to defend the moral absolute that carrying a weapon was always wrong in a context of the high level of threat faced by many young people in the local area. Some teachers focused on the broader senselessness of youth violence, bypassing pupils' very real anxieties altogether. Others emphasised the serious consequences of getting caught. Few were prepared to allow the frank discussion the groups sometimes attempted to engineer. But beyond these moments of resistance, pupils become surprisingly literate in the language of emotional competence, diagnosing their feelings and sanctioning others. This performativity bore little resemblance to everyday relations outside of this artificial arena, which remained spontaneous, emotionally volatile and largely unreflexive. In fact, circle time was described quite uncritically by one pupil as 'mind games'.

Alongside regular circle time activities pupils worked on self-reflexive projects, celebrating sanctioned values and identities, and in two of the schools, drawing self-portraits. Regular 'anger management' sessions also ran in all three schools, delivered by staff that had undergone specific training. There was a certain irony to this given that so few of these staff members could be said to be good role models for SEAL principles. Schools are, perhaps inevitably, highly emotional places. The disconnect between policy rhetoric emphasising stress reduction and calm self-reflection, and the fraught and emotionally demanding environment of daily school life was at times striking. Against the backdrop of institutionally governed ideals of 'emotional skill', unregulated and uncontainable feelings ran high among pupils, parents and staff.

From early on in the project we encountered staff members breaking down in tears, making rude personal remarks about particular colleagues or pupils, and even levelling serous allegations about conduct within the school. As was outlined in the previous chapter the different pressures, allegiances and personal investments could set mainstream and specialist behaviour staff against each other, resulting in acrimony and feuds. And aside from institutional politics, mainstream school staff could feel overwhelmed by frustration, anger and irritation when engaging with persistent misbehaviour, often in the context of a strong commitment to teaching and learning. Many felt strongly that disruptive pupils did not belong in a mainstream classroom and that it was in no one's interest to persevere in trying to assimilate them.

It was not unusual for teachers to lose their temper, use bad language, and make provocative comments or aggressive threats towards pupils. Several teachers in our research admitted feeling, at times, driven to near violence. Indeed, in Meedham, a male teacher was dismissed for a violent attack on one of the girls involved in our research. After an altercation she was slammed against a wall and partially strangled. Perturbingly, this was not, as far as we could ascertain, reported to the police. While this was an extreme incident it highlights just how far the schools stood from the calm, reflexive, emotionally flat ideal SEAL embodies. At Hailingbrooke, Dave Stirling was well known for shouting and for what often appeared to be a highly strategic and somewhat theatrical loss of temper to rein in chaotic acting out or to break up a fight. Yet he frequently delivered the anger management classes, much to the amusement of the pupils. We also once observed the complete meltdown of an anger management session when the mentor co-delivering it lost his temper and stormed out.

Pointing this out is not to brand anger management training as worthless or even to suggest it is directed at the wrong side of the desk. Many young people did find the methods taught useful. Counting to 10 (a standard technique) became something of a functional trope within the units. Sometimes pupils would do it out loud to signal their mounting irritation over something. However, as I discuss in Chapter 4, the expression of anger is often contingent and is always deeply socially embedded, limiting the effectiveness of learned techniques.

Personalising inclusion: vulnerability and resilience

Having described some of the routine activities pursued within the units I want to shift the focus to the characteristics of the young people attending them, and to give some sense of their lives and the particular challenges they faced. All three schools were based in deprived catchment areas and the effect of poverty and its attendant problems was very evident day to day. Most of the BSU pupils came from low income families who were struggling to make ends meet. In some cases it was possible to directly link experiences of deprivation to their BSU referral, though the personalisation of 'inclusion' very effectively masked this connection.

For example, 13-year-old Jake ended up in the Hailingbrooke BSU after, in his words, "throwing wobblers and running away from teachers". He was white (of Eastern European heritage), slightly overweight and his clothes were tattered, worn and sometimes a bit dirty. His mother, a lone parent, struggled to keep him in a school uniform and he often wore tracksuit bottoms and tee shirts instead. In the first session he attended I was struck by how subdued and deeply unhappy he appeared to be. He was sullen and abstracted, wandering off during a group activity to play with some drums that were being stored in the corner of the drama studio. I followed him and tried to strike up a conversation but he affected not to hear me.

Jake really troubled me before I got to know him. His face was grey and etched with anxiety in those early days, but over the course of the term he seemed to become much happier. From what I could gather he had gained a new stepfather, whom he seemed to revere. Things clearly improved financially for him and he began to regale the group with stories about his stepdad's attributes (he owned a shop and was an accomplished wrestler). While he maintained a close relationship with his biological father, visiting him weekly, Jake enthusiastically and somewhat romantically embraced a new step-family of brothers and sisters. They lived in Bedfordshire, a place Jake experienced as a bucolic paradise in comparison to his own neighbourhood, which he described as violent, noisy and full of druggies and rubbish. He professed to hate his housing estate so much that he refused to draw it during a 'map your neighbourhood' activity (he drew a dragon made up of lots of joined up dots instead). He harboured a hope that he would eventually move to Bedfordshire with his mum.

Jake had previously been excluded from the first primary school he attended. He described being relentlessly bullied by two boys in particular, although from his account it seemed he had become targeted more generally in the playground because poverty marked him out as being different.

> "One day I come in, because, like, my clothes are dirty, I come in in stripey dungarees, like and I was in year one, and one of them was laughing. There was this train thing, and he climbed to the top, and I kicked him off. And after that he stopped bullying me. And another one say, 'Just because you beat up one of my friends, don't mean I'll stop

bullying you', and then he, he laughed at me, he laughed at my dungarees and said, 'Where did your mum get that? Oxfam?' And then I punched his teeth out. But after that day, no one bullied me."

The price of Jake's freedom from bullying was frequent aggressive outbursts in the face of any provocation, in order to maintain his belligerent reputation. While this shifted the power balance in the playground it compounded his difference and made for a troubled school history, tarnished by numerous exclusions. It was his volatile temper and general disengagement that precipitated his referral to the BSU. Beneath this antagonism though, lay his fear, anxiety and sense of vulnerability. He found transferring to Hailingbrooke from primary school unnerving and frightening.

"Meeting new people, and older people, because when I come here, I didn't know no one, a couple of people. And, like, then I see what happens, like people get mugged and when I see fights, everyone bleeding and everything, not like the stuff in that primary. And girls fighting and everything. That's nothing like primary."

While he had clearly struggled in the mainstream school, Jake resented his transfer to the BSU. He complained about the bad behaviour of the other unit pupils, claiming they "say F... Off and eat sweets and everything". He pleaded to return to the mainstream classroom, where "you get more education". Over time he reluctantly joined in BSU activities and was extremely well behaved outside of his occasional volatile outbursts. In our group sessions he became very talkative and animated. He had an impressive talent for mimicry, often combining this with crazy dancing to render the whole group helpless with laughter. He also enjoyed any opportunity we gave him to act, throwing himself wholeheartedly into the scenes he produced. While we were working with him Dave organised for him to begin attending selected outside lessons as part of a reintegration strategy. The following term Jake returned to the mainstream school, and despite a short blip that saw him briefly reassigned to the unit, he stayed there (at least as long as we did).

Jake was a BSU success story, but in the context of his improving circumstances at home and, more specifically, his mother's ability to buy him a proper school uniform, it was hard to gauge what impact his time in the BSU actually had. He certainly became more confident, and his BSU association with many of the hardest pupils in the school undoubtedly equipped him with a new status in the classroom. But as is well demonstrated in relation to adults living in poverty, the socially mediated experience of shame can render public encounters into arenas for humiliation and ostracism (Chase and Walker, 2013). People suffering hardship often withdraw from social situations in anticipation of shame rather than face such an assault on their dignity. Jake of course was not able to physically withdraw but instead disengaged psychologically, especially from circle time activities that routinely required painful self-exposure. Eventually he became better equipped to claim an entitlement to belong, engaging in what Barrie Thorne (2008) has described as 'shame work' to conceal his poverty.

A concentration of the travails of disadvantage within the unit may also have helped Jake. He was far from the only BSU pupil to experience grinding poverty, although he was more ground down by it than most. It was not uncommon for pupils to arrive at school in torn, outgrown or excessively worn clothes, and on one occasion a pupil was forced to stay at home because he had no trousers to wear. Shame work remained crucial in managing these indignities, although it often exacerbated conflict with teachers. For example, Max, Jake's BSU classmate at Hailingbrooke got into trouble for his aggressive refusal to take off his coat in the classroom and had been sent into the corridor. He arrived early for our group session in the drama studio and sat glowering at me. "I'm not taking my coat off", he barked. I assured him I had no intention of even suggesting it. When he had calmed down I asked gently why it mattered so much and he lifted the front part of his coat up to reveal an extensive rip in his shirt.

Interestingly, there seemed to be an economy of dignity, in that cheap, ripped shoes were considered more shameful than worn clothing. Hats were similarly important. And while knowledge about quality brands and technology could be mobilised to mask a lack of desirable possessions, getting it wrong could be deeply shaming. A shared experience of poverty did not neutralise the humiliation of exposure and pupils could be extremely cruel and contemptuous. Those subject to shame for their poverty often mitigate their feelings through constructing others as more shameful (Chase and Walker, 2013; Shildrick and MacDonald, 2013). Yet shame work was also commonly accepted and supported within the unit, with few challenges, even where claims to status were clearly of a dubious quality. For example, Armani (13) frequently bragged about things he clearly did not own (expensive motorbikes, brand name clothes, etc) but we never saw him called out on it. In Jake's case though he arrived in the BSU lacking the resources for even the most rudimentary shame work and was made to suffer for his very visible poverty.

At Meedham Girls, extreme poverty was less discernible although many of the pupils were coping with poor housing and low family incomes. But like Jake, 12-year-old Angelina was marked out by embodied disadvantage. She was a tiny white girl with long brown hair and a strong London accent. Her oversized uniform hung off of her painfully thin frame and she wore the same grey complexion and tense expression as Jake had initially. During our time at Meedham she was the only white girl in the BSU and was generally separate from the everyday banter and chatter. She often seemed preoccupied and lost in thought and was frequently absent from the unit, although she enthusiastically took part in the research group activities when present.

Angelina had been excluded from primary school for slapping a teacher. She described how this teacher would get angry and grab and pull pupils by the arm. Angelina was extremely sensitive about being touched and reacted forcefully. She confessed this with some embarrassment, but was also defensive, claiming she had only done what the other children had wanted to. When I interviewed her at the end of the term she veered between expressing contrition and righteous anger about her experiences. She was similarly conflicted about being asked questions in the first place. She was very flattered by the interest I showed in her, and fascinated by the tape recorder, but also very wary of saying too much. The result was a prickly interview crammed full of opaque references to the difficulties and deprivations she was experiencing. The following exchange illustrates how easy it was to blunder into delicate territory.

> Angelina: I don't know. You know when you're first there [in the unit], when people touch you, you just feel a bit nervous and you just start acting a bit weird and stuff, I felt a bit like that. But I don't really feel weird now.
>
> Val: Did people touch you in here then?
>
> Angelina: What do you mean touch me?
>
> Val: You said, "when people touch me".
>
> Angelina: They didn't touch me.

Val: No? Okay. You just said that the other teacher pulled you around.

Angelina: Oh yeah, yeah, yeah!

Val: I thought you said the teachers were doing that here as well but they don't?

Angelina: No.

Val: Okay.

Angelina: They will never dare touch me!

Angelina's interview contained many other confusing and worrying fragments, and I was unable to piece together a clear narrative. I doubted that Angelina could either. She talked about not being able to see her father but then went on to refer to him in the present tense. When I asked if there was anyone she disliked and preferred to keep away from she asked if I meant in her family. After listing some family friends she hesitated and said there was someone else but she didn't want to talk about it. It was, she stated firmly, "confidential to me and my Mum and my brother". I backed off quickly, aware her family was receiving ongoing support from social services and keen to respect her privacy. But the question about avoiding people clearly resonated. As she explained, her movements were restricted by necessity not by choice.

> Angelina: We don't really play out because (pause) I don't know why (pause) they don't allow us. One day there was a big, a TV and a microwave outside my door, like in a bonfire, exploding, and they blamed my brother. Then now they not allowing my brother to go out because they think he will start (pause) you know?
>
> Val: Who's 'they' Angelina?
>
> Angelina: People think my brother started the fire. He never, that's why my mum said (pause) if we were allowed to play out (unclear) there's nothing for me to go out for. There's only tyres and little, just you know the swings, put up and down. They will put them up in a couple of years

time but in a couple of years time I'll be (pause). There will be no point.

Val: How old is your brother?

Angelina: Eleven.

Val: Eleven. Right. So your mum said you can't play out now?

Angelina: No, my mum wants me to play out but I just can't.

Val: You just can't, okay because of people.

Angelina: Yeah. My mum arranges me going on day trips and stuff.

Angelina clearly adored her mum and was fiercely protective of her. Her referral to the BSU had been made because of her 'issues with anger' and she described how insults to her mum made her particularly furious. As I outline in Chapter 6, this was a very common trigger point for the young people in the research. Like Jake, Angelina's anger and aggression was matched with fear. She described school as 'scary' and found the toilets particularly intimidating. Yet school was also a place she valued very highly. She had been able to play football in the playground, had learnt how to play guitar and really appreciated the school food (as did Jake). She was also very attached to particular members of school staff, both inside and outside the unit. A mainstream teacher, Mr York, had started a chess club in the school and taught her to play. Discovering an aptitude for the game she soon developed a passion for it, glowing with enthusiasm whenever she talked about it.

Chess skills became an important source of pride and accomplishment for Angelina. Mr York had suggested that she play in school tournaments and she could barely contain her excitement at the prospect. She fantasised about winning trophies that would improve the school's status. She was acutely aware that the school had a poor reputation and was anxious about its survival in the future, fearing that teachers might leave if the intake fell. Like the other girls in the unit she had clear ideas about what should be done to improve the school. She suggested a complete rebuilding programme (with a regular cleaning schedule), changing the playground, enforcing strict school rules and getting professional chefs in to cook the food.

"What I'd do. I'd go down to BBC radio and what I'd do.
I'll do like an advert for the school and say, 'Our school.
Richest school. Come here if you want nice teachers and
Jamie Oliver to cook for you every day'."

While Angelina's disadvantage had impacted severely on her education,
she remained enthusiastic about the prospect of learning. She was
allowed out of the unit to attend lessons in core subjects, but as one
of the mentors acknowledged, she was unlikely to 'graduate' back to
mainstream with the rest of the girls. Instead she was identified as a
long-term 'project'.

Connectedness and separation

Poverty and disadvantage was lived through a wide range of anxieties,
indignities and deprivations. Often the circumstances jolting a family
into poverty resulted from a trauma that was in itself painful and
disorientating. For example, a number of pupils had lost their fathers
because they were put in prison or deported. Illness of family members
was another common experience linked to poverty. Thirteen-year-
old Tiffany from Gravensdale described how her father had been the
victim of a brutal attack after a football match, leaving him severely
injured. He had spent three months in a hospital 20-odd miles away
from their home, ensuring their family faced an uncertain future on
benefits while also needing to cover the costs of regular visits to see
him. In other cases, pupils, their mothers and siblings had fled from
domestic violence and found themselves having to cope with the
insecurities of temporary housing and the benefits system.

Significantly, these experiences tended not to be discussed at any
length by the pupils themselves. Personal traumas, hardships and
worries were more commonly normalised and talked about as if they
were everyday annoyances. For example, during a group activity
at Hailingbrooke four boys sat chatting while they sketched their
neighbourhood. Thirteen-year-old Sanchez revealed he no longer
lived locally and that he had moved to the outskirts of London with
his gran after his dad had 'gone crazy'. This passed without comment
and later on in the session BM (also 13) casually mentioned that his
family were about to be evicted because of rent arrears. He was glad,
he calmly said, to be leaving the flat but had no idea where they would
move on to. Affect rarely featured in the telling of these experiences,
with pupils ignoring emotional consequences and preferring to present
themselves as in control.

This stoicism contrasted with the volatile emotions these young people could display in the classroom. Highly visible, angry acting out tended to obscure some quite remarkable abilities to repress and contain feelings. As I will develop further in this chapter, the young people participating in the research demonstrated sophisticated social and emotional skills and a level of determined resilience that would underscore any definition of 'character'. In some cases young people were coping with serious anxieties and pressures without ever mentioning them at all. Twelve-year-old Lindon was one of the first pupils we worked with at Hailingbrooke. He was a slim black British African boy with a steely gaze and an air of confidence. He dominated in the group and often sought to police it for us, although his own behaviour could sometimes be very difficult to manage. He was enthusiastic, extremely charming, good humoured and often touchingly kind. He was also whip sharp with a deeply felt sense of social justice. He challenged things that he felt were unfair or senseless, and this regularly got him into trouble. He loudly expressed disgust at a display of British Prime Ministers in the corridor outside the head teacher's office, demanding to know why none were black. He also led a small revolt in the BSU, when the subject of the missing English child Madeleine McCann came up. Resisting the teacher's entreaties to display empathy, he pointed out that a poor black child would not receive anything like the same concern and media coverage (see Gillies, 2011).

Lindon really seemed to enjoy our research sessions and while he was wilful and sometimes volatile he had never seemed particularly troubled. Consequently, it was a shock to discover, on contacting his mother for an interview, that she had been seriously ill in hospital. Lindon was an only child and lived with his mother in a small flat. He had been visiting her in hospital every day before school, while being looked after (in the loosest sense of the word) by his uncle. Lindon's mother produced heartrending letters he had written, revealing just how worried he had been throughout the period we were working with him. His mother was eventually discharged from hospital but was still weak. Her sister had taken Lindon to live with her, but he had run away and lived with friends until he was allowed home again. We knew nothing of all this turmoil. While his emotions could bubble up into problematic displays of frustration or over exuberance he made it to school every day, participated eagerly in BSU activities and was popular with other pupils. He vociferously contributed to circle time, but clearly censored far more than he ever shared. For Lindon, suppression and lack of reflexivity appeared to be an effective coping strategy. In fact, it seemed that Lindon valued school, precisely because it provided respite from, rather than a forum for his difficult feelings.

Jamal was in the same research group alongside Lindon. He also had a very sick mother, but was utterly confused about the whereabouts of his father, who had been suddenly deported shortly after they arrived in the UK from Jamaica. Jamel had discovered that his father had travelled to Germany and remarried but struggled to make any sense of this. By the next term, Jamal's younger brother, Curtis had also been transferred to the BSU (alongside Jamal). We included Curtis in our next research group and were intrigued to find he regularly spoke of his father as if he were still at home. On interviewing their mother we found out that their father had briefly visited but had returned to his new wife, leaving Curtis distressed and angry. In the BSU Curtis maintained the fiction that his father was still at home, while Jamel tacitly offered support by remaining tight-lipped.

Transnational ruptures: migrant experiences

Censoring out traumatic events seemed to be a particularly common practice among pupils from refugee backgrounds. In some cases this may have been because the horror was something they hoped to leave behind them in another country. For example, we were told by teachers that Sanchez (13) had been a child soldier before being brought to the UK (via Portugal, Spain and France) at the age of 11. Sanchez himself professed to have no memory at all of Africa and said he had even forgotten how speak his language. But he was able to describe, in a very matter of fact way, his current troubled relationship with his father. After developing a drinking problem Sanchez's father became violent and began to physically neglect his sons. Sanchez went to live with his grandmother after his father attacked him with a knife. He was clearly deeply hurt and preoccupied by this turn of events. His mother had remained in Africa and whenever he produced an artwork during our group sessions he asked to keep it so he could send it to her.

A significant number of pupils taking part in our study had not been born in the UK, and many, like Sanchez, Jamal and Curtis, were relatively newly arrived in the country. This resettlement was characterised by particular challenges for pupils that often became obscured behind broader concerns about personal conduct and social and emotional skills. Schools retained sparse knowledge of their pupils' migrant backgrounds, unless they were new entrants. Yet pupils often transferred from London primary schools while still in the process of adapting to their new lives in the UK. For some this meant starting secondary school with a reputation for being troubled or troublesome and encountering very little understanding of their situation and past experiences from teachers.

For example, 12-year-old Max and his family had arrived as economic migrants from Portugal. Max started primary school halfway through year six, but spoke no English and found the other pupils hostile and mocking.

> Max: The kids, like, because I can't speak English, the kids was, like, taking the mick out of me. So I end up fighting.

> Yvonne: Wasn't there anyone that you could talk to, within the school, about that?

> Max: No. Because I didn't have ... I couldn't speak ... I didn't know how to speak it. I didn't know, I couldn't tell no one, so that's, like, why I was, like, I saw them last, like a month ago, I saw the guy, the guy from the primary school I used to go, and, like, I ask him, "Why, was it like that? Do you remember me?" He was, like, "Yeah, you're the kid from the primary school, I was taking the mick". I was like, "Yeah", I was like, "Why you don't take the mick now?" Because I can speak English, and he just walk away. They just take the piss out of you, I hate them. And I got, I got excluded from it, I got excluded from the primary school. Because no one believed me, I couldn't speak, so they thought I was the one taking the mick out of them, not excluded, but I got into loads of trouble. Every time I was, like, in the corner, sitting down with no friends.

Max learnt to speak English at great speed and was word perfect by the time he started at Hailingbrooke a few months later. He retained no trace of an accent and sounded exactly like his London-born counterparts. Nevertheless, his record for being difficult followed him to secondary school, ensuring he was marked out as a potential problem from the beginning. Like many pupils at Hailingbrooke Max was involved in low level disruption in the classroom. He was mischievous, impulsive and quickly gained a reputation. Before his first year at Hailingbrooke was out he was facing the threat of permanent exclusion. A Spanish teacher misheard something he said in Portuguese and accused him of being abusive. Outraged and indignant, Max hotly denied he had ever said the alleged phrase, but the school claimed to have a tape recording of the incident. Believing him, Max's parents challenged the accusation and demanded a copy of the tape. They were told it was expensive and that they would have to buy a copy. Undeterred, Max's parents offered the money and attended a governors' meeting to defend him, despite speaking very little English themselves. The threat of exclusion was lifted when no tape was produced.

Max returned to school deeply resentful, and was back in hot water shortly after for throwing a snowball at the head teacher. At this point Dave Stirling had stepped in and offered to work with him in the BSU. He had been in the unit for over a year when he began participating in our research. As the example of Max highlights, pupils from migrant families often found themselves having to manage hostility from peers, on the grounds of their status as newcomers. Developing a thick skin and the social resources to deal with abuse and incitement were crucial in these circumstances, but as a strategy it could place them at the centre of conflict, heightening their visibility in the classroom. The following exchange unfolded as part of a group discussion at Gravensdale between four 13-year-old boys. James was second generation Irish, Bond had been resettled into a London primary school when he moved with his family from Serbia. The other two boys (Luke and Alfie) were white English.

> James: I think Bond would like to be English and have a passport for once and not be an immigrant.
>
> Bond: James is lying miss he's just being James.
>
> James: Where's your passport?
>
> Bond: It's at home actually mate…
>
> Val: So why do you all keep going on about immigrants?
>
> James: Because he is one.
>
> Bond: I ain't. They just say that to me because I'm from Serbia and they think it's funny 'cos they're all English boys and have fry-ups in the morning.
>
> Val: Is everyone English?
>
> James: No.

Bond: The English population's like less English people in England than…

James: Too many foreign people's coming in our country.

Bond: I reckon Ireland's the country to live in. You walk round the corner, if you see someone with new shoes you can have 'em you just got to knock him out, fight for the shoes.

Val: Have you ever been to Ireland?

Bond: No, but I've heard all about it, heard all about it.

James: Oh, but look at your country, you, oh I'm not even going to explain how you catch your dinner.

(Luke and Alfie laugh)

James: What dinner do you have in Serbia – go on? Rice and beans (shouts) IMMIGRANT – ON THE BACK OF A TRUCK. (Talking over Bond and directly into the tape recorder) I clearly state that Bond Janev came to this country on the back of a van.

Luke: That's recorded. They'll get you.

This was a highly charged and unpleasant exchange that Bond handled relatively confidently and with some bravado. James, realising he had been 'caught' on tape, stormed out of the room in tears. I went after him to reassure him we were not intending to pass any material on to teachers. When I returned to the room Bond was bantering about football with the other boys. He was very skilled at using humour to manage situations and was often extremely funny, but he also frequently overstepped the line. His trademark was heavy sarcasm, innuendo and feigned innocence, which many teachers found maddening. He was known in the school as a loud, self-assured, attention-seeking boy, but as this excerpt demonstrates, his brash classroom persona was relational and shaped in response to often hostile classroom encounters.

Migrant experiences were also often characterised by instability, insecurity and loss. Angel had been brought to the UK when she was eight, but her parents had split up and her mother had returned to Jamaica. Angel missed her mother desperately and resented her father's new partner. The conflict she was experiencing at home spilled over into school and she was referred to Meedham BSU for sullen rudeness. On a more practical level, migrant families could find it difficult to settle and establish a secure and safe base, meaning many of the pupils we worked with had experienced multiple moves. This was hugely disadvantaging given the significance geographical knowledge commanded. As I will outline, later on in this chapter, violent crime was a routinely navigated hazard (particularly for boys). The pupils lived with a heightened sense of territory and built identities around their postcodes. Movement outside of these areas of belonging was termed 'slipping' and carried risks unless protection was provided by postcode natives or through identification as belonging to a particular 'clique' (a gang like association.

Lack of local knowledge and social connections inevitably disadvantaged newly arrived pupils. Peer popularity and earning a tough reputation could assume great importance in that context and pupils were hyper aware of the dangers they might inadvertently face by displaying vulnerability. Drawing on Bourdieu, Simon Harding (2014) describes these dynamics in terms of 'street capital', referring to 'an amalgam of street knowledge and street skills (cultural capital); internalised behaviours and ways of being and thinking (habitus); local history, family connections and networks, relationships (social capital), reputation, status and local recognition, honour and prestige' (p 6). The acquisition of street capital was regarded by many of the boys as essential for survival, with particular ethnicities often forming protective alliances, which left them prone to accusations of gang membership (Alexander, 2004).

As well as adapting to new power dynamics and social expectations, pupils from migrant families might also be managing anxiety about what was happening in their home country in their absence. Twelve-year-old Damien had arrived from Jamaica and was living with his older sister. He wore a large diamond stud in his ear and seemed to exude an effortless air of cool. He was handsome, good at football and very popular with girls at Hailingbrooke. But he was frequently involved in fights and ended up in the BSU after being defiant and abusive to teachers. He was not the most forthcoming participant in our research, but one particular activity provoked a powerful articulation of his thoughts and feelings about Jamaica.

I had found some coloured cardboard sticker shapes in a pound shop and brought them in with a range of old magazines and some plastic scissors. The idea was for pupils to create a life story collage. Most did not get further than cutting out some pictures, but Damien ignored the magazines and the others in the group to produce a written stream of consciousness on the sticker shapes (see figure 1). In the top right hand orange jagged star he wrote: 'My uncle died in Jamaica. He got shot 12 times and I was angry. I felt like I wanted to kill someone'. Next to this he drew a cross and 'In memory of my uncle'. In the bottom right-hand green star he wrote: 'I was born in Jamaica and I went to school. I had lots of friends and my sister and cousins'. On the left-hand side, beneath the orange star bearing the Jamaican flag, he placed a pink star stating: 'I don't know if my grandparents have died. I really want to see them'. I was quite taken aback by this, particularly since he had barely contributed a word in previous sessions. When he had finished, I gently probed about when he had last visited Jamaica, but he clearly did not want to talk about it. Instead he began dribbling a ball around the drama studio. I respected his silence and backed off, grateful for this small insight into his experience of dislocation. He never did elaborate on anything he wrote that day.

Pupils from migrant backgrounds could also be forced to adapt very rapidly to profound cultural change. This could disrupt established coping mechanisms and lead to confusion and conflict. For example, while still very young, Manny had fled his West African village with his family when civil war broke out there. They took refuge

Figure 1: Collage created by 12-year-old Damien

in a neighbouring country and returned several years later, only to become caught up in further violence. Manny's mother took his two younger brothers and set out ahead for England to find safety. After being moved around the country in temporary accommodation, they were housed in London in a small bedsit. Manny, his father and older sister eventually travelled from Africa to join them. By the time he was enrolled in a full-time school place Manny was almost 10 years old. He was 12 when he participated in the BSU research. His family of six remained living in one room for years, desperately lobbying the housing department for larger accommodation. According to his mother, Manny, spent very little time at home because he was unable to bear the overcrowding.

Manny learnt to speak English quickly but described the culture shock he had experienced and how he had struggled to make sense of the new rules he found himself bound by. He regaled the research group with tales of his life in Africa, describing how he used to supplement his family's diet by trapping birds. He was proud of his technique and when he saw London was populated with a mass of pigeons, he mistakenly thought he had a transferable skill. On his way back from school, and feeling hungry, he managed to catch a fat pigeon only to be picked up by police and brought home in a squad car. He told this story in a self-deprecating way to emphasise how green he had been only a year ago. The others in the group laughed along with him, wincing at the idea of eating a London pigeon. But Manny's problems extended beyond this initial cultural dislocation. He was not able to read or write and he struggled to make sense of what was expected of him in the classroom. After several months shuttling between the BSU and the off-site provision, he was eventually permanently excluded for outbursts of frustration and fighting. Mr Phillips, his year head, had reflected that he simply did not belong in the school.

Violence and vulnerability

As I have already alluded, violence and crime were very real backdrops to pupils' lives across the three schools. The vast majority of the boys in our research and many of the girls had fallen victim to street robbery and/or violence, often repeatedly. Journeys to and from school could be experienced as particularly hazardous. As I have mentioned, the everyday experiences of the pupils were shaped by territoriality. For boys there were some positives as well as strong negatives associated with the attribution of ownership rights to particular regions. As Kintrea et al (2008) found in research across British cities, boys and young men could emphasise territorial boundaries to strengthen identities and develop friendship. There was a clear status and value gained from belonging to a particular area, even though personal feelings towards neighbourhoods could still be ambivalent. The boys participating in our research were particularly attached to their postcodes. These were often worked into the art they produced. When we used the video camera in Hailingbrooke the boys introduced themselves with their postcodes, drawing on hand signs and colours that they told us were associated with local gangs.

But beyond the identity pride, the same boys were also bitterly cognisant of the negative consequence of this partitioning. Territoriality generated fear, anxiety and could severely restrict movement. It was a particular problem for BSU pupils because they often lived outside of their school boroughs. Some had been previously excluded from their local school and were placed in the only school that could be found to accept them. Others had been in temporary housing and had remained in their original school when they were moved. Either way it was common for BSU pupils to have to travel, sometimes long distances across boroughs to get to school. This was less of an issue for girls, although they too could feel apprehension at being out of place. But for the boys, journeys to and from school could mean exposure to extreme danger. As well as the high incidence of street robbery, the co-ed schools were located in areas where teenage stabbings had become worryingly common. During the course of our fieldwork three teenagers known to our research participants were fatally stabbed while two of the participants themselves were hospitalised with knife wounds. Some pupils also had personal experience of extreme violence or even murder in their family. For example, Jamal and Curtis's older brother had been shot and nearly lost his life in a street altercation in a neighbouring borough.

The fear that such incidents precipitated was seismic in the schools. Dark threats and rumours about gang affiliation and who would be next circulated at a pace and were taken very seriously. One of my most disturbing memories of Gravensdale was waiting in the reception to be escorted to the BSU while a terrified boy begged to be allowed home. He was white, slightly overweight and clinging desperately to his mother. He explained, through sobs, how he had received a death threat. He was so distressed he could barely stand up. BSU pupils though, were considerably more stoical about the risks they faced. Most had developed strategies that allowed them to move more safely, either by avoiding particular places, claiming a friendship with someone from the area or claiming membership of an alternative 'clique' with a violent reputation. Again, this highlights the significance of social relationships and the extent to which developing strong social bonds could become a priority.

Some boys were particularly preoccupied by staying safe. Bringing weapons into school was not uncommon. Sanchez was excluded when he was discovered with a screwdriver. For Keishawn (13) violence was a clear and present danger. He was a small African-Caribbean boy and had been attacked several times on his way home from school. He lived a considerable distance from the school and as a result was identified by association with a clique several boroughs away from Hailingbrooke, leaving him with restricted mobility as a result. As written in my field notes from a session we ran with a performance poet, street safety was at the forefront of his mind.

> When Charlie [the poet] got them to brainstorm ideas for writing poems, Keishawn was very vocal. He talked about the safety issue again. He said that [his home town] and the countryside were the only places he was safe. Charlie questioned him and asked, "Even if you're not involved in anything?" He said yes, he'd get moved on [attacked] because he'd be with people recognised not to be local.

Later on in the term we encouraged the pupils to bring in music that meant something to them and talk about it. Keishawn came with a track he had helped produce. An 18-year-old rapper who lived close by to Keishawn performed and titled it 'Red and Blue Make Colour Purple'. It was a reference to his neighbourhood, in which the local gangs were designated by the colour blue. According to Keishawn, 'Blue and Red Make Colour Purple', describes a time when that part of London was united, in contrast to the brutal reality of the situation as it stands. It was not the clearest recording and heavy slang was used throughout, but we could pick out references to the LA gang wars in the 70s and the phrase 'kids and girlfriends in the graveyards'.

For Keishawn, though, the message from the song was that 'you have to do what you have to do' to protect yourself and survive.

> "I don't, I don't, I don't ... like, the 'Shank in the balls' [weapon down trousers]... I don't really do all that stuff... But like ... stay in [blue neighbourhood] if you're from [blue neighbourhood] stay in [blue neighbourhood] don't go nowhere else ... if you're gonna go anywhere else go with your man, boy ... that's all I'm saying ...

'cos if you're moving by yourself and not bear [loads of] [blue neighbourhood] boys you're gonna get moved to [attacked]."

The difference between 'cliques' and criminal gangs was quite hard to distinguish. As Aldridge and Medina's (2008) ethnography of British street gangs demonstrated, such associations are complex, fluid and operate on a largely informal basis. It appeared that criminal gangs in the areas could sometimes function within looser territorial-based associations or 'cliques which could then become known and associated with the gang'. As a result, a young person might become identified with a notorious gang without any involvement in criminal activity. Gangs and cliques seemed to operate through the same territorial, mixed age structure with 'youngers' and 'elders' but there was a world of difference between an association with a criminal gang and a clique.

Kieran (14) had been repeatedly victimised while travelling to and from school until he was directly approached by a gang member and offered protection. He ran errands for the gang, often carrying drugs, or 'shotting' as he called it. Kieran was a quiet, sensitive mixed-race boy who was clearly acutely uncomfortable with his involvement. He liked the money he made and had capitalised on his reputation in the school, to the extent that his sinister threats had landed him in Hailingbrooke BSU, but he felt trapped. He had been involved in some sickening violence on the street and was deeply troubled by it, as the picture he drew in one of the sessions powerfully conveyed (see figure 2). He wanted out but could see no safe way of disassociating himself.

At 14 years old Kieran epitomised what John Pitts (2008) has termed the 'reluctant gangster', 'a product of, and an actor in, a world demarcated by poverty, sociocultural and racial exclusion, illegitimate opportunity, and big city corruption' (39). Teachers knew about Kieran's gang involvement (a mainstream teacher interviewed for our project described him as 'evil'). An interview with Kieran's mother revealed her patchy knowledge of the situation and profound anxiety. Like ourselves and the professionals we consulted, she had little idea of what to do. Informing the police would have been dangerous for him and a betrayal of his trust. Youth services were shockingly thin on the ground at the time. The youth counselling services in his borough had unfeasibly long waiting lists. Though provision was better around the Hailingbrooke area he was not officially eligible to use it because he was not resident in the borough. We managed to argue successfully that he should be seen on the basis that he attended a school in the borough, but all we could do was pass on the number and hope he rang it.

Figure 2: Kieran's portrait of his neighbourhood representing drug dealing and violence

Foregrounding the social and structural

As I have outlined in this chapter, BSU practices centred on personal rehabilitation. A referral carried the judgement that a particular pupil was lacking in the psychological capacity to cooperate and learn alongside other pupils. The therapeutic style activities were positioned as equipping the excluded with the means to participate. Consequently, the physical dislocation of young people, who by their very existence challenge narratives of fairness, was reframed as an active 'inclusion' project. This is achieved partly through a denial that minds are located in socially and structurally situated bodies.

Closer examination of the struggles of the young people in this study reveals the material and relational dimensions that make actions, responses and resistance intelligible. Managing often multiple life challenges set them apart, shaped their values, practices and strategies for survival. More specifically, these experiences highlight the extent to which mainstream classrooms have made learning contingent. There is no place for the vicissitudes and burdens of poverty and discrimination. Disadvantage has become envisaged as a psychological barrier to learning through a conflation of poverty with personal deficit. This has been further ingrained through a neoliberal appeal to self-optimisation and responsibilisation, enshrining and naturalising values of achievement and competition. Teachers are now forced to endorse a normative model of human capital, grounded in the deceit that who you become can and should have nothing to do with who you are. In the following chapter I explore in more detail how teachers and other school staff made sense of challenging behaviour and contrast these dominant constructions with the self-reflections of the young people themselves.

FOUR

Damaged boys, needy girls

The previous chapter shone a spotlight on the everyday workings of the BSUs and illuminated the stories and experiences of a range of young people referred to them because of their behaviour. In this chapter I explore how teachers and other school staff made sense of challenging conduct from within a dominant ideal of 'inclusion' that was built around psychologised assessments of individual competence and wellbeing. In particular, I show how a distinctly gendered discourse of risk orders the way young people are understood and targeted as suffering from personal deficits or particular conditions. I also examine how such a therapeutically inflected curriculum shaped the way the pupils themselves narrated their lives and articulated their difficulties.

I begin with a general analysis of the way concepts of risk have colonised inclusion agendas, de-contextualising and reifying experiences of exclusion. I then show how references to psychological disorder or 'damage' by school staff positions boys as potentially dangerous or 'risky'. I explore this process through a specific focus on anger and its expression in the classroom. As the previous chapter made clear, anger and its consequences very commonly precipitated BSU referrals. Pupils themselves also often located their anger at the centre of their problems, but as I will show this belied considerable ambivalence, as well as the socially situated nature of the emotional expression. For girls, constructions of developmental immaturity and 'neediness' shaped school encounters. A theme of 'vulnerability' was drawn on by school staff to trivialise the acting out of girls and normalise gendered scripts. As such, I highlight the passive collusion of staff within a normative cultural production and privileging of particular kinds of masculinities and femininities.

At risk of being risky

In contemporary western societies, concerns around individual dangerousness and imminent threat have been largely replaced by a broader category of potential risk (Castel, 1991; Rose, 2010; Lupton, 2013). In other words, we have seen a shift away from identifying and containing 'the mad and the bad' to an embrace of the concept of risk profiling and the statistical calculation of harm. The effect is to more precisely locate potential risk in larger numbers of people through a focus on recognisable dangerous characteristics, behaviours and lifestyles. Profiling reveals marginalised groups (the poor, minority ethnic children and young people, care leavers, etc) to be most 'at risk'. This calculation then works to project anticipated negative trajectories into the future, effectively masking the enduring social and structural causes (Pica-Smith and Veloria, 2012). Risk becomes a de facto characteristic attached to particular groups, to be managed accordingly.

Nikolas Rose (2010) highlights the comments made in 2008 by Gary Pugh, the then director of forensic science and DNA spokesman for the UK's Association of Chief Police Officers. Pugh called for primary school children exhibiting bad behaviour to be placed on the UK National DNA Database on the grounds that early issues with conduct often progressed to criminal activity in later life. This controversial recommendation was widely reported in the British media alongside a report from the Institute for Public Policy Research (IPPR) titled 'Make Me a Criminal', which recommended screening at ages of five and 12. The report's author, Julia Margo, advocated targeted behavioural therapy and parenting programmes, claiming, 'You can carry out a risk factor analysis where you look at the characteristics of an individual child aged five to seven and identify risk factors that make it more likely that they would become an offender'.[1] In a stroke, the multiple antecedents and complex biographies underlying school difficulties are disappeared through a focus on managing and containing the risks inherent in challenging behaviour. As Brid Featherstone and colleagues (2014) cogently articulate:

> A new rhetoric of governance argued for the lessening of risk, not the meeting of need. This is of considerable importance as a diverse cast of people and issues become known only through the language of risk. (p 22)

Rose (2010) identifies this paradigm of risk as a distinct change in mechanisms of governance: 'not so much "discipline and punish", but "screen and intervene"' (p 97). He also notes how it operates through a dual sense of risk, encompassing risk to others and risk to the self. Concerns to classify and 'treat' those who are likely to present a future risk to others become conflated with the aim of identifying those with a susceptibility to conditions or harmful outcomes. The segregation and management of risk is reframed as a benevolent practice designed to protect individuals and society alike. This mode of governance can be traced across public institutions through the growth of what has been termed the 'preventative state' (Parton, 2006). The identification of 'at risk' groups within the population to be targeted for intervention reflects a wider objective of predicting and heading off social problems before they have even manifested.

The categorisation of 'at risk' pupils, ostensibly 'for their own good', operates within a highly moralised agenda. The targeted are worked upon with the aim of equipping them with risk management skills which they are then required to utilise. Risk is reframed to encompass judgement and self-care, mediated and operationalised through the active sphere of the personal. The 'at risk' label comes to connote those needing to embrace their individualised citizenship and become 'responsible risk takers' (Giddens, 1998). As the description of circle time activities in the previous chapter outlined, this involves recognising thoughts, feelings and actions as wrong and substituting them with 'prosocial' tropes and personal optimisation techniques. Yet in the face of this intense subjectification, persistent misbehaviour and 'risky' conduct continued largely unabated, leaving school staff struggling to make sense of such behaviour from within the dominant framework of the rational self-interested individual. As I demonstrate in Chapter 6, inadequate parents (more particularly mothers) are most commonly evoked to explain deficits in personality and self-management skills.

'Emotional behavioural deficiency': Damaged goods?

In the fast pace high-pressure environs of the schools, particular pupil actions or behaviours could seem provocative, incomprehensible or even mindless to school staff. During the course of our fieldwork we were often left similarly bemused, irritated and exasperated ourselves. But our role as researchers gave us the space and a privileged vantage point to reflect carefully on the complex situated dynamics framing incidents and flashpoints. We were able to collect multiple perspectives (from mainstream teachers, BSU staff, a variety of pupils, and parents). We were also able to observe over time and come to recognise common trigger points and sensitivities. For example, it was possible to apply an analytical lens of 'face work' (Goffman, 1959) to situations where conflict erupted seemingly from nowhere.

Taunts, put downs and other affronts were commonplace in banter between boys in the units, with humour largely defusing any aggression, if not always the hurtful meaning. As Mary Jane Kehily and Anoop Nayak (1997) note, humour plays a constitutive role in young men's performance of masculinity. But humour was often misjudged, hitting a nerve or embarrassing the subject so comprehensively that he was unable to institute an appropriate comeback. Comebacks, no matter how lame, were important face-saving mechanisms, allowing some dignity to be restored. But they could also mark an escalation point if the original slight was particularly stinging. The comeback could up the ante, stretching its jokey presentation to breaking point. This might provoke an inflamed hurling of an unambiguously nasty comment, which (particularly if it concerned family members) could cause an exchange, hovering in tense dangerous territory, to go nuclear. Violent conflict in the co-ed units was rarely predictable and tended to unfold fast, rendering complex exchanges to a blur. While it was not uncommon, it was jarring and upsetting for all concerned. Even some boys who had worked hard to cultivate a tough image cried after fights and were clearly shocked by the turn of events.

For many school staff this behaviour illustrated the pupils' lack of emotional and social skills. Boys who often got into fights were seen as deficient in control and unable to establish healthy relationships. Very commonly this was talked about as if it were an organic condition. Sometimes it was mapped onto formally and informally diagnosed special educational needs. Speculation was rife about which pupils had undiagnosed ADHD, and boys were frequently described as being 'on the spectrum' for autism. Beverly, the manager of the short-term behaviour support at Hailingbrooke, was not untypical in her reflections on her predominantly male class.

> "A lot of them are EBD – sort of Emotional Behavioural Deficiency – which is another type of special need… I mean, it's one of these new ones. I think that, within schools, I've been hearing – since I've been teaching, it's been something that's been bandied around – and it is a specific behavioural deficit kind of syndrome, but my understanding of it, it can, I mean, a lot of the kids are hyperactive in some way, but I think a lot of it. I think the reason they use 'emotional' is that it's possibly come from home in a certain way, so whether it's in parents who haven't done a lot of parenting, or that have had drug problems, or, or the related other problems, you know, or they're very young, you know, all those various ways that they've been damaged in certain ways."

This concept of 'damage' was a key explanatory framework across the schools, drawn on to make sense of what many teachers regarded as nihilistic tendencies. Behaviours tended to be interpreted in terms of irrationality and hyper arousal and viewed as evidence of psychological impairment. While many school staff saw their role as attempting to repair this damage, others adopted a more deterministic perspective, emphasising the irreversible nature of the condition. For example, Mr Phillips, a year head, repeatedly stressed the pointlessness of attempting to engage minds that were beyond redemption. Mr Phillips was a committed teacher and expressed a strong sense of responsibility to pupils he recognised as demonstrating potential, but he was fatalistic about the rest.

> "I was told that when I first started teaching 'accept the fact that 5–10% of the kids you will NEVER get through to and they WILL fail'. I did my training next to one of the biggest housing estates in the country and really rough... You know, 'some of the boys are really frustrating me' and [the head] said, 'you've GOT to accept it, 5–10% you will NOT get through to and there are systems in place for them but don't kick yer own ass about it, it's just the way the system works!' It's really hard to deal with that though because you start off all idealistic and I am still a bit idealistic but I know there are certain kids I can't get near and I don't get pissed off with it anymore and just work with the ones that I can."

Mr Phillips articulated a strong construction of 'impossible learners' (Youdell, 2006). From his perspective, up to 10% of a class are damaged beyond hope, even if through no fault of their own. They do not, he concluded, belong in a mainstream setting. His reference to other 'systems in place' for them, positioned their mainstream inclusion as a cruel act both for the damaged pupil and for those whose education they disrupt. This amounted to more than theoretical musings. By all accounts Mr Phillips actively contrived to remove troublesome pupils from his classroom. A large number of BSU pupils self-identified as victims of a Mr Phillips-directed conspiracy, describing how they had been set up, wrongly accused or entrapped. According to these pupils, he continued to issue dark threats vowing to see them excluded from the school. The persecutory practices of Mr Phillips were also acknowledged by the 'well behaved' pupils in the Hailingbrooke focus group (chosen by Mr Phillips himself).

Only too aware of the injustices being perpetrated, Dave Stirling (the BSU manager) sometimes explicitly challenged Mr Phillips' version of events, winning reprieves for particular pupils. For example, a play fight had broken out in an unsupervised mainstream playground between boys from different form groups who were nursing a largely good-natured rivalry. It got out of hand and one of the boys got cut by another boy brandishing a ruler. Although it was a relatively minor injury, the police were called and Mr Phillips took the opportunity to implicate one of his troublesome unteachables, Buggs (14). Dave defended him, drawing attention to the eyewitness accounts implicating someone else. Buggs avoided permanent exclusion (and prosecution) but ended up in the BSU on the grounds that he was an alleged ringleader.

Anger issues

The 'fight' and the anger that Buggs expressed at being wrongfully accused were neatly slotted into the emotional and social deficit model framing the BSU interventions. Buggs was immediately signed up to an anger management course. Loud, defiant, aggressive behaviour from boys in the school was generally designated as an 'anger management problem', ensuring the socially embedded meanings framing conflicts were bypassed for a focus on personal dysfunction. The preoccupation with anger gave staff and pupils alike a broad, flexible diagnostic label where behaviour did not fit other kinds of medicalised disorders (like ADHD or autistic spectrum disorder). Large numbers of pupils defined themselves as having an 'anger management problem' describing their struggles to keep their temper at bay. These accounts were mildly confessional as if disclosing an addiction at a support group. Subsequent probing around the actual experience of anger and the circumstances in which it was expressed revealed considerably more ambivalence and contradiction than this apparent self-identification first suggested. At a social and relational level, being known as an angry person had many positives for these boys. While often associated with serious consequences, anger could generate heady, if temporary, feelings of power and could allow them to exert greater control in difficult situations.

For example, Marcus, a 15-year-old black Caribbean pupil at Gravensdale BSU described himself as 'working through' his anger issues. He readily identified as a having a control problem and emphasised how dangerous this made him.

> "Like when I'm angry, people can't stop me, they have to just let me do what I do, because I'm gonna switch on you... For some reason when I'm angry, and I have to do something, I will do it, and then I will calm down. I cannot

calm down and not do it… I don't have, er, like, er, second thoughts. I don't think of any. Once something is in my mind, once I have a task to do something, I'm doing it, I'm not gonna , I'm not gonna worry about this, or worry about that, I will just do it. I don't know … it's like I don't have no fear, I don't know, I just go into a different world. Everybody knows that. 'Don't touch Marcus.'"

As this excerpt reveals, the mysterious compelling force driving his anger has a liberatory effect, lifting him beyond uncertainty and anxiety. According to Marcus, his fury triggers determination, purpose and fearlessness, while the lack of control removes him from any immediate accountability for his actions. Marcus had been referred to the BSU because he was regarded (by the head teacher in particular) as aggressive. He had been involved in fights outside of school with boys from a neighbouring institution, ensuring that amidst anxiety about teenage stabbings he was flagged up as an 'at risk' pupil. From the head and deputy head teacher's perspective Marcus was dangerous and very likely to be involved in gang activity. He was watched carefully inside the school and suspected of being behind any violence or bullying incidents.

But the Marcus we came to know during the research sessions was very different from the antisocial thug this institutionalised concern presented him as. He was highly self-reflexive and thoughtful in our research sessions. He could be loud at times but he was also very well-mannered and good humoured. He had a slight speech impediment and found reading and writing very difficult, but despite struggling academically he was liked by many of the mainstream teachers and had developed a particularly close relationship with the black male mentors in the unit. He was a talented athlete and football player and had won trophies for the school. He also enjoyed looking after his younger siblings and had managed to get a job teaching an after school dance class at a primary school.

Marcus explained how he had stepped up in a street argument, inflaming an ongoing feud with boys from a neighbouring school. Rumours of a larger fight between the rival schools began to circulate and groups of boys started gathering outside Gravensdale until they were dispersed by the police. This incident earned Marcus a formidable reputation among other pupils and potential contenders on the street, offering him some protection against the kind of victimisation so many boys experienced routinely. As Marcus discovered, white-hot fury in the context of serious threat could be experienced as a valuable strength, as his account of being confronted with a knife demonstrates.

> "Outside of school, like, if stuff happened, I'm gonna try and defend myself. I'm not gonna stay there and… 'Cos, one time, when we was at a bus, one boy tried to stab me, so I had to try to defend myself. He barge into me, and I just looked at him and went 'what?' It's just like people that wanna start hype [trouble]… Because me, like, if someone says, like, 'I'm gonna stab you,' that's like taking my life, so I'm just gonna … I go berserk … he's showed me his knife. So then I've come after him, and he, like, once he saw my, my reaction, he's backed away. I mean, I was. I went for him, and he just ran off."

Jake, the white boy struggling with the demands of poverty I discussed in the previous chapter, articulated a similar sense of protective power in his description of punching his bully's teeth out and enjoying the untouchable status he earned in the process. Jake had continued to lose his temper regularly at secondary school, often in response to goading from other pupils. In one orchestrated incident a group of pupils had been throwing pens at him until he exploded and punched his computer screen, leaving his knuckles battered and bleeding. Another similar incident saw him excluded when he retrieved the pens and furiously threw them back, narrowly missing a teacher.

Going berserk meant owning a potentially dangerous psychological flaw that prevented self-control, yet both Marcus and Jake were clearly able to exercise restraint when necessary. In fact, Marcus could have been said to display impressive levels of self-discipline in the context of repeated provocation from the head teacher and (as I discuss further in Chapter 6) the police. Suspicion that he was involved in gang activity ensured he was under constant surveillance. He was often implicated in trouble he had nothing to do with and forced to repeatedly endure being searched and moved on, in the playground and in the street. Despite never having been temporarily excluded he was very aware that his place within the school was tenuous.

> "I haven't really been in trouble in this school, but like you know what I mean, like, teachers are just waiting for me to crack, or, (pause) or for them, like, to get something on me, to get me out the school. But I just keep my head down. I just keep my head down."

Many of Marcus's friends had been excluded but he expressed determination not to rise to any bait.

> "Some of the teachers, like, we have, like, teachers that have come to the school that are drunk and stuff, and tried it. One of my friends, the teacher gripped [held] him so he gripped up the teacher and he got excluded for a couple of weeks. Because they're teachers they can get away with stuff. But I don't know. That's how the school is … I mean, even the teachers knew what (pause) they just keep their mouth quiet, if you know what I mean. But, yeah, he's, he's tried it on me. In the playground, he's come and spoke to me, tried, 'Come on,' he's pushing me, and I'm like, 'Move. You've been drinking. Move from me.' If he touches me, I'm gonna hit him. But I know that I'm gonna get in trouble, because he's gonna lie. So I just leave him. And when he pushes me, I'll be like 'I'll punch you, move'."

This account suggests that Marcus's threshold for pathological anger is either reassuringly high or he has considerably more control than he is prepared to acknowledge. Similarly, Jake's angry outbursts might be viewed as more conditional than driven by emotional deficit. For example, after returning to the mainstream classroom Jake got a girlfriend.

> "I met her when she threw a pen at me… By an accident. Then I got angry. And then that's when she started to like me. I was going to flip the table over, but I thought, 'No, calm down!' I was like, 'She's a girl, and she's beautiful!'"

Jake's ability to quickly shift out of an unbounded display of rage, again suggests his anger is more consciously deployed as a social weapon than felt as faulty autonomic response. That is not to suggest that anger was never experienced as a lack of control, but instead to highlight the way social investment may mitigate against routine regulation of emotions. In fact, prevailing interpretations of anger as a psychological pathology could even intensify its significance and effect. Some pupils seemed to actively cultivate the image that they were 'mad' or unhinged. Daniel (13) was particularly proud of his wild, volatile behaviour viewing it as intrinsic to who he was. He had even developed his own graffiti tag displaying his nickname: 'crazy kid' (see figure 3).

Figure 3: Daniel's graffiti tag

But, investing in this kind of intimidating identity could be a very risky strategy. Displays of apparently unboundaried anger not only led to school exclusion, they could also raise the stakes in physical conflicts. Shortly after we had completed our research with Marcus he was confronted and stabbed in the street. This happened just up the road from the school gate in the middle of the day. The expression of anger as a protective force relies on its impact to overwhelm and frighten, in turn encouraging ever more extreme displays of anger and power in response. Marcus had been very conscious of his vulnerability and his options in terms of becoming more closely involved with organised crime activities in the area. As I discuss in Chapter 6 it was something he feared his poor future prospects might push him toward. Ironically, had he become more closely affiliated with a criminal gang he may have avoided the street attack (albeit whilst becoming more vulnerable to other threats). From the school's perspective the stabbing was vindication of their suspicions that he was a gang member. Marcus recovered in hospital but did not come back to school.

Contextualising anger

The example of Marcus demonstrates very effectively the way in which conceptualisations of anger as a personal pathology rely on a simplistic account of wrongdoing in which behaviours are divorced from a broader context of injury and injustice. BSU pupils were generally treated by the mainstream schools as perpetrators requiring intensive support to mend their ways, with little consideration given to the often multiple ways in which these pupils were also being challenged, hurt and intimidated. Marcus was under intensive surveillance by teachers, CCTV cameras and the police, both inside and outside the school, but his reputation as aggressive and dangerous obscured the very real risk he was facing to his life. Similarly, Kieran, the boy involved with a criminal gang discussed in Chapter 3, was identified as a threat to be contained rather than as a vulnerable 13-year-old managing in an unsafe environment.

At a more prosaic level anger was most commonly tied to an experience of injustice. Attempts to maintain discipline often revolved around encounters that end up belittling or humiliating troublesome pupils. Mainstream teachers had a tendency to read malice into bad behaviour and often attributed considerable power to those able to disrupt lessons. This elicited anger in the teacher and an inability to recognise what might be at stake for the pupil. But from the pupils' perspective teachers appeared all-powerful and were, of course, able to wield huge influence over their lives. In some cases, encounters with a hostile, furious teacher led the pupil to anticipate the worst in terms of punishment. Angry responses towards school staff could be driven by an unfocused but potent mix of distress, anger and resentment. If a pupil assumed that the worst that could happen would happen (exclusion, or even a call home to their parents) they had little incentive to control their anger. Teachers commonly assumed that pupils cared very little about their place in the classroom, but expressions of anger were very often provoked by anticipation and extreme fear of expulsion. As I show in Chapter 6, school exclusion was invariably a devastating experience for the young person concerned, regardless of their behaviour.

More fundamentally, anger was usually experienced by pupils as an entirely justifiable response. In the artificial space of a BSU anger management class, amidst all the technical focus on breathing, counting to 10 and imagining traffic lights, the script of anger as a problematic personal flaw reigned, but back in the real world it was more commonly related to fairness. Expressing anger was often explained in terms of standing up for yourself and establishing a claim to dignity. The following quote is from Luke, after attending his anger management course.

> "I've still got that anger, though. I've still got it. But I've got... Don't really fight any more ... because everyone knows, everyone knows, like... Like everybody, like normally... Well, don't do that to Luke, because Luke won't take it, and this and that, and they know. But some kids, some kids just take it, and I don't like bullies either. I don't like seeing people bullied, because, like, when I was in primary, I did used to get, like some kid did used to try and bully me, and one day, my dad said to me, 'I've had enough. You stand up for yourself, otherwise I'm going to beat you up myself', like, and then basically I just stood up for myself, and then he didn't do it again."

There were very few BSU pupils that did not frame more specific accounts of their angry outbursts within a narrative of social justice. Tales of being wrongly accused, singled out and humiliated commonly accompanied descriptions of losing their temper and there was an evident satisfaction that came from fighting back. Sometimes a sense of feeling wronged hung in the air, feeding into and compounding already existing problems. Max, the Portuguese speaker falsely accused of making abusive comments (as discussed in Chapter 3), hung on to deep resentment at the way he and his parents had been treated. His impulsive decision to lob a snowball at the head teacher after his exclusion threat had been lifted was problematised as irrational and uncontrolled, but the sentiment behind it was not difficult to understand. And significantly, anger was often felt on behalf of others. When Marcus was targeted by the boys from another school he had been touched to find he had a solid contingent of Gravensdale boys ready to fight alongside him. In fact, some of the more serious incidents in the co-ed schools were associated with a strongly felt sense of solidarity and group injury.

Within the BSUs there was a shared experience of stigma. All were very aware of their low status within the school and there was a strong sense of being unfairly discriminated against, or 'tarnished' as one boy described it. But there were few outlets within the co-ed schools to articulate any sense of grievance or injustice. Even circle time discussions of topics with clear political connotations were expected to be conducted in a flat, largely dispassionate way and were most often used to demonstrate correct and incorrect ways of relating. As Beverley Skeggs and Vik Loveday (2012) contend, emotions are only effective for understanding power when they are connected to an idea or source that renders injustice comprehensible as a social problem. This seemed to be precisely what circle time groups were designed to prevent. The message that there is no legitimate place for pupil anger in the classroom was clear, effectively delegitimising even the possibility of righteous passion firing political commitment and beliefs. As Guy Claxton (2005) asks, 'If we all develop our Emotional Intelligence, and we restrain our aggression and deploy our empathy, will there be anyone left to ask hard questions about what is going on around us?' (p 22). This concern was not lost on BSU staff, but their capacity to meaningfully engage with it was limited by the emotional skills model they were expected to adhere to and promote.

Developmental deficits: challenging girls

Interpretations of problematic behaviour within the schools were heavily gendered. Boys were considerably more likely to be referred to the BSUs in the co-ed schools, and reflecting the national picture, were much more likely to be excluded. While challenging conduct from boys tended to be understood in terms of damage and disorder, troublesome girls, in the main, elicited considerably less concern. School staff discussed the developmental struggles girls were undergoing and often described feeling protective towards them. For example, Kate Blackman (head of Gravensdale BSU) talked about needing to 'mollycoddle' girls and emphasised the emotional difficulties they faced in achieving maturity. Keely, a participant in our group, was acknowledged to be on the edge of exclusion, but was described as a frightened little girl.

> "She's put this great big stupid hat on that's not hers, and it worked. In year seven she got badly bullied, so she created the big girl image, and it worked, and she's sticking with it, no matter what. So, 'I'll be the big toughie, and I'll ...' and 'you can't'. As soon as you begin to take that hat off, she doesn't know where to go, because then she's little fat Keely again, and she doesn't like that, so she doesn't want to go back to it. The other person is more popular, gets her own, you know, gets what she wants, and it kind of works for her. The other thing is, she's a big girl, right. So by year nine, she'd be more their size, so rather than being the great big girl... Because we've had other girls, like Ellie is a girl who did exactly the same thing, but come

year 11, she said to me, 'Miss, the boys are talking to me like I'm all right. They're approaching me. They're not scared of me anymore. I've got a boyfriend, I can be nice, I can get back on with my school work', and I just said to her, 'They've, they've reached you. You know, they've all grown up, and now you're the same, you're, you're not so unusual and scary'."

Keely's behaviour was challenging. She repeatedly walked out of classes, openly smoked and had told the head teacher to 'fuck off', but her actions were interpreted as part of a bumpy developmental trajectory towards womanhood. Kate regarded boys and girls as having 'very different needs', and drew attention to the 'bitchy' interactions girls needed to be able to navigate. Troublesome boys, according to Kate lacked social sophistication and self-awareness often because of an organic deficit. She was prone to making informal diagnosis of undetected disorders in boys, drawing on this as an explanatory framework. Even dyslexia was regarded as a limiting condition in boys. For example, in discussing Luke she drew attention to his reluctance to come to terms with his dyslexic self.

"I think that all stems from him not accepting himself, and, you know, not allowing himself to be dyslexic. And once he overcomes that, I think he'll be happier and not, you know, compete with everyone, because he can't."

By all accounts, Luke's behaviour was less overtly troublesome than Keely's. He had been involved in fights outside of school, been aggressive at home and had punched a wall. This earned him the epithet of 'angry young man', in contrast to Keely's 'frightened little girl'.

Girls' behaviour was generally viewed as far less threatening to teachers in comparison with boys, with concerns centring in the main on rudeness, stroppiness and lack of cooperation. Girls were also very commonly referred to as 'children'. Separate groups for girls were established in the co-ed schools to deal with behaviour that was much more likely to be understood from within a normalised framework of adolescent girl troubles. These groups tended to centre on raising self-esteem and increasing confidence, with school staff implicating hormones, friendships, boys and anxieties over weight and appearance in their understandings of challenging conduct in girls. Replete with gendered meanings, these sessions produced and reinforced the invisible template of heterocentric knowledge and practices through which the girls came to make sense of themselves and their own behaviour (Butler, 1990).

The trivialisation of girls' behaviour was often articulated in terms of them having come off the developmental rails. The deputy head at Meedham girls, Miss Jennings, talked about the importance of supporting girls though having 'conversations' they may not be having at home. Problems could go beyond 'PMT or growing up' if something changed at home, but Miss Jennings claimed to instinctively know if that was the case. By far the most common word used to describe girls' challenging behaviour was 'inappropriate', echoing centuries-old judgements of 'respectability' levelled against women and girls (Skeggs, 1997). Much less commonly applied to boys, 'inappropriate' most often meant too loud, rude or of unsuitable appearance, reflecting the particular embodied nature of these gendered troubles. For example, Rita, a mentor at Meedham BSU, articulated her frustrations at the improper conduct of the girls.

> "I notice that with quite a number of girls. And their whole inability to not see that the way they speak and the way their body language and their manner is not appropriate... I far prefer to work in this building where it's controlled much more and if a student comes in and they're NOT in an appropriate uniform they get sent home. If they're wearing jewellery they're not supposed to then they'll get sent home. It's very difficult. If you go over there [the upper mainstream site up the road] they'll be using their mobile phones; they wear inappropriate footwear; they've got different colours in their hair; they've got jewellery on and it's not picked up on."

Inappropriate also often referred to sexualised behaviour in girls, either in terms of inferred sexual relationships or talk about sex. For example, the deputy head at Meedham expressed shock at the precocious 'awareness' of some girls. As Jessica Ringrose (2013) notes, in terms of sexuality, contemporary girls are positioned between the binary categories of postfeminist empowerment and moral panic over the hypersexualisation of children (particularly girls). At Meedham, the latter concern dominated through an emphasis on respectable asexual femininity, practised through attention to a proper appearance, social skills and deportment. There was much chat within the unit about babies and children. Lots of the girls had young sisters or cousins that they cared for (we were quizzed about our marital status and how many children we had), but there was relatively little everyday talk about boys or romantic relationships.

It was very different at Gravensdale where the girls were preoccupied by their relationships with boys. As I alluded to in Chapter 2, there was a serious problem of sexual bullying directed at girls in both co-ed schools. Our attempt to run mixed gender groups at Gravensdale brought the issue into sharp relief. While the boys used the sessions as a forum to showcase their verbal sparring skills, the girls laughed, pulled faces and remained for the most part tight-lipped. Sometimes the humour appeared to be directed at one or two of the girls in particular, and although deliberately pitched above our heads, it was clear something nasty was being communicated. If we explicitly asked questions to the girls in the mixed sessions they would look down, shrug their shoulders and mumble "I don't know".

At the end of the second session, we caught up with some of the girls outside the room and asked what was going on. They described feeling self-conscious in the group and said the boys would 'take the piss' if they spoke out. They also said they felt physically intimidated, claiming that boys would often hurt them in the playground. One of the girls, Amy, rolled up her sleeve to display extensive bruising all up her arm. They hurried off again, leaving us feeling shocked and bemused. I watched as they caught up with a gaggle of boys in the corridor, laughing and shouting as they went. Outside of our sessions the girls did not behave like powerless victims in the playground or classroom. They bantered with the boys, teased them and often appeared to be sharing intimate exchanges. But these relationships operated within the constraints of an aggressive, patriarchal, heterosexualised framework in which the boys were very clearly top dogs. By the third session we were segregating the group by gender, operating in opposite corners of the room. The boys were furious at this development and protested loudly by bursting into the girls' space or sneaking closer and trying to hear what was being discussed. In this separate space the girls talked largely about the boys, describing the ways in which they were annoyed by them, how it was fun to wind them up and which ones were worthy of attention. For example, Tiffany described how boys made her life difficult.

> "I don't know, it's like going through their hormones.
> They're like ... probably like you know, 'Ah, big boobs!'
> and everything. It's like I've got, like, the biggest boobs
> out of all my mates as well, and so it makes it even worse,
> because the boys are like, 'Boo' [pokes herself]. And even

if you wear, like, baggy shirts, they still go. And my mum's like, 'Why are you wearing baggy shirts that are, like, too big?' And I'm like, 'Oh I gotta'."

But the impact of this 'hassle' was quickly minimised by Tiffany as being manageable and she went on to reflect on how she generally preferred boys to girls. Girls were 'bitchy', she claimed. Attempts by the boys to gatecrash the girls' space was met with rolling of eyes, smiles and giggles. There was a status associated with attention from the boys, reflecting the extent to which the girls were invested in a competitive heterosexualised matrix of power relations (Ringrose, 2013).

In contrast, the boys at Gravensdale talked relatively little about the girls. If girls were mentioned it was usually in the context of an opaque and obviously snide aside. For example, during one segregated session, Luke mumbled to Bond with a smirk, "I could tell you a thing or two about Amy, mate," triggering raucous laughter from the others.

There is a considerable body of literature exploring this kind of 'laddish' behaviour and the intricate ways in which gender identities are negotiated and enacted within schools (Reay, 2001; Haywood and Mac An Ghaill, 2003; Jackson, 2006; Archer et al, 2010). In particular, Mac An Ghaill's (1994) account of the 'hypermasculinity' cultivated by working-class boys in response to the insecurities and injuries of school, offers a compelling framework for understanding this often theatrical display of gender power. The boys were clearly invested in relationships with the girls, but routinely used them to celebrate their superiority and dominance. As Haywood and Mac Ghaill (2003) note, school acts as a 'masculinity making device', producing and legitimating practices that mediate relations of power. In the context of Gravensdale, BSU boys acted into an aggressive, heterosexualised framework that allowed them to position girls as weak and low in status. In one of the segregated sessions, I asked some of the boys at Gravensdale what they thought about single sex schools. Their alarm at the concept was revealing.

Luke: In a boys school it's a bit weird, you walk around and there's just all boys. That's how people turn gay, you know what I mean?

Val: Is it really???

Bond: I read it in a magazine, too many boys turns you gay.

James: Boys can be really aggressive.

Alfie: Yeah and cause lots of fights.

James: I reckon girls bring a bit of peace to the school.

Luke: Girls calm you down. They never like seeing you fight. They're like [high pitched voice] oh, oh, like they scream and everything. They always start screaming and everything.

Val: Do you think girls feel the same way about that?

Luke: An all-girls school is very bitchy as well.

Val: Is it?

Bond: Very bitchy. They talk about each other all the time.

Val: How do you know that?

Bond: In this school it's bitchy 'cos girls talk about boys.

Val: But boys talk about girls. You've just been talking about girls.

James: [sings] Boys will be boys.

Bond: But we have a little laugh, but we don't really bitch as much as girls.

Luke: Yeah girls are like moaning. You say one little thing and they'll go off in a strop.

Just as our segregation of the group was met with dismay and anger, the idea of a boys only school was deeply threatening. The suggestion made by Luke and Bond that boys might turn gay highlights, not only a performative homophobia, but also the fragility of their 'powerful' identities. The claim that girls are a crucial civilising influence returns the conversation to a more comfortable essentialist account of brutal pugnacious males pulled back from the brink by weak, hysterical females. The focus then turns to an attack on girls, depicting them as 'bitchy' and 'moaning'. Luke's 'bitchy' comment came five minutes or so after his unambiguously malicious reference to Amy, but this was categorised as having 'a little laugh'.

The construction of girls as 'bitchy' claimed a solidity that made it almost irrefutable, ensuring it could be used to problematise any female solidarity that cut across the gender hierarchy. Girls forming a clique, hanging out together and resisting the attention of boys were at risk of acquiring the label. Some girls (like Tiffany) sought to prove they were not 'bitchy' by prioritising friendships with boys above girls. This problematisation of girls' friendships was embedded in Gravensdale BSU with activities designed to help girls manage 'bitchiness'. As such, 'bitchiness' was naturalised as a feature of being a girl. The gender patterned nature of bullying and the often sophisticated relational nature of aggression among girls has been well documented (Osler and Vincent, 2003; George, 2007; Ringrose, 2008). However, research exploring the complex power dynamics contextualising girls' friendships points towards the gendered, classed and racialised micro-politics framing such conflicts (Hey, 1997; Brown, 2003; Ringrose, 2008). Bitchiness as a discourse reinforced a set of meanings that exacerbated disputes among girls, silenced resistance and made principles of heterosexual competition normative (Ringrose, 2008).

This is particularly well illustrated by returning to the example of Amy. Small, white and 14 years old, Amy had been referred to the BSU for her troublesome behaviour in class. Though she was generally quiet and calm, she drew on subtle but very effective methods for disrupting lessons. She often refused to take part in activities (providing a whole range of implausible excuses) and was very good at provoking reactions from others. During our group sessions she sometimes enthusiastically suggested pursuing a specific activity, only to resolutely decline to join in herself. She was also prone to telling outlandish stories, swearing they were true. Amy was often the butt of the boys' jokes, although she seemed torn between feeling flattered and upset. Slim and pretty, she was heavily invested in her femininity, using her body as a 'tool of attraction' (Swan, 2013). She wore extensive, carefully applied makeup and a 'customised' school uniform. She kept the hem of her skirt short and deliberately frayed, and adorned her blazer with a selection of badges and buttons. But Amy was at the centre of a nasty feud with a group of girls who had formerly been her friends. The root of the problem, it seemed, was rivalry over Luke. Amy claimed to have gone out with him (denied by Luke himself), sparking anger and a schism among her friends.

The consequences of this were major for Amy. She had been ostracised by a best friend, threatened, attacked on the street, and persecuted on social media. Her mother described how a group of girls befriended Amy to take her shopping, only to surreptitiously fill her bag with unpaid for items and wait for her to trigger the store alarm. When another girl in the school was attacked, Amy was deliberately implicated, resulting in her being arrested by the police and questioned until the CCTV cameras that plastered Gravensdale proved her innocence. Amy fantasised about leaving the school, but remained defiant.

> "I ain't gonna move because of what they're doing to me. Because it's not me. They're thinking that it's getting me, so they're going to win, but I'm not. I'm not gonna play their silly little games. It's not bothering me, I ain't gonna play the game, and basically they're just trying to get back at me because Kim's going out with Luke, and Luke turned round to her and told her that he don't like her, Luke does not like her, Luke told her over and over again he does not like her, but because I went out with him, she gets jealous. But I'm not playing her silly little game no more. She can go out with him, I'm not bothered. But I'm not playing her silly little games."

Amy received very little support from the school despite being a victim of what was clearly a concerted and orchestrated bullying campaign. Kate Blackman made no mention of the harassment Amy was suffering and was instead quite dismissive of her as a vacuous teenage girl obsessed with boys.

> "Amy really wasn't a problem until year nine and boys came on the scene, and now the 'Mm-mm', you know, if you've got Luke or Alfie there, she's okay, because she'll just be listening to them, otherwise there's not much to engage with. (LAUGHS) That's about Amy for you. You know, she's not going to be a beauty queen is she!"

This was an unusually cruel comment from Kate Blackman, expressing contempt over Amy's low horizons and lack of potential. There was no sense that school should or could aim to inspire any alternative talents. In fact, Kate was brutal in her assessment of the future prospects of girls like Amy.

"Oh, it's all they have [their looks]. So she'll get, she'll have her kids, get married, and, you know, that's what she'll do well."

Though this quote sounds as though it comes from a different era it is contextualised by a postfeminist construction of equality as a given, and girls as agents freely choosing to trade on their looks and settle for domesticity (Gill, 2008; McRobbie, 2008). Kate even feels able to assess Amy's erotic capital, "She's not going to be a beauty queen". Sensing her susceptibility to being dismissed as only fit for motherhood, Amy emphasised antipathy to ever having children and talked instead about wanting to become a writer. But ultimately her place in the school was untenable in the context of the unresolved bullying and after spending time at the school's off-site provision she was eventually permanently excluded for fighting.

While Amy received particularly harsh treatment, there was genuine sympathy and understanding particularly from female teachers of the pressures that girls might be facing. Girls were regarded as vulnerable to losing their way on the path to adulthood, becoming loud, stroppy or even promiscuous in the process. Again, these are highly gendered constructions that were rarely applied to boys. The lost soul story was readily adopted by the girls themselves to emphasise their status as needy rather than badly behaved. For example, Chanelle from Meedham Girls:

"Well, in the beginning, she [mother] wasn't happy, because they ... Miss Bridge didn't, like, exactly tell my mum why I was (pause) she just basically told my mum the bad things – why I'm going to BSU. But when she had the meeting, she understood that it's not because I'm bad or whatever, that (pause) just extra support. And she was alright with it."

Chanelle's attempt to normalise her BSU referral reflects the compelling regulatory pull of the developmental narrative. Chanelle and others present themselves as essentially good girls in need of support to find their way. This resonates with the observation made by Archer et al (2010) that girls involved with school conflict often struggle to present themselves as 'good underneath'. Such stories are constructed from and embedded within taken for granted assumptions about normal and acceptable girl behaviour, encouraging a commitment to working towards conformity. And this drive to conformity was deceptively sharp edged. As I explore in the next chapter, the troublesome adolescent girl discourse enforced normative boundaries, which if breached could situate a girl beyond the paternalistic pale. The consequences of this could be brutal. Girls transgressing feminine norms risked losing the protective support of BSU staff, resulting in them being sent to male-dominated behaviour support initiatives. As I will outline, such girls were subject to severe harassment, and even physical and sexual abuse.

Girls were less likely than boys to be seen as lacking in social and emotional skills, but they were more commonly infantilised and portrayed as 'spoilt', over-indulged and lacking in potential. This tendency to trivialise and downplay the acting out of girls in the classroom ensured that while permanent exclusion was less likely, specific, socially located difficulties and barriers to mainstream inclusion were rarely considered. Audrey Osler and colleagues (Osler et al, 2002; Osler and Vincent, 2003; Osler, 2006) have shown how girls are given low priority in school planning for behaviour management, with their needs overshadowed by concerns about boys' antisocial conduct.

At Meedham Girls there was a very overt drawing in of feminised practices into BSU activities, including knitting and embroidery, cushions and cakes. At Gravensdale, conversations were often more explicitly focused on relationships with boys, rehearsing a characteristically narrow form of institutionally sanctioned hetero-gendered sexuality (Mellor and Epstein, 2006). At Gravensdale, femininity, or more accurately, lack of appropriately performed femininity, could be quite unambiguously placed at the core of the problematized personal. As Kate Blackman's earlier quote about her "frightened little girls" suggests, not being recognised as feminine enough could be as problematic as Amy's low aptitude femininity. Keely's and Ellie's difficulties were partly attributed to their intimidating size. More specifically, according to Kate, things improved for 'big' Ellie when her proportions became more appropriate and she got a boyfriend. To emphasise the point, Kate even paraphrased Ellie's response.

> "Miss, the boys are talking to me like I'm all right. They're approaching me. They're not scared of me anymore. I've got a boyfriend, I can be nice. I can get back on with my school work."

At Meedham there was less emphasis on shape and size and more of a preoccupation with deportment (correct uniform, walking not running, politeness). Anger management training was referred to as 'conflict management' and the deputy head expressed concern that the girls were 'louder' than those in other schools. There was also an apparent oversensitivity to displays of aggression among girls. For example, pursuing their drama interest in the playground, the BSU girls had staged and filmed a play on their mobile phones. The scene involved bullying and featured a mock fight. Despite quickly establishing the fight was not real, the police were called in to issue dark threats about the dangers of fighting. As the girls reflected:

> "We were just being silly. It was like a play really. We were just acting, somebody had glasses and the other people were just people who was bullying them and we was just fighting, not using hands, just like making it look real and some people was video recording it. And the teacher saw us 'cos some other students went and told the teachers but we was only, 'cos we don't have anything to do in the playground, no equipment or nothing so, we got in trouble for that and then the police come into our school." (Natasha)

> "We were pretending to, um, we was videoing each other, but we was pretending to, like, fight, and videoing everything... And then we got in trouble, then they ... we had to have a meeting. All of us, like 10 of us, and our parents came in, and the police was talking to us, saying it was wrong. It was a game. They was just saying even if it wasn't real, that you would get in trouble, and if you do it and it is real, you could have got, you can get a, I forgot what's it called, a criminal record." (Charpane)

The way this incident was dealt with may have reflected the risk-averse culture at Meedham, but it is also important to note that the girls from Gravensdale were white while those from Meedham were predominantly black. Issues of race intersect with gender to position girls' behaviour in particular ways (Mirza, 2009). Expectations and interpretations of femininity are highly racialised with concern about appearance, loudness, and aggression more likely to be directed at black girls (Connolly, 1998; Morris, 2008; Rollock, 2008). The deputy head at Meedham, Sarah Jennings, alluded indirectly to the racial makeup of the BSU (and the school) in her reflections on the challenges of working at the school:

> "We're exclusively a working-class school, and that's fine but that brings with it certain lacks of influences and the impact of these 'special school'–type students is enormous!

...You've got the girl in year seven whose parents won't really work with us because of their own issues and their own education background. Girls who are inappropriate in terms of their awareness of how (pause) I just sometimes look at these girls open-mouthed at how they have that confidence to say what they do. It's very, very [worrying] I think it's an inner, an inner city problem maybe?" (Sarah Jennings, Deputy Head at Meedham Girls School)

Class is drawn on quite explicitly here to rather bluntly explain the personal deficit model driving BSU interventions. However, race is also heavily encoded in the phrase 'inner city'. As I explore in the next chapter, this euphemistic turn of phrase reflects a more general taboo operating in schools around the subject of race, and the discomfort it generates among teachers. More specifically, I show how race, class and gender seamlessly intersect to produce particular problems and solutions within the schools, rendering some pupils 'unincludable' in the process.

Note

[1] See 'Put young children on DNA list, urge police', *The Observer*, Sunday 16 March 2008, http://www.theguardian.com/society/2008/mar/16/youthjustice.children

FIVE

Dynamics of disadvantage: race, gender and class

'Inclusion' as an approach is founded on a morally infused stand against discrimination. Commitment to support all learners as being equally entitled and valued carries the implicit recognition that pupils may be treated differently because of the social and structural classifications they occupy. Yet 'inclusion' policies tend to be characterised by a one-sided preoccupation with celebrating diversity and promoting equality, with this positive message all but drowning out more critical assessment of the day-to-day practices that lead to the very clear patterns of disadvantage I noted in Chapter 2. As I will outline in more detail, discourses of inclusion in schools operate within the interstices of ingrained and unreflected-upon categories of difference, with enduring disparities concealed beneath the feel good gloss of diversity.

I begin with a focus on race as a key site of discrimination in the schools. I take a closer look at the racial dynamics driving encounters at Gravensdale, highlighting and exploring how systematised prejudice was routinely justified and defended by school staff. Broadening the analysis out to include the other schools I show how race issues operate under the surface, silently shaping encounters and making certain outcomes more likely than others. I then move on to explore how race intersects with gender to produce differently inflected risks and solutions. I also take a closer look at interactions between boys and girls and expose the ugly but normalised culture of sexual violence governing relations in the co-ed schools. The chapter concludes with an explicit consideration of class, drawing on the example of the only middle-class boy participating in the research.

Gravensdale: Not racist but...

As I've outlined, race was a particularly fraught issue at Gravensdale. Allegations of racism were common alongside a curious tolerance of racial abuse that set it apart from the other institutions. All three schools were similar in terms of their ethnically diverse intake. At Gravensdale and Hailingbrooke the main ethnic groups were white, black African, black Caribbean and Turkish alongside a very wide variety of other ethnicities. Meedham was similar but lacking any sizable Turkish population and with more black African and Caribbean pupils. All three schools proudly acclaimed this multicultural array, but as I'll demonstrate, a fundamental unease penetrated the celebratory veneer of diversity at Gravensdale. Racial tensions were high among pupils and staff, yet there appeared to be no outlet to discuss or address this in any meaningful way.

The frequency with which jokey racial insults were hurled in the playground was among the first signs that relations in the school were troubled. It was profoundly shocking to hear white boys using the 'N word' to describe black fellow pupils and to realise how often playground humour revolved around crude ethnic stereotyping. This often went on under the nose of school staff, yet no one seemed prepared to call it out as offensive or problematic. The pupils themselves seemed unfazed and described it as normal reciprocal knock-about humour. But there was an unmistakably nasty edge to much of the banter and the air often crackled with tension. For example, before we gained access to the second BSU mentor group, Anita (the behaviour support manager) organised a small group of young men to participate in the research. On the day the session was scheduled Anita seemed very surprised see any of them turn up (we later discovered they were persistent truants). Three white English boys attended the session and another boy from Mexico (Jo) came in late. There was lots of engaged discussion with the white boys until Jo's entrance. The white boys then became visibly hostile, mocking his accent and making snide comments. Jo began to angrily challenge them and in an attempt to sidestep a full-blown fight, Yvonne appealed for respect and an end to accent mocking. This provoked fury from the white boys. "Are you calling me a racist?", one of them spat back at her. That marked the end of the session and we abandoned any further attempt at groupwork with that particular configuration of pupils.

After this uncomfortable experience we became aware of loosely racialised playground factions operating within Gravensdale. Pupils were identified as, and described themselves as 'Safes' (black pupils), 'Sweets' (white pupils)[1] or Turks. The black boys at Gravensdale were particularly adamant that racial insults should not be taken seriously, but as we discovered, a previous attempt by the head to crack down on conflict in the playground had seen them hauled out and accused of racist behaviour towards the Sweets and the Turks. The tendency for white pupils to be positioned and to position themselves as the victims of racism was something we encountered repeatedly at Gravensdale.

For example, Luke justified his use of the 'N word' on the grounds that some of his best friends are black, and racist themselves.

> "I think it's funny, like, because, like, most of the black people in my year, like they go to me, 'Oh, I like this white guy'. Because I'm funny, because I, like, have a joke around with them. And they go to me, 'You white this', and I go, 'What, you this/that?' and we joke around and everything, but, like, they don't really take it personal. They don't go, 'What do you say? You're racist'. Like they joke around. I take it for a joke. I don't, it don't really bother me if people go, 'You white this and white that'. …Like in football as well, like when you do a tackle, they go, 'You white this' … it's a colour. So you live with it… Like football, I went and shook a boy's hand, he went, 'Move your white hand away from me'. I went, 'You're a mug'. He went, 'You people'. I'm not being funny, it's not always the white people are doing it. I went, 'It's evenly matched now, isn't it?' It doesn't bother me if people go, 'You white this', 'you white that', I just think, 'Yeah, right, good for you, mate. Yeah, whatever. If that's your opinion, that's your opinion. I'm white, this is it, isn't it!' I do actually probably know more black people than white people."

Luke's account of how he bears the burden of whiteness abuse relies on the detachment of racism from any conception of power, privilege or systemic discrimination. Stripped from its social, structural and historical context racism becomes little more than a form of personalised hurt, equally felt by any racial group. The ready identification and calling out of reverse racism by pupils at Gravensdale was compounded by the positively antagonistic stance school management maintained toward allegations of racial inequality. The school had been beset by claims of racist incidents against black pupils. Significant numbers of black parents had complained and the school was being monitored by the local authority because such a disproportionate number of African-Caribbean boys had been excluded.

The head and deputy head were resolute in their denial that racism was operating within the school and seemed genuinely bemused, hurt and angry. They approached the allegations as if they were a personal attack against the integrity and morality of individual staff members. The incidents themselves were investigated on those grounds, with the head concluding that any such suggestion was 'rubbish'. As David

Gillborn (2008) notes, discussion of racism can provoke a defensive recoil, shutting down consideration of the subtle and dispersed ways discrimination operates. At Gravensdale, any acknowledgement of the existence of institutional racism was regarded as a dangerous admission of guilt. Instead, all efforts were channelled into justifying the unjustifiable. For example, Mr Wickes described the previously high numbers of black pupils excluded as a statistical 'spike' and emphasised the mediating factors.

> "Because when I had a meeting with the inclusion/ exclusion person at the borough a couple of years ago, he was sort of praising me for my statistics… I don't really do a quota for, you know, ethnic groups and so forth. However, obviously I've got a duty of care to look out for, because of institutional racialism, for example, or whatever it might be, so I make sure I do look after the issues, but looking at the issues last year, it looks like there's 80 black Caribbean students in the year group, of which I think about 17 or 18 at some point were excluded. So we obviously analyse it carefully, and we're keeping an eye on it, and this year we're noticing that they were down. …And you also refer back as well to other data, like attainment, because black Caribbean/black African are all achieving significantly above expected in the school, whereas the white working-class are achieving significantly below expected in the school, so, you know, that would kind of knock back any issues of racism."

Mr Wickes and Ms Sheldon put significant effort into 'knocking back' allegations of racism. As well as countenancing and pursuing complaints of reverse racism to demonstrate the even handedness of the issue, they defensively attacked what they viewed as malicious and calculated accusations. Ms Sheldon expressed indignation at the very notion that racism could operate in a multicultural school, and as this quote highlights, blames the opportunism of black mothers.

> "Spend the rest of the years of my life working in schools like this, why would I do that if I was a racist? I know, for instance, a colleague of mine has gone to deal with a mum today, who wanted to see me, but I hadn't dealt with the incident, so there was no point in her seeing me, but I've made sure, you know, there's a black man and a white man

sat there, you know, so that she's not going to sit in front of a white figure of authority, because she'll do that, you know, at some point she might if she doesn't feel it's fair, she'll go, 'You're being racist'. No, we're not. You know, 'Your son's badly behaved', it doesn't matter whether he's, you know, turquoise!"

Ms Sheldon's logic that racists would not choose to work in her school combined with fury at the perceived injustice of white teachers facing false allegations form a powerful and impenetrable block to any critical reflexivity. She purported to maintain an unbiased colour blind approach claiming not to see race, yet the language of diversity and difference simultaneously tripped off her tongue. Ms Sheldon emphasised the multicultural credentials of the school and described the intake as 'genuinely inclusive'. From this perspective, welcoming diversity works to neutralise the troublesome issue of race. The contradictory stance of valuing diversity while claiming not to see race reflects the extent to which current inclusion agendas depoliticise race, partly through the abstraction and personalisation of difference. Symbolic representation of ethnic diversity can be celebrated without reference to the way this difference is experienced as inequality. Meanwhile, racism becomes reframed as a weapon used by black accusers to wield power over white professionals, through deployment of 'the race card'.

Yet Gravensdale was adept at playing its own race card to deflect attention from the sustained and systematic inequalities disadvantaging black students. As the above quote from Mr Wickes demonstrates, discussions of racism commonly prompted a singling out of the white working classes as at greater risk of educational failure and the social problems associated with it. This claim functioned not just to undermine or 'knock back' potential allegations of racism within the institution, but also to distance the speaker from the problematic personal identifications associated with their 'whiteness'. In spite of her declared colour blindness, the white working class were apparently very visible to Ms Sheldon.

"You know, we reflect society, it seems to be a bit of society which has just dropped out, it doesn't have a place, doesn't have an identity, and because it is (pause) because it is the white working class, nobody wants to talk about it, and it's possibly because – between you, me, and the tape recorder – they're not necessarily very nice. You know, they're small-minded, racist ... I mean ... you know what I mean! And nobody wants to say, 'Oh, look at them, they have a problem', because they're also thinking, 'Well, they shouldn't have a problem really, should they', you know, 'it's all at their fingertips', you know, they haven't got a language problem."

As Lawler (2005) points out, this specific othering of the white working class has become a recognisable feature of middle-class identity. She describes a racialising move to hyper whiten the working classes ensuring their emblematic whiteness becomes central to their continued disparagement. While once associated with racial 'impurity' and condemned as 'not white enough', the white working classes are now likely to be portrayed as 'too white', embodying, and to some extent, containing, all that is troubling about whiteness. One effect is to construct racism as a predominantly working-class problem deflecting attention away from middle-class-run institutions. Gillborn (2010) also notes the fluid and highly contingent ways in which the white working class are invoked through the discourses of degenerate and victim. While they are portrayed as feckless, ignorant racists they are also commonly positioned as having lost out to race equality initiatives that have gone too far.

'Do you want to be in this school?'

While Gravensdale remained resolutely focused on their 'white kid problem', racist practices and assumptions continued to systematically disadvantage non-white pupils, black Caribbean boys in particular. The dismissal of the disproportionate exclusion rates as a 'spike' concealed the alternative measure taken by the school to remove black boys unofficially. None of the black boys we worked with in our second term at Gravensdale were ever officially excluded, but equally none saw out the end of the school year. Instead, they were all dismissed on early study leave many months before they were officially eligible to leave. As a report by the Children's Commission details, this form of illegal exclusion is not uncommon and appears to impact disproportionately on those groups most likely to be formally excluded (Children's Commission, 2013).

Mr Wickes, Ms Sheldon and others at the school were not racists in the sense that they deliberately set out to disadvantage black pupils. In contemporary UK society few people draw on a biologised category of race to assert their superiority, highlighting the need for a more nuanced and sophisticated understanding of how racism becomes ingrained in social practices and institutions (Gillborn, 2008). While staff at Gravensdale saw themselves as impartially following procedures, safeguarding and protecting the best interests of pupils, the black boys found themselves positioned as intrinsically threatening the very authority underpinning these practices. Their embodied difference was routinely read as a dangerous challenge to the 'cultural arbitrary' (Bourdieu and Passeron, 1977). As Deborah Youdell (2003) details, blackness becomes censured through routine, and unreflected upon interpretations of youth/street black identity as inherently undermining the institutional fabric of school.

> The school's constituting interpretations of Black sub-cultural identities as intrinsically anti-school and a challenge to authority are tacit. It is unlikely that any racialised or racist intent underpins these constitutions. Rather, the racialised and racist nature of these constitutions can be understood in terms of common-sense and institutional racism. Such racism operates through the historicity – the sedimented meanings – of unrecognised and unacknowledged organisational and common-sense discourses which cite and inscribe the biological and/or cultural deficiency, hypersexuality, deviance, and threat of Blackness – the discourse of a Black challenge to White hegemony. (p 24)

This process operates at the micro level of everyday interaction, with performative embodied identities fashioned through interaction with racialised institutional discourses to render some undesirable or even impossible learners (Youdell, 2006; Rollock, 2007).

At Gravensdale, black street identities were explicitly linked to fears about gangs and gang violence. As Ralphs et al (2009) show, merely living in gang active areas could result in young people being labelled as 'high risk', triggering greater surveillance and police harassment. They also note the significance of ethnicity in informing perceptions of those most likely to be gang members. Public speculation about gangs and gang membership is quite unambiguously 'viewed and projected through the lens of race and ethnicity' (Berkley, 2011). Crude and simplistic media accounts of street violence among the young paint it as a problem rooted in the black community, sustaining a long history of moral panic about violent black criminality (Joseph and Gunter, 2011). Black young men have an increased susceptibility towards becoming victims and/or punished perpetrators of gang violence, but this can only be understood from within the context of endemic racism and the severe disadvantage it inflicts. Violent youth offending predominantly occurs in profoundly economically deprived urban areas (Pitts, 2008), while the racially biased practices of the police are well documented (Bowling and Phillips, 2007; Sharpe and Atherton, 2007).

The staff at Gravensdale were understandably very anxious about the violent street culture affecting a large number of the pupils. A 15-year-old boy from the school had lost his life in a stabbing incident shortly before we commenced the research and several other pupils had been hospitalised with knife wounds. Staff were vigilant and worked closely with police, quickly reporting any concerns over gang activity. But teachers' suspicions were ordered by dominant, racially inflected gang member stereotypes. Black boys' behaviour, already marked out as antagonistic, became hyper visible. Marcus, Will, Shane and Mica (all 15 years old) complained of feeling that they were under constant surveillance. They were moved on whenever they gathered as a group in the playground and were held responsible for random misdemeanours in the school. In a group discussion with Chireal (who shared their sense of injustice through association), the black boys described feeling under siege, resentfully clinging on to their precarious place in the school.

> Marcus: You can't argue back. You argue back and you end up in his office and you don't come back.
>
> Will: Someone gets robbed, yeah. And the next minutes we're the suspect.
>
> Marcus: [Put's on head's voice] "What's going on?" you know...
>
> Mica: Half the people right here got named out. He searched our bags.
>
> Marcus: He grabbed us out, yeah. Took us in the hall, yeah, "pockets, pockets" everything on the floor. [barks] "Alright then", and he just walked out.
>
> Shane: His name for it is... (All together): "Do you want to be in this school?" (all laughing) And he'll do things on purpose, he wants to provoke you. He even told us, "Oh I'll be so glad when you lot leave".

Chireal: He said we're all going to fail GCSE in science.

Marcus: I feel so angry towards the school.

Shane: I feel like I want to beat him badly.

Chireal: I hate this school.

The boys were scathing of the notion that they were gang members and extracted much humour from the accusation made by the head that Marcus was the gang leader. But the consequences of the head's suspicion were no laughing matter. As Ralphs et al (2009) show, police often mistakenly label young people as gang associates, subjecting them to severe persecution and harassment. All of the boys were forced to endure regular stop and search measures while Marcus was frequently followed by a leering, plain clothed police officer. When their schoolmate was murdered Marcus was initially marked out as the chief suspect after Mr Wickes informed the police of his suspicions.

> Marcus: My friend Mark got stabbed right and he died and I got criticised for that. You know police come, searched my house. Apparently I done it. We was playing the game we always play in the changing rooms and Shane said they started it and I said yeah and I finished it. He was like, "You finished it, you finished it". I was doing my mocks and he hauled us out. "You killed Mark, didn't you? You killed him. Don't lie I heard you."

> Shane: He said you killed him?!

> Marcus: "You said you finished it." I was playing a game for God's sake. Next day my mum's on the phone, "Marcus come home the murder squad are searching our house."… They had a warrant and everything. They took my phone. I said who told you this. They said it's classified.

> Mentor: It was Mr Wicks.

> Marcus: I'm in the system now because of him.

Mr Wickes' suspicion over the murder was solidified when he confiscated Marcus's phone and discovered a text that read 'RIP Mark'.

Mr Wickes' own confusion and horror at the brutal and senseless killing was no doubt to the fore when he read sinister intent into such a common bereavement platitude. Despite the police quickly ruling Gravensdale pupils out as suspects, Mr Wickes remained suspicious and even began following Marcus on to the bus at the end of the school day. Yet this sustained level of surveillance and harassment did not prevent Marcus himself becoming a knife crime victim so close to the school. This bitter irony was not lost on Shane, who was vibrating with anger and distress after the attack. He was furious that, despite threats openly circulating, no one from the school or police had tried to protect Marcus. Shane, Will and Mica's relationship with the school deteriorated sharply after Marcus was attacked. Early study leave was arranged and Ms Sheldon dismissed them and their complaints of racism with impassioned disgust.

> "But the kids who opt out, or choose something else, like choose a gang. Just that makes me really angry. That's why I'm really angry with those three boys who have gone home, because they've chosen (pause) one of them came in with his mum today, and he's got a tee-shirt that says, 'Stop snitching' on it! I just. I don't really. I'm really angry! It almost made me violent, and I just, I get so angry about it. You know governments and all the sociological reasons that's what it's a hangover from, but you know, it's not like that anymore. I hate this, you know, 'We won't talk to the police. We won't talk to the authorities', I hate being called a racist, I hate it! It makes me really angry.

It was Shane wearing the tee-shirt. There seems little doubt that this was a deliberate and considered act of resistance on his part. And this provocative action was contextualised by the circumstances surrounding Shane's original referral to the BSU, which occurred after his best friend (also black) was excluded for threatening a teacher. The police were involved and Shane was pressured to make a statement. As Ms Sheldon noted earlier on in her interview, he point blank refused.

> "Shane was either there, or he was one of the ones who told about it, and he wouldn't sign, he wouldn't make a statement, and, you know, sort of went downhill from there really. Never high level round the corridors, never classroom disruption, he's clever. It's the out of school, 'I'm a hard

man. I'm the gang, you can't tell me what to do' sort of stuff, on the edge, with Shane." (Ms Sheldon)

This incident cogently illustrates, not only how poorly understood trigger points or grievances were within the school, but also the hidden emotional drivers behind actions and reactions. Ms Sheldon seemed oblivious to the anger and turmoil behind the tee-shirt wearing gesture and instead reads it as a straightforward affirmation of gang values. Her own fury at mindless gang violence is projected onto Shane, blinding her to the deep and ingrained prejudice that sees a boy pathologised and pushed out of school on the basis of mere conjecture about his street profile. Shane did not have a criminal record, despite the police harassment, and as Ms Sheldon acknowledged, his behaviour in school was never particularly problematic. That this was interpreted in terms of cunning and a clever propensity to escape detection reveals much about Ms Sheldon's unconscious fear of black young men.

Invisible racism

The race issue at Gravensdale was institutionally ingrained but severe enough for outsiders to draw attention to it. At the other schools similarly racist outcomes derived from considerably more subtle and embedded practices. At Hailingbrooke the disproportionate numbers of black young men referred to the BSU and/or excluded was certainly exacerbated by Mr Phillips, as discussed in the previous chapter. His claim that up to 10% of any class are unteachable concealed the racialised values through which particular pupils were categorised as such. Notably, almost all of Mr Phillips' 'unteachables' were black or mixed race. Yet any attempt to apply a charge of deliberate or intentional racism would quickly flounder. Mr Phillips was respectful, supportive and appreciative towards high achieving black students and would no doubt be appalled by any suggestion that his actions resulted in racism. However, he drew unreflexively on a particular model of an engaged versus a disengaged student, which in practice worked to disadvantage black and minority ethnic students. As David Gillborn (2008) established, classroom learning is framed by very particular and racialised conceptualisations of a good student or 'ideal client', which shape and direct teacher student interactions.

Mr Phillips not only gave up on those he branded unteachable, he also set about actively removing them from the classroom using whatever means necessary. This inevitably resulted in black and mixed race pupils experiencing serious injustice at his hands. Mr Phillips' fabrications were well recognised by Dave Stirling, who often explicitly challenged his account of events and advocated for his victims. For example, Keishawn (13) found himself in the BSU after an altercation with Mr Phillips in the corridor. He described how he and his friend had been sent out of a lesson for talking in class. Noticing Mr Phillips was walking towards them and recognising they were in danger, the boys had quickly moved in the opposite direction. Mr Phillips caught up with them. He accused Keishawn of being abusive and marched him to the BSU. According to Keishawn, there was something of a confrontation between Dave Stirling and Mr Phillips, with Dave demanding to know exactly why a referral was appropriate and in the end suggesting Mr Phillips 'just leave'. Keishawn told this story many times painting Dave as a strong principled hero.

Keishawn was a small African-Caribbean boy and an absolute joy to include in the research. He was enthusiastic, highly perceptive and very open and unguarded. He talked easily and unselfconsciously about hopes, fears and his relationships with others. Before starting at Hailingbrooke, Keishawn had a troubled and disruptive experience of primary school. His mother took him out of the first school he attended because she felt he was being victimised. It was a predominantly white school and incidents of bullying were not being taken seriously. Keishawn's grandmother had some savings and put them towards a place at a Jamaican-run private school close to their house at the time. This school was run on strict discipline principles, enforced with corporal punishment. Keishawn struggled and ran away from the school prompting his mother to place him in a third school. By the time Keishawn moved to Hailingbrooke his grandmother was suffering from advanced cancer. He and his mother cared for her while she underwent chemotherapy but the course of her illness was brutal and distressing. Keishawn felt her loss deeply.

Keishawn carried a diagnosis of dyslexia and ADHD into Hailingbrooke. He received no extra literacy support and he remained unmedicated for ADHD because his mother refuted the diagnosis. There was certainly very little evidence of his attention deficit or hyperactivity in our sessions. He was for the most part calm and well behaved albeit with a very mischievous, childlike sense of humour. After two terms Dave organised for him to slowly rejoin mainstream, much to Keishawn's dismay. He felt protected and comfortable in the BSU and feared the consequences of returning to the classroom. His apprehension was justified given that he was permanently excluded shortly after. Mr Phillips was not involved but the circumstances, gleaned from his mother, were perturbing to us.

Hats were not allowed in the playground at Hailingbrooke, although this was a rule commonly broken. Keishawn was very self-conscious about his hair and wore a hat as often as he could get away with it. Keishawn's favourite hat ended up being confiscated. It was not unusual for items to be confiscated and they were usually handed back at the end of school. This particular hat was expensively branded and Keishawn had saved up for a long time to buy it. When the hat was not handed back, Keishawn's mother suggested he ask for it to be returned. His repeated enquiries were met with indifference from teaching staff and in frustration he claims to have shouted "I'll get my mum to come to the school and sort it out". The teaching assistant heard this as a threat to shank [stab] her and approached another staff member to report it. By the time the incident reached the head teacher's office Keishawn was additionally accused of shouting, "I fucking hate all white teachers".

While it is never possible to categorically know the truth of contested incidents like this one, we really struggled to believe Keishawn had said either of these things. While I could imagine many of the other boys issuing violent threats, Keishawn had a particular sensitivity to street violence. He had been victimised several times and while like all the other pupils he lived within the constraints of violent territoriality, his main concern was survival and keeping his head down. He did, however, often draw on a variety of slang words, which could easily have been misinterpreted[2]. What is more, his mother certainly was a force to be reckoned with and probably would have retrieved his hat very quickly.

The anti-white sentiments were even harder to imagine coming from Keishawn. He was generally quite dismissive of the concept of racism, declaring in one particularly memorable session that Nelson Mandela had sorted the problem out years ago. While it is entirely possible he developed resentment towards white teachers in the months following his return to the mainstream school, it is just as possible to believe that school staff heard what they were expecting to. In an emotionally fraught environment where teachers are primed to recognise black boys as risky, Keishawn came to ask for a brand name hat that, from the school's perspective, symbolised gang violence and an anti-school mindset (Rollock, 2007). It seems reasonable to consider whether his expressed frustration would have been interpreted very differently had he been a white girl.

Racism operated at a more subtle, subterranean level at Hailingbrooke, (at least in comparison to Gravensdale) and crucially was recognised as such by Dave Stirling in the BSU. Dave was able to contextualise and reflect more broadly on behaviour and identify the particular way black boys were being disadvantaged, as this quote from him demonstrates.

> "The attitudes towards certain groups of pupils in school was very, very negative, and you start thinking, 'Hang on a minute. These people are not being treated fairly ... there was a group of probably about eight or nine young men – this is year nine – African-Caribbean men, boys, who were getting into lots of trouble, at risk of exclusion and all this sort of thing, when fundamentally, yes the behaviour was challenging, nobody had really, I don't believe, honestly sort of kind of thought deeply about why these kids might be behaving like that... If you're, you know, 13, 14 years old, and you've got another probably white male telling you what you've got to do and why, not really entering into a dialogue about it, or trying to see your perspective, or where the conflict actually lies."

Dave made links with a range of outside organisations including African-Caribbean supplementary schools and worked closely with the black mentors in the unit. Dave was also assertive in calling out and challenging institutional racism when he recognised it as impacting on BSU pupils. For example, he talked about a boy who was about to be referred in to the unit.

> "Why is the head teacher going 'Der ... der' and giving the name of this kid? And you think to yourself, 'Well, alright, it's because he is about a foot taller than everybody else out there, he is a young black man. He is quite defensive in the way that he responds to authority', and those are the reasons why, I think, that it's, you've got locked into this situation where he is always the one who is being called, yet there are people around him behaving badly and all this sort of thing... At no point was I making excuses for this kid's behaviour, and neither was his father. However, the idea is, how can you enter a dialogue with the boy? You know, unless you're straight with him, and say, 'Look, I think I understand what you're saying'. I understand that there is this situation. Yes, racism exists. Yes, there are racist practices going on in school. Our job really is to unpick those in your favour. This is your entitlement, your education ...

it's empowerment, it's advocacy, it's actually standing up for some of these people."

Dave's determination to stand up for the pupils won him much affection and respect in the unit but his influence was inevitably restricted. He was often very convincing in recounting a pupil's side of the story and overturned a number of punitive decisions, but he riled a great many mainstream staff in the process. As a result, Dave remained isolated in the inclusion unit like a troublesome conscious.

Gender hierarchies and sexual violence

As I discussed in the previous chapter, low-level disruptive behaviour from girls tended to be normalised and treated as a feature of stormy adolescent development. But if girls were perceived to transgress the bounds of feminine adolescent normality they could find themselves situated beyond the paternalistic pale. This was particularly evident in the co-ed schools, where girls unwilling or unable to take up a subject position as vulnerable faced harsh consequences. For example, behaviour perceived to be violent or threatening from girls could result in them being sent to male-dominated behaviour support initiatives, often as the only female. The unequal resources targeted towards boys, driven by a notion that girls' behaviour is naturally less problematic, both masks the particular needs that girls may have while also ensuring that those receiving referrals are vulnerable to being stigmatised as highly aberrant.

Again, there is a racialised dimension to the categorisation of unacceptable behaviour from girls. As Nicola Rollock (2007) argues, concern over the disproportional exclusion rates of black boys can obscure the fact that black girls are twice as likely to be permanently excluded compared with the total school population and their white female peers. At Hailingbrooke the small number of girls placed alongside the boys in the BSUs were almost exclusively black, suggesting little may have changed since researchers noted how teachers were more likely to view black girls' behaviour as loud, unfeminine and challenging (Wright 1987; Mirza, 1997).

Observing group dynamics at Hailingbrooke BSU when one or two girls were present was an ugly and disturbing experience. The girls faced a barrage of abuse and harassment from the boys, much of it sexualised. The highly charged nature of these interactions and the insults that were hurled reflect a more general dynamic through which normative heterosexuality is enforced (Mellor and Epstein, 2006). The boys acted up in a very different way when a girl was present, displaying a level of hostility that shocked and confused me. As adult females, Yvonne and I were often subject to jokey sexist comments from the boys in the group sessions, which we quickly brushed off. More than occasionally sexualised language or references were made, forcing us to develop the mantra 'keep it clean'. This was remarkably effective in closing down descriptions of pornography or macho bragging around sexual conquests. But all semblance of order broke down the one and only time a girl joined one of our research sessions at Hailingbrooke.

Nikita had been attending one of the separate groups for troubled girls at Hailingbrooke, but her behaviour was regarded as severe enough to see her transferred temporarily to the BSU. There had been no advanced plan to include her in the research, but when I arrived at the unit to set up in the drama studio I was met by a harassed-looking Dave Stirling, who asked if it would be possible to take a couple of extra pupils. I tentatively agreed and set out some extra chairs. When I looked into the BSU classroom I could almost smell the testosterone. There was a rowdy atmosphere and the boys were gathered around a computer screen having accessed a soft porn image of a naked woman. Dave was nowhere to be seen but a mentor was half-heartedly admonishing them, declaring the image to be 'disgusting'. Nikita sat sketching quietly in the corner.

When the boys came filing in for the research session I was perturbed to see Nikita among them. Her presence was met with unbridled antagonism from the boys. Nothing I said had any impact, including my threat to bring the session to a close. The boys referred to her as 'it', called her Nicolas, claiming she looked like a boy and levelled a number of nasty, sexualised insults at her. Nikita remained impressively stoic and laughed good-humouredly through the malicious onslaught, until the boys began passing round a picture someone had drawn depicting her as an elephant. She asked if she could go to the toilet and did not come back until the end of the session. I heard later that she had been found wandering the corridors, acquiring an 'absent without permission' charge against her already troubled record.

This response from the BSU boys was indicative of the wider misogynistic and highly sexualised culture prevailing within the co-ed schools. This could, and indeed did tip into serious sexual violence. There were disturbing incidents of sexual assault in both co-ed schools, which I only became aware of because they involved BSU boys participating in the research. At Gravensdale, one of the boys in our research (Tom) had received a week's temporary exclusion and a BSU referral for his part in a particularly nasty collective attack on a Turkish girl in the playground. She was beaten and sexually assaulted by up to 10 boys after she gained a reputation for bullying and throwing her weight around. Small, shy, quiet and awkward, Tom was far from the most likely suspect in the BSU. He described the incident as a 'group attack', perpetrated because the girl was hitting boys. He claimed the school was not addressing her violent behaviour, and that the attack was orchestrated in an attempt to redress this injustice. He did not mention the sexual assault. School staff were keen to play the incident down and there appears to have been none of the zealous involvement of the police characterising other far less serious episodes. A mentor acknowledged that it was an ugly and unacceptable incident but emphasised the provocative behaviour of the girl involved.

At Hailingbrooke, Kari (12 years old and on a phased return to the mainstream school) and another boy had been repeatedly caught persecuting an Eastern European girl in the playground. We discovered the details of this quite by chance. Yvonne was interviewing Kari's mother (Linda) at her home when the phone rang. After establishing it was the school Linda helpfully placed the call on speaker phone. It was the year head calling to report his general concern about Kari's aggressive sexual propositioning of the girl, and more specifically about an incident occurring that morning. The year head explained that the girl spoke very little English and had been alarmed by the aggressive tone and gestures the boys had subjected her to. But despite warnings from school staff, Kari and the other boy had been seen 'repeatedly rubbing their hands up and down the girl's bottom, continuously' leaving her in a very distressed state. The teacher went on to say that had the incident occurred outside of the school it would have been deemed a sexual assault requiring police involvement, but because it happened in the playground he had chosen to reprimand Kari himself. The call concluded with the warning that if the girl 'complains to her parents' the matter may be out of the school's hands. The phone call left Linda shaken and disturbed.

As far as we could gather there were no further repercussions for Kari. He was not even temporarily excluded, despite receiving this sanction many times before for incidents considerably less serious than a sexual assault. Given that the police were routinely called in for trivial playground incidents like play fights or verbal threats, the reluctance of the schools to view sexual violence as a criminal justice matter was telling. I am not making this point to suggest Tom and Kari should have been criminalised. The singling out of individual 12 and 13 year olds as perpetrators would merely detract from a much wider and deeper problem. The determination of the schools to overlook, normalise or deny gender hierarchies and sexual violence was at the core of the issue.

This raises the question of why the schools were so inured to an endemic gendered culture that exposed girls to intimidation, domination and violence. As emerging research on the extent and prevalence of child sexual exploitation reveals, the problem extends far beyond schools, encompassing institutions designed to support some of the most vulnerable children in the country. A high profile report by Alexis Jay (2014) described how 1,400 girls in Rotherham alone were victims of multiple organised crimes including rape, abduction and violent intimidation by adult males. As the report starkly details, police, social services and schools were aware of the abuse but did little to prevent it. Instead girls were commonly viewed as complicit in their own trafficking, having made a lifestyle choice. Indeed some victims of gang rape were even arrested and charged with prostitution.

The long history of women and girls being blamed for provoking violence from men endures despite the comprehensive critique of gender dynamics offered by second wave feminists in the 1970s and the apparently greater legal protection introduced. Indeed, many of the teachers working with the girls in the schools would likely have regarded themselves as drawing on feminist liberatory discourse in their attempts to address gender discrimination. The focus on raising self-esteem and increasing confidence pursued in the single-sex girl groups drew heavily on values of choice, authenticity and empowerment. Rosalind Gill (2007) describes this approach in terms of a post-feminist sensibility underpinned by a 'grammar of individualism' (p 17). As a cultural phenomenon, post-feminism is also marked by a move away from concepts of sexual objectification, towards notions of sexual subjectification in which women and girls are encouraged to internalise and agentically project back male fantasies. Gill points to the,

> pernicious connection of this representational shift to neoliberal subjectivities in which sexual objectification can be (re-)presented not as something done to women by some men, but as the freely chosen wish of active, confident, assertive female subjects. (p 11)

Pointing to significant rises in breast augmentation surgery among teenage girls and Brazilian waxing to resemble porn stars, Gill highlights post-feminist representations of women pleasing themselves and boosting their self-esteem, with little attention given to underlying social pressures. The absence of this more critical dimension was very noticeable in the schools, with choice being prioritised both as an explanation of behaviour and a goal. Hence (as discussed in the previous chapter), Amy's investment in relationships with boys was contemptuously dismissed as a (poor) choice and beyond intervention.

But to critique the post-feminist ethos informing gender politics within contemporary institutions is not to suggest the girls in the co-ed school should be viewed as passive victims of male dominance. There was a considerably more complex dynamic at work, with girls often wielding extensive power in day-to-day interactions. As Simon Harding's (2014) ethnography of London street gangs demonstrates, the central role of girls and women in such hypermasculine cultures is often overlooked. In his social field analysis, girls are viewed as 'players' in their own right, albeit occupying a lower status and more risky position in the hierarchy. Girls have the capacity to undermine, ridicule or enhance boys' reputations and are often highly strategic in manoeuvring to achieve particular ends (like the expulsion of Amy). In the mainstream playgrounds it was commonly girls who acted as look outs to warn illicit smokers, gamblers or fighters of the impending presence of a teacher, suggesting they had many secrets to keep and to trade. This power likely underpinned the boys' investment in securing the girls' silence, and may help explain both the reticence of the Gravensdale girls to confide in us, as well as the furious opposition of the boys to the gender-segregated groups.

Class, distinction and the case of Ethan

While the enduring injuries of race were papered over with the celebratory language of diversity and the lexicon of personal choice was offered to empower 'vulnerable immature' girls, the framework of class was strategically retained to position white, poor, low status individuals. Class was rarely explicitly discussed unless it was tied to the epithet 'white working class'. In this context, the 'white working class' were constructed almost as an ethnic group in their own right, and as such the only ethnic group that could be subject to explicit pathologisation. Yet class disadvantage marked out almost all of the pupils participating in the research. This fact was not lost on teachers, but it was rarely explicitly acknowledged. Instead coded references were made to the particular areas or estates pupils came from, or that their parents were drawing welfare benefits. This relative silence around class as form of inequality reflects the assertion made by the Department for Education that poverty is no excuse for poor performance[3]. Denying clear and extensive evidence of attainment gaps between rich and poor, Ofsted has worked to implement a 'no excuses culture', stressing aspiration, opportunity and social mobility. Peter Brant, a government advisor on social mobility and child poverty, put it more bluntly, claiming that 'working class children must learn to be middle class to get on'.[4]

While the schools participating in the research had largely working-class intakes, they also included pupils from more privileged backgrounds. London is well known as a city where poverty and affluence live cheek by jowl. And as explored by Diane Reay and colleagues (2011), some middle-class parents actively decide to send their children to their local comprehensives. In terms of the BSUs, only one boy stood out as unambiguously middle-class. His story very effectively illustrates how class dynamics operate in educational settings, and more specifically, the struggles characterising different sites and places within diverse comprehensive school settings.

Ethan was a white 13-year-old boy referred to the BSU for truancy and impulsive behaviour. He had a tendency to walk out of lessons and out of the school gate without saying a word to anyone. Ethan was thin and pale, with long, dark hair. He was extremely polite and had a very well-spoken London accent. His mother was a TV producer, his father was an artist and he lived in a wealthy part of the borough. Ethan was conspicuous in the BSU, in that his sense of place or 'habitus' was clearly at odds with his surroundings. Pierre Bourdieu has used the term 'habitus' to refer to socialised ways of being and doing which constitute 'the internalised form of class condition and of the conditioning it entails' (Bourdieu, 1979: 101). Habitus is acquired, not through conscious learning but through lived practice, and is deeply ingrained in material dispositions such as walking, talking and speaking, as well as thinking and feeling. Ethan's embodied middle-class habitus set him apart from the other pupils.

But habitus only makes sense in the local context in which it is formed. Bourdieu terms this social arena, the 'field'. Ethan's habitus was mismatched in the BSU and he was made to suffer for it. His long hair and effete mannerisms were ridiculed and he was subject to relentless homophobic abuse. He was knocked over, had balls kicked at him and was physically silenced with a hand over his mouth at times. Two boys in particular, BM and Daniel, found Ethan intolerable although neither was able to properly articulate why. BM was nearly excluded from the research session several times because he became so angry when Ethan tried to contribute to activities. Daniel displayed a slightly cooler level of contempt but still put Ethan in a headlock twice. Ethan often looked really frightened during the group sessions, meaning we instinctively went out of our way to protect and support him, further infuriating the other boys.

But Ethan was no passive victim. He was charming and resourceful. He refused to be silenced and he made no attempt to blend in with the other boys. He spent much of his time sketching, producing an abstract drawing of a female torso, which he explained represented his mother. From Bourdieu's perspective, habitus is pliable, reflecting the new and different experiences in the field (Reay, 2004). But habitus is also constituted through access to particular kinds of social and material resources. From this perspective, class can be understood in terms of 'capital movements through social space' (Skeggs, 1997). The configuration of this social space is highly stratified, with class positions determined by forms of capital that translate into power, control and influence. Capitals include economic (income and wealth); cultural (dispositions, taste, cultural knowledge, credentials); social (resources based on networks and relationships); and symbolic, which is the form other capitals take once they are perceived and recognised as legitimate (Bourdieu, 1986).

Ethan's access to capitals mediated against any 'sense of place' in the BSU. Instead he drew strength from his difference and sense of superiority. He was limited in his ability to draw value from his cultural capital in the working-class-dominated field of the BSU, but he enjoyed precious moments of personal legitimation in day-to-day interactions. For example, when BM announced he was moving from a good area closer to the school, Ethan expressed mock amazement that anyone could think that had been a good place to live. To emphasise this point he reminded the group where the wealthy parts of town were (this included his own neighbourhood). I was on guard during this exchange, waiting for BM to retaliate but the intent seemed to go right over his head. Similarly, in a conversation about holidays Ethan told me about his trip to Florence and Rome, with a knowing smile, aware that I would read the cultural significance. This is not to suggest that Ethan was smug or arrogant. He was earnest, respectful and kind in the midst of being victimised by the other boys. But while the other boys were made to experience their difference as a deficit, Ethan could recognise his as a resource.

As Beverley Skeggs (1997) notes, different fields are associated with very different power dynamics in that the working classes have no institutional sites to assert their legitimacy. Structures built around the law, education, health and the media devalue working-class cultural worth and confine its value in wider capital arenas. Sanctioned cultural capital allows value to be attached to the self through identifications and dis-identifications. While Ethan's status was low in the BSU, he had access to capitals that could be recognised in that wider arena. This aided his reintegration back into the mainstream school, although he continued to truant. Mr Phillips, the punitive year head, was unusually tolerant, describing Ethan as "just not of this world" and concluding that the walking out of school was "just something he does". Also striking was the sympathy he directed to Ethan's mother as a parent managing a son lodged on another plane of existence. As I show in the next chapter, this was an aberration in the context of a more general conviction that bad behaviour and personal deficit were indicators of incompetent parenting.

Notes

[1] We never discovered the origin of Safes and Sweets.

[2] Skeen, meaning OK, was one of his favourites.

[3] For example see 'Poverty no excuse for poor exam results, says children's secretary', http://www.theguardian.com/politics/2009/jan/16/ed-balls-academies-exam-results

[4] See Georgia Graham (2003) 'Working class children must learn to be middle class to get on in life, government advisor says', *The Telegraph*, http://www.telegraph.co.uk/education/10671048/Working-class-children-must-learn-to-be-middle-class-to-get-on-in-life-government-advisor-says.html

SIX

'Yo momma ...': foregrounding families

"Without your mum you're nothing." (Tanisha, 14)

As the previous chapters have illustrated, schools rely on a model of deficit and disorder to make sense of challenging behaviour in the classroom. The root cause of this personal deficiency is firmly assumed to lie in the home life of the problematised pupil, with responsibility directed at mothers in particular. In this chapter, I show how constructions of inadequate parenting framed and justified the very existence of BSUs as inclusion centres, with practices orientated towards countering and compensating for presumed negative family influences. By focusing on specific examples I highlight the way misunderstandings, conjecture and moral pronouncements could combine to obscure complex socially dispersed difficulties, while simultaneously poisoning home–school relations. As I will illustrate, far from representing a negative force, the young people in the research positioned family at the very centre of their lives. Relationships with parents, siblings and other family members were the source of enormous, pride, passion and pleasure, alongside more difficult emotions, often associated with separation. Illuminating the perspectives of parents themselves reveals the intensive emotional and physical labour they engaged in to address their children's problems, and the extent to which this was completely invisible to the schools.

Blaming the parents

"Where it goes wrong consistently and regularly over long periods of time is where there is poor parenting. It's a challenge because people are not shown to be parents or what to do when X, Y, Z situations occur in their children's lives ... but I'm expecting them to be experts at something they haven't been trained in. Whereas I'm an expert at my job, I've been trained for this and I trained hard and long before I even got the job. But parents are expected to be experts straightaway ON the job. So, where there's poor parenting you will find difficulties... Rarely do you hear of a child who has poor parents and makes a success of themselves... So I will parent them according to my set of rules or we, as a school, parent them but the parent relationship they value the most is a poor one ... that's the window they will view the world through, so if that relationship is abusive or it's full of violence or shouting or aggression or it's not full of anything much, it's just there. There are no boundaries with nothing there and no substance to it, that is how they see the world and so I'm forever fighting against a tide, you know if they see the world through a window of poor parenting it's near impossible ... near impossible." (Miss O'Conner, Hailingbrooke)

This quote from the deputy head at Hailingbrooke was among the more moderate reflections on the foundational role of parenting in determining educational success or failure. Similar, and at times less measured sentiments were expressed by staff at all three institutions, equipping an explanation of troublesome behaviour with a logic seemingly as powerful as gravity. It is worth unpacking Miss O'Conner's claims in detail given that in the space of one quote she pretty much encapsulates a hegemonic parenting deficit model. First is the observation that, "Where it goes wrong consistently and regularly there is poor parenting". From this perspective a BSU referral automatically flags up parental failure ensuring the scope of the problem is confined to the subjective development of the pupil. All of the complex social dynamics, power hierarchies and structural deprivations I have described in this book are vanished from view. Instead, troubles are projected onto the visible and ready stigmatised form of the poor (often minority ethnic) mother. She embodies the personal lack the BSU's activities seek to address by failing to attach value to herself or her child.

Second, Miss O'Conner expresses some sympathy for parents who are expected do a job without adequate training. This comment draws on an instrumentalist policy construction of parenting as a 'skill' that must be learnt. The deeply relational, situational and value-specific experience of parenting is transformed into an exercise that can be assessed as 'good' or 'poor'. Detached from any appreciation of structural context, culture or values, good parenting is presented as a set of neutral and natural techniques, with love and intimacy reduced to mere mechanics. From this perspective the disadvantaged should not be blamed, but upskilled instead. Miss O'Conner's contrasting of amateurish parents with her own 'hard and long' training emphasises her authority and ability to pronounce and act as the superior 'parent'. In lacking this objectivity and skill, parents could be viewed as caring too much about their children, to the extent that it clouded their judgement and precluded rational behaviour, or caring too little, or at least failing to demonstrate the caring actions deemed appropriate by the schools (Gillies and Robinson, 2013). June, the mentor at Meedham Girls, even expressed a preference for dealing with foster carers rather than parents because of their greater professionalism.

Third, Miss O'Conner asserts, "Rarely do you hear of a child who has poor parents and makes a success of themselves". This hard-core parental determinism reflects a more general cultural shift towards what has been termed 'parentocracy' to describe the increasing significance accorded to parental involvement in education. Mapping the beginning of the process, Brown (1990) described how an emerging commitment to the 'wealth and wishes of parents' in the arena of education was displacing more traditional concerns with children's abilities and potential. A preoccupation with maximising school choice under the Thatcher government of the 1980s morphed into a New Labour consumerist framework reaching deep within the arena of childrearing (Gillies, 2014). Good parenting became associated with choosing, accessing and continuously evaluating products and services (food, toys, childcare, parenting advice, etc). More specifically, this form of parenting became positioned as the key determinant of future success, articulated though the policy trope 'it's not who you are that matters, it's how you parent' (Hartas, 2014). In other words the choices your parents made in raising you determine future success regardless of the level of privilege you experience.

Leaving aside the evidence that quite contrary to this claim, educational success is clearly linked to parental status rather than parenting practices (Hartas, 2011; Hartas, 2012; Hartas, 2014; Dickerson and Popli, 2012), this myth assumes a level playing field. The wide differentials in the resources rich and poor parents can access are simply not factored into the equation. Freedom of movement and choice correlates with economic capital. Money can buy, among other things, extra tuition, educational equipment (iPads, computers, books), outings, and educational assessments when things are not going so well, and above all a house in a good catchment area. Middle-class cultural capital equates with well-educated parents who are academically confident, relatively familiar with the expectations framing school curriculums and able to teach and steer their children towards attainment. Middle-class social capital can also be brought to bear, with parents accessing useful contacts in their social networks (teachers, academics and other influential professionals) for advice, help with homework and work experience placements.

And as the example of Ethan in the previous chapter demonstrates, in the context of troublesome behaviour, middle-class recognition generates symbolic capital, securing a level of respect and power denied to working-class parents. The bad parent discourse is not just inaccurate and oversimplified, it is insidious, stripping parents of authority and agency whilst also justifying the writing off a child from the 'wrong' kind of background. As Miss O'Conner's comments indicate, education has come to be seen as an adjunct to parenting, structuring entitlement to state provision. Rather than emphasising the importance of an education system able to include all children, a parent's responsibility to ensure their children are includable becomes the core focus for concern. Zena, a mentor at Meedham Girls, expressed this more explicitly.

> "Basically we should be carrying on what parents are teaching at home; we shouldn't be teaching and then parents carrying it on. Parents need to bring, before their child even steps into school, they need to have been educated at home already and we just need to be continuing what they've been taught and going with that. But it has to be the right teaching because certain parents aren't teaching their children and it's almost like they're too scared to teach their children."

The concept of 'school readiness' structured the rationale of Miss O'Conner, Zena and many other school staff, positioning full participation in learning as contingent. The notion that children from poor backgrounds lack the necessary foundation for education is cemented in policy and practice through a preoccupation with early years and the 'home learning environment'. In a government-funded review of health inequalities, Michael Marmot (2014) made the startling claim that almost half of all five-year-olds are not 'school ready'. This attracted much publicity and was met with broad consternation about the unmet need for parenting support. Few appeared to question why schools were apparently unable and 'unready' for 50% of children. Marmot's report prompted reaction from the Department for Education, with a spokesperson quoted as saying, 'No child should start school behind their peers'[1]. This highlights how far understanding of education has moved away from the aim of providing opportunities for all children regardless of their ability or background. Instead, children without the requisite learning already in place are rendered, in the words of Miss O'Conner, "near impossible" learners.

In effect then the children of the poor are subject to the kind of pernicious social determinism parenting interventions purport to challenge. With no acknowledgement that childrearing practices are grounded in socio-economic circumstances, a singling out of parenting merely echoes a centuries old preoccupation with lineage. The key difference is that parents are held personally responsible for their children's disadvantage, while the more privileged claim the moral high ground. Education becomes about entitlement; my child does well because I have put the groundwork in and made the right choices. Worse still, children from disadvantaged backgrounds are denied any entitlement in their own right (beyond a possibility of 'training' for their parents). Being born into a family where parenting is deemed to be 'poor' gets conceptualised as a life sentence unless the parent can be persuaded to 'repent' and imitate middle-class practices. Indeed, the life sentence is increasingly inscribed onto the brains of the disadvantaged through a focus on the neural implications of poor parenting (Edwards et al, 2015). 'Impossible learners' becomes an explanatory category, simultaneously branding those positioned within it as hopeless and inadequately loved. In the quote, Miss O'Conner articulates the characteristics of bad parenting most frequently levelled against the poorest in society; abusive, lacking in boundaries, neglectful ("no substance"), and above all, ignorant of children's needs. Miss O'Conner did not direct her accusations towards any parents in particular but many members of staff across the three schools did. This provides a perfect opportunity to examine the common assumptions made about parents in more detail.

Reaching parents: the centrality of mothers

Accessing parents' perspectives was a key feature of the research design, but the process was characterised by a sharp learning curve. Initially we attempted to contact parents through central records, but it quickly became clear that school offices commonly held out-of-date information. At Hailingbrooke we turned to Dave Stirling, who passed on current mobile phone numbers. But while some parents consented to an interview through this cold calling method, most did not even pick up. At Gravensdale, school staff were scathing about the very idea of parents participating and it took months just to be allowed entry to the unreliable central school database. By the end of the second term we realised that by far the most effective method of accessing parents was to ask the young person themselves to set up an interview. Most pupils seemed really keen to have their parents involved with the study and only one parent approached in this way declined to take part. The downside to this method was that large numbers of the BSU pupils were excluded or sent to off-site provisions before we had a chance to negotiate access to their parents. It is also worth noting that a not insignificant number of the participants had parents living abroad. By the end of the fieldwork we had managed to interview 22 parents, most of them mothers. Contrary to the predictions made by Gravensdale's staff, parents were interested in talking to us. In fact, many had burning resentments about the way their children had been treated, with some deliberately disengaging from the school because of their sense of powerlessness.

Interviews with parents were particularly illuminating, not least because they were conducted in the family home. The pressures deriving from disadvantage and hardship became highly visible to us, with some families forced to cope with damp, overcrowded, temporary housing. The pupils themselves were often at home during the interview and keen to give a commentary on the area or show off treasured possessions. Significantly, parents filled in gaps in our knowledge, and sometimes made us aware of crucial contextualising information we had not previously been aware of (Lindon's turmoil around his mother's illness for example, as discussed in Chapter 3).

At a fundamental level, every parent we interviewed expressed deep concern for their children's welfare, giving often poignant accounts of their struggles to address problems and their fears for the future. As has been the case in other qualitative studies of troubling and troublesome youth (Hillian and Reitsma-Street, 2003; Squires and Stephen, 2005; Nixon and Parr, 2006), families bore no resemblance to prevailing policy and practice stereotypes of incompetent, indifferent or uncaring parents. This emotional investment appeared to be reflected in the very high estimation pupils themselves tended to hold, particularly of their mothers. Almost all described a warm, loving, if at times fiery relationship with their mothers (fathers were not always present). In the interviews we asked what pupils considered to be their most important possessions and discovered a high number unblinkingly cited their mother. Some pupils emphasised their closeness.

> "Well, my mum, she's like my older sister, because I can tell her anything and she'll understand." (Charpane, 13)

"Me and my mum, we've, oh I'll tell her everything. I tell her everything. I ain't got nothing to hide from her, I don't see any reason to hide anything from her." (Alfie, 13)

Others articulated a sense of obligation, recognising sacrifices and efforts their mothers had made for them.

"I want to be good for my mum in school and that, because of what she's done for me." (Bond)

"She brought me into this world, no one else." (Angelina)

"I get on well with my Mum, anything she tells me to do I just do it. [The] stuff she had to go through when she was young ... because my Nan had too much children that she couldn't handle ... so most of them either went to live with their dads, my Mum went into care and stuff ... back with my Nan when she was older. Even though she had us quite young, she never gave up ... she used to be bad in the school and stuff like that but she made sure that she got her job and a good job as well because she works for the council." (Natasha)

As this last quote suggests, mothers (alongside other family members) were often identified as role models, exhibiting admirable qualities, or as in the case of Alfie's mum, offering the wisdom of hindsight.

"My mum just sat me down and went, 'Look Alf, you've gotta either stop now and get your education, or you're going to carry on and you're going to miss school. You're going to get excluded before you finish school'. And she sort of said like, 'this is your chance now. Sort it out', because like she said how she could have had a better job at the moment, but no, she decided to talk in class and not learn, and she's just trying to put me in the right direction." (Alfie)

Mothers tended to be portrayed with some affectionate humour as a force to be reckoned with, getting them to school in the first place and checking their behaviour. Mothers also appeared to be viewed as relatively powerful. They broke up fights, provided protection on the street, brokered peace deals and confronted unreasonable teachers. The value attached to mothers was also experienced as intensely personal and precious. Keishawn wrote a poem about how much he missed his mother when she took a temporary job abroad. And as I mentioned in the previous chapter, Ethan spent some considerable time sketching an abstract picture of his mother during our research sessions. As Martin Robb (2011) notes, research on masculinities has tended to overlook the importance of maternal relationships for young men in particular, focusing instead on the significance of fathers and 'male role models'. Yet mothers clearly play a central role in the lives and identities of their sons. This was certainly recognised by mentors in the co-ed schools, who sometimes challenged boys' troublesome behaviour by pointing out how they were letting their mothers down. If accomplished sensitively it was a surprisingly effective tactic, although it could easily backfire, triggering emotional volatility.

The subject of mothers was widely recognised within the units to be a highly delicate one. Cussing mothers was neither acceptable nor tolerated by boys or girls unless it was very overtly framed in the spirit of a 'Yo Momma' joke, thereby expressing 'ritual humour' (Kehily and Nayak, 1997). This taboo was well understood but could be strategically breeched in arguments, particularly between boys, to up the ante and inflict serious hurt. Mothers, whose ever they were, occupied a venerable status with perceived slights necessitating retribution. Demonstrating fierce loyalty to family could be a matter of personal pride. For example, Marcus (discussed in Chapters 3 and 4) cited his mother as the most important thing he owned and articulated an aggressive protectiveness as part of a sense of masculine duty.

> "If someone hurts her or touches her, I'll just go mad. Even though we have arguments and stuff, like ... it makes me angry. If someone touches my mum, I'll probably kill them... Because that's my mum, okay, like, if they [brother or sister] got hurt, I'll hurt the person. But if it's my mum, it's a different thing, because I think more anger comes out of me."

While Marcus, drew on this patriarchal, hyper macho account of his mother as valuable property to be protected, she was clearly a very powerful figure in his life. He explained how she restricted his movements and refused to let him out if she thought he was up to no good. He also claimed he only made it to school because she would not let him lie in bed and threatened to walk him there. He listened to and valued her advice, and had relied on her to argue his case when was falsely accused at school and by the police.

Family first

During a relatively early stage of the fieldwork at Hailingbrooke I became pregnant. It felt awkward to make an announcement so I just gradually expanded before the boys' eyes until Daniel (13) stared hard at me sideways on and asked if I was having a baby. I discovered, to my amusement, there had been speculation that one of the supply teachers was the father. Again it was Daniel that broached the subject, making reference to Mr Henson as my 'babyfather'. But rumour aside, my pregnancy introduced an interesting dynamic, highlighting the particular reverence motherhood inspired. I became the source of paternalistic concern for the boys, told to sit down, not to move chairs and tables and gently chastised for taking part in ball games. I stopped trying to break up fights but my presence in the room was used by the boys to shame those sparring: "What are you thinking of, there's a pregnant women who could get hurt". But above all I was touched by their interest and concern. They asked lots of questions, shared the experiences of their mothers and sisters and made suggestions for names (mostly their own names). When I returned to the school after having my son they continued to ask after him, begging me to bring him in for a visit.

While I had been surprised by the boys' reaction to my pregnancy it resonated with their parents' descriptions of caring practices towards younger family members like cousins or brothers or sisters. It also made very visible the strong significance attached to the ideal of family relationships. The pupils passionately and consistently described family as the most important thing in their lives. Probing what seemed like a rather romanticised account, we proposed the idea that friends might be more supportive, leaving many pupils aghast that we would even question such a natural order. This response from the white boys at Gravensdale was very typical.

Luke: Friends are more supportive than family? I definitely disagree with that.

James: Family first.

Alfie: Family, family definitely family.

Luke: 'Cos family, they brought you up and everything, they brought you up yeah, they was there for you, you meet friends half way through your life. You might have friends all through your life and stuff, but basically your mum, your mum like brought you into this world and if you disrespect that then basically how you gonna make your mum feel like. She loves you very much. She wanted to have you and everything.

Similar sentiments were expressed during a group discussion between an ethnically mixed group of boys at Hailingbrooke.

Daniel: I listen to my mum like every time, obviously she's the one that feeds me, I stay at her house yeah obviously I'm only 13 but...

Max: Of course.

Daniel: These kids that don't listen to their mum yeah, some rude people. How can you not listen to your mum yeah she's the one that gave birth to you.

Conor: Yeah like 'cos the government didn't give birth to us, he didn't push us out of his arse.

Behind these deeply held values around family and mothering in particular, there often lay considerable hard work by parents to keep their children safe and ensure they were not written off by the school.

Situated parenting: fighting your kid's corner

In interviews, parents tended to stress the strengths, talents, kindness and humour of their children alongside a general sense of injustice, frustration and anxiety. In most cases mothers were the key allies and advocates for their children when they got into trouble at school or with the law. Returning to the example of Marcus, the account given by his mother, Dawn, highlights the struggles and worries, contextualising their family life. She explained how, when Marcus was still young, they had been forced to flee from domestic violence. Marcus's father developed an addiction to crack and had become abusive. Finding a safe place to live was difficult and she had been obliged to temporarily leave Marcus with relatives and go into hiding. After spending some time in a bed and breakfast, she and Marcus moved to a secure family home. Dawn began a new relationship and had two more children. Another crisis point came when both her parents died and she split up with her partner. Worried about the potential effect on the children, she referred them as a family to their local child and adolescent mental health services for a six-week course of counselling. She was assured by the counsellor that they had come through it well as a family. She had also voluntarily attended parenting classes.

Dawn was generally happy with Marcus's primary school, though she was worried about his educational progress. He had been considered to have special educational needs related to speech and literacy but there were few concerns about his behaviour.

> "He was fine in school. He was fine in primary. He would have a few tantrums, but I was never ever, ever called in to the headmaster. I was never called in to the teacher, to say that, you know, I mean, I work [in a school] I see children that have to be taken out for lunchtimes because they're so disruptive, that are always at the headmaster, my son's never had that. Even in Gravensdale I've never been called in by the head teacher for my son's behaviour. Never. But he is known as one of the, the thugs, in the school. My son's never been suspended. Yes, I have got letters home that he's been disruptive in the lesson, and he's going to get a detention. But that's standard. I don't believe that he has behavioural problems, that he comes from a dysfunctional family or whatever. He doesn't. He's very much loved... At every parents' evening, careers, careers evening, anything, I am there. I'm there... That's why I was a bit upset when he was put in this group without my knowledge, because if you're working on him, you don't really know my child, you know?"

Dawn had been shocked to find Marcus had been referred to Gravensdale BSU. He had been attending a mentoring group in the unit for several years before she found out from Marcus himself. She was angry and resentful that she was not involved or consulted before Marcus was labelled as having behaviour problems and was worried about the implications of this for his future. She was particularly furious to find he had been missing IT lessons at school to follow the BSU programme. She had contacted his head of year and demanded he rejoin the class, but heard nothing back. One of the most common complaints from Gravensdale parents was the inaccessibility of teachers and their unresponsiveness. For example, Amy's mother, Tina, vented her frustration about the school's reluctance to discuss the bullying her daughter was suffering. Worse still, after Amy was sent to the off-site provision, Tina found that her phone calls were being completely ignored. She had been concerned about Amy missing out on her education and had wanted to know when she would be able to rejoin the mainstream school.

> "I was trying to get through to Miss Sheldon, the lady that suggested all this [off-site placement], and every time I left a message, she wouldn't get back to me. In the end, about two weeks later, I got a letter, and all it was, was an invoice of how much they – Gravensdale School – pays for Amy to go to that place. And I thought, 'You know what? They're just being rude'…All they can do is send me a bill of what it's costing them to send her there, where she's learning nothing, she's missed out on all kinds of stuff – her work experience, everything … they never returned none of my calls. I went up the school the other week … I said, 'I wanna see Miss Sheldon now. She's never returning any of my calls'. It's just, it's just plain rudeness. 'How do you expect the children to behave if you can't even behave proper with a parent? I mean, you're not returning … I've left untold messages, don't tell me you're not getting them'. And still I went there, she said, 'Miss Sheldon's busy, someone else is dealing with what's going on with Amy'. I said, 'Well, then I'll speak to them, then'… So still no one came to me. I said, 'Well, I want someone to phone me … now, basically'. And still no one's phoned. You know, they don't care."

Sending a copy of the administrative invoice was a blatantly contemptuous act designed to depict Amy as a drain on the school finances and position Tina as over-demanding. In her interview, Ms Sheldon was excoriating about those she viewed as incompetent parents, exclaiming they should "do their bloody job".

> "I mean, I meet parents all the time. It's not necessarily my favourite thing to do, I don't think it's one of my strength areas, if I can pass it on to somebody else, I will… A lot of the families are completely dysfunctional. I mean, I don't

just mean the men have gone, I mean the women are also struggling to find their roles. A lot of them are drunk or addicted to drugs – I mean a lot. So the girl we're trying to talk to today, you know, I actually had to lay it on the line and say, 'Look, we know you didn't have any parenting basically'."

But in many cases it was the schools rather than the parents who could be accused of not 'doing their job'. Behaviour problems were often linked to a failure to address particular learning needs. Marcus had been considered by his primary school to have special educational needs related to speech and literacy, but his entitlement to extra help was withdrawn when he transferred to Gravensdale. Dawn met with the head to challenge this decision but was assured there were children worse off and that Marcus was coping. When she suggested applying for an official statement she was told it was 'too late'. She was also led to believe that only very dysfunctional families received statements. Dawn blamed herself for not having had the knowledge to instigate the process while Marcus was still at primary school. Like Dawn, many mothers recognised their children were struggling and tried hard to get extra help in the classroom. But few had succeeded, even when their children had diagnosed special educational needs.

Armani transferred from primary school straight into Hailingbrooke BSU with a diagnosis of ADHD, dyslexia and dyspraxia. While he had a statement of special educational needs detailing the learning support he was entitled to, it was not forthcoming. Dave Stirling was clearly very troubled by this neglect and he raised it often, quoting the school's legal responsibilities. By the time Armani had turned 14 his academic failure was severe, much to his mother, Tracey's, distress. She angrily and assertively challenged the school and was instrumental in negotiating a more vocational route for him, securing a place in a scheme working with cars three days a week. Armani's father and eldest brother were in prison, ensuring the family was quickly stereotyped as 'troubled'. This status effectively worked to delegitimise Tracey's protests. School staff quickly positioned her as having 'issues' with parenting, conveniently overlooking the 'issues' they appeared to be having with educating.

Peter (12) was in Hailingbrooke BSU alongside Armani. He also had a longstanding diagnosis of ADHD and had transferred into the unit from primary school. He had begun his Ritalin medication much earlier than Armani and this had impacted on his growth. He was tiny, cheeky and at times very challenging. He could not sit down for very long, was very impulsive and he swore at teachers with abandon. But he was also very bright, funny and well liked within the unit. He had experienced a particularly difficult time at primary school, where he had been physically restrained and pinned to the ground, with teachers kneeling on his legs. He was quite traumatised by this and mentioned it often in our group sessions. Dave Stirling had promised him it would never happen at Hailingbrooke and he repeated this promise back to us as if it was a protective mantra.

In spite of his difficult behaviour, Peter was gifted at maths. He loved number games and had impressive mental arithmetic skills. He enjoyed showing this off during group sessions by demonstrating complex number tricks or accepting sums as challenges. In the early days there had even been some discussion of fast tracking him for a GCSE but the poor maths provision in the unit left him bored and frustrated. During what passed for maths lessons he would push the worksheet away vehemently declaring how much he hated the subject. Peter's mother Louise had struggled for years to get Peter statemented, but his maths ability was seen as evidence that his ADHD wasn't impairing his learning. When he was due to transfer to secondary level, Louise did her research and found him a school that specialised in ADHD. He was initially accepted, but then had the offer withdrawn when he did not receive the statement.

Peter lived with Louise, his brother and sister and stepfather in a flat on an estate nearby to the school. Because his behaviour was often very provocative he received regular fixed-term exclusions. He was also sometimes sent home just because there were staff shortages in the unit. This was devastating for Louise. When pupils are excluded from school parents are legally obliged to keep their children at home for the first five days. If their children are caught in any public place during this period parents can be prosecuted or receive a fixed penalty notice, and this rule applies even if children are accompanied by their parents. Louise worked during the day delivering newspapers and selling products door to door, but having to care for Peter in school hours, repeatedly and at short notice, was making employment untenable. While Peter had a good relationship with his father, he was not able to take much time off from his full-time job. Stacks of undelivered newspapers were piled up in Louise's flat and she was anxious about what would happen when her bosses realised just how behind she'd got.

Although Louise had built a very good relationship with the staff at the BSU, Peter's time at Hailingbrooke was relatively short. He got into a fight with another boy just as the school head and deputy head were walking past the unit's playground. In the general uproar Peter told the head to 'fuck off'. The head's response was to try and restrain Peter, which he fought with all his strength. The police were called and several riot vans arrived at the same time as Louise. As she observed, this was somewhat of an overreaction for a tiny 12-year-old boy. Peter was sent to the off-site provision and was then eventually permanently excluded.

As these examples demonstrate, parents often made strenuous efforts to address their children's problems and secure the best outcomes, but their role as advocates could put them on a collision course with the school. Parents were painfully aware that, despite their claims to the contrary, schools could not be relied upon to protect the best interests of their children. The best interests of the school took priority over meeting individual needs of troublesome pupils, resulting in vulnerability to scapegoating, marginalisation, and in some cases, demonisation. The interventions of parents were crucial in confronting and highlighting such injustices but school staff hurled accusations of complicity and ignorance to delegitimise any challenging of their authority. As the following quote from Sarah Jennings, the deputy head at Meedham, demonstrates, a paternalistic discourse was drawn on to depict parents as naughty children acting out.

> "I think increasingly we have parents now who have themselves been in centres, been permanently excluded. We have a year seven student who we can't make any progress with because her father was permanently excluded himself. He knows exactly the steps that we have to go through to permanently exclude, you know the hierarchy of referral and … also their 14-year-old has got a statement of SEN … I think there needs to be more work done with families but they've got to be captive and I think there needs to be, and I don't know why the government hasn't thought about it … there needs to be some kind of contract where if you have a child and you want them educated in the education system here you also have to learn and you also have to attend… I often preface meetings with students or I'll see a parent first without the child and say … 'Look, before we have this meeting, I want you to understand that I believe that it's important that YOU DO listen to what your daughter is saying and you HAVE to keep that rapport and that relationship BUT if you allow her to drive a wedge between us … you are really building a very difficult situation for yourself for the future'."

The bad faith attributed to the challenging parent lacks empathy for the distress families threatened with exclusion face. There was little acknowledgement from Sarah Jennings that a caring parent would do everything possible to resist such a devastating outcome. Instead, the father mentioned at the beginning of the quote is depicted as playing the system (acquiring a statement for his daughter in the process). In fact, Sarah Jennings appears to feel parents should be contractually obliged to attend school as pupils alongside their children, submitting to the superior knowledge of teachers. This cuts right across market-based education reforms that have positioned parents as consumers, choosing and evaluating schools. The attitudes expressed by school staff more generally, reveals the strong social class differentials shaping the way parents are able to exercise power. While middle-class parents are expected to take up the consumer role, impose their own definitions of a situation and exert their influence, working-class parents continue to occupy a client-based model, in which they are expected to demonstrate passive deference (Edwards and Gillies, 2011).

But much to the schools' disgust, parents often did fight hard against the decisions they saw as disadvantaging their children. Sometimes this led to a complete breakdown in home–school relations. The parents of Will, Mica and Shane, three of the persecuted black boys at Gravensdale, were scathing in their description of encounters with the school and had quite deliberately disengaged. At Hailingbrooke, Fredrick, a father, described how he had given up on the school and was keeping Joshua (13) at home while he negotiated a 'managed move', a process where a pupil at risk of exclusion voluntarily moves to another school. Fredrick was a well-educated, black African lone father, caring for Joshua and his two sisters (11 and 16). Joshua had found himself in Mr Phillips' cross-hairs and, like many other boys, was being explicitly provoked, steeling his father's determination to sever ties with the school.

> "I don't want him to be here. He doesn't want to be here. And 'you don't want him here'. You know, why be somewhere where you don't want to be, or they don't want you? You know, so yes, I could force him to go back to the school, but they had it in for him, you know … particularly his head of year at the time, a guy called Mr Phillips … who, in my opinion, didn't have the correct CV for that job, you know he definitely didn't have the aptitude to be doing that job in my opinion. You know, he was threatening Joshua. He had been goaded by a teacher.

You can't have that, you know. And why is he gonna make that up? He's not the sort of person to make that kind of thing up. But basically, this teacher was goading him, you know, to do something … there was no way I was gonna put up with that, so that's why I said I need to get him out of that school."

Fredrick's outrage at Mr Phillips' harassment of Joshua was marked by a quiet determination that this could not be tolerated. While the experience of black working-class parents was often characterised by a sense of institutional powerlessness, Fredrick deployed his stock of middle-class cultural capital in an attempt to defend his son from false accusations and claim an entitlement to education. Most notably, he is able to phrase his objections in terms of the school's incompetence, pronouncing on Mr Phillips' lack of 'aptitude'. He positions himself as a knowledgeable consumer finding the school to be wanting. But while he was able to draw on middle-class cultural capital to exercise agency and resist the victimisation of his son, ultimately, like many other black middle-class families, he was only able to minimise the effects of racism (Rollock et al, 2011). Joshua was forced to leave the school, despite his father's best efforts to challenge the discrimination he was facing.

"He got into trouble once before, they accused him of starting a fire… For that, I had to go to the governors, present my evidence to the governors, and debunk, basically, what they're saying. And, of course, the governors said, 'Yeah, what he's saying is right', so he's back in the school. But it would have been something else, and I just wasn't prepared for that."

Fredrick, with the support of Dave Stirling, took a proactive role, incriminating the school and demanding a better alternative. But parents without the requisite cultural capital would have risked contemptuous indifference and potential prosecution by education welfare officers for keeping their child off school. Instead, working-class parents relied on a range of other strategies for managing their children's difficulties. These included scraping together money for outside tuition, bringing in other family members or friends to act as mentors, exploring vocational options and/or researching further education colleges as a potential second chance at gaining an education. These practices were largely invisible to school staff who often interpreted lack of institutional engagement as a lack of concern for the pupil's welfare. This meant the parents of BSU pupils could find themselves in a catch-22 situation; interpreted as complicit and irresponsible if they challenged the school over injustices, or alternatively regarded as uncaring and neglectful if they withdrew and sought solutions elsewhere.

Minding the gap

As I have outlined, school staff tended to paint their own pictures of the home lives of pupils to make sense of troublesome behaviour. These assessments were almost always highly speculative and made with very little grounded knowledge of pupils' actual home circumstances. There was often a huge gap between teachers' perceptions of parents as culpable and the complex and nuanced reality contextualising problems. For example, Mr Phillips articulated a simple and uncompromising account of parents who fail to fulfil their responsibilities.

> "The parents get let off very lightly when it comes down to responsibility a lot of the time. If parents want to stick their heads in the sand – these are the same parents – oh bless their hearts – I'll hold sympathy with them but the same kind of parents that when the kid gets shot in the street 'cos he's been messing about with gangs, will sit there and go, ' My boy was a good boy!' Really, why was he running around the street at 2 o'clock in the morning with guns then? If one of my boys got caught for something then they'd be dealt with, simple as! I'm the parent and it's my responsibility. I've actually had a phone call with a parent before, the boy was really kicking off in class, I phoned the parent and the parent said, 'The government pay my benefit, the government can sort him out'."

The comment about benefits seemed like an unlikely thing for a parent to say. On probing, it became clear that he was talking about the mother of Kari, a participant in our research. Kari was 12 years old and African-Caribbean. His mother, Linda, had already been interviewed as part of our research. She gave a powerful account, conveying anxiety and distress about the difficulties Kari was experiencing at school. She was particularly worried about his future prospects and emphasised the struggle she had encountered to access meaningful help. She was grateful he had been referred to the BSU and felt the input from the mentors was very useful.

"I'm just trying every avenue there is for my son's life. Because you know what, because if he carries on like that, he will be going to prison. He might be that person that pulls that trigger, and he might be that person who receives the bullet, so I'm desperate for him, and I'm grabbing every which way to get help… I feel I'm getting all the support there is… Unless there's more support out there that I don't know about, but it might … yeah, I'm getting support from the school. I love the fact. I know this might not sound good on the tape, but I love the fact that the mentors in the school that Kari's with and so forth, are black, because it's, it's different, in'it?"

Linda's reference to the significance of race is made tentatively, reflecting the sensitivity black parents had to being labelled as 'playing the race card'. As research has demonstrated, black parents are likely to avoid citing racism as a problem for fear of provoking antagonism, meaning race becomes a subtle and unnamed feature of interactions (Vincent, 2012). As the previous chapter outlined, naming race could actually work to invalidate perspectives, positioning parents as irrational and unreasonable. Linda's disclaimer that it, "might not sound good on the tape" points to her perceived lack of entitlement to raise an issue of central significance to herself and her son. In fact, Linda had a relatively good rapport with Dave Stirling and the BSU mentors, but her relationship with the mainstream school was strained. Like many other parents, she was subject to measures designed to force her to accept greater accountability for her son's troublesome behaviour. These included frequent daytime phone calls reporting on his conduct, and expectations that she would attend school meetings at very short notice. Linda had been trying to hold down a job as a temporary administrative worker, and had struggled to take the frequent personal calls. Sometimes, she was called to the phone just to be told Kari had been well behaved during the school day. When her temporary contract came to an end she contacted the school to inform them she would be at home and available until she found new job. Clearly though, it was the message that Linda was back on benefits that filtered through to Mr Phillips. His dismissal of her as a welfare scrounger intent on dodging her responsibilities highlights how wilfully misconstrued parents' actions could be.

Linda explained how Kari's problems stretched back to primary school. He had complained of bullying and Linda felt that teachers had singled him out as a problem. Again, she tentatively implicated race, suggesting that other black mothers had similar problems. She felt Kari had eventually become angry and decided to fight back. His behaviour started to became violent and extreme. He punched a boy in the mouth, knocking his teeth out, cut a girl's ponytail off, and vandalised the school. Eventually, he was excluded in the final year of primary and a move to a pupil referral unit was suggested. Linda visited the unit with Kari but was horrified at what they saw.

> "When we was there, we saw a fight, it wasn't a fight, it was about four or five teachers trying to control this boy. When Kari looked out the window, he goes, 'That's my friend! That's my friend! What are they doing to my friend?' So he's charged down the stairs, I've had to charge after him, and I said, 'Kari, keep out of it. Keep away of it'. So he shouted to them, 'What are you doing to my friend? That's my friend' … this boy used to go to the same school as Kari, but he's been taken out and gone to the unit. But one of the workers said that he wanted to go home and he wasn't allowed to go home, so they was trying to restrain, but obviously the temper and everything, and it took four or five of the staff to hold this child. But they did put him in a car and take him home. And when I saw that, I thought, 'No. This is not the place for Kari. If Kari ends up going here, he's going to be worse.' That kind of place doesn't work for a child. How can they do, that's like a mini prison. That's not gonna work. The child's already got anger problems, and you're making the situation worse with this child. I didn't like it. And I thought, 'If Kari comes here, I've lost him. I've lost him'."

Linda got Kari a place at Hailingbrooke instead and although his challenging behaviour quickly saw him transferred to the BSU he was generally very calm and withdrawn in the unit. In fact, we often found him to be unnervingly self-contained. He was strikingly articulate and argued frequently with teachers, often tying them in verbal knots. His independence and self-direction appeared to set him apart from the other pupils who generally seemed to dislike but slightly fear him. Kari was very good at making sinister threats, which the other pupils took very seriously. Linda was relieved at the improvement in Kari's behaviour but like many of the parents we interviewed, she felt she was fighting on two fronts. Keeping Kari on track in school was a battle, but keeping him safe on the streets was another struggle requiring different strategies. She was concerned that Kari seemed to know so many boys on the street and realised he was developing an interest in postcodes.

> "He was with my mum one time, and he said to her, 'Nanny, what is your postcode?' And she goes, 'Why are you asking me that? What do you mean, what's my postcode?' …I think he was just checking out. Because I know, from my nephew, he can't easily walk and see my mum… Because my sister was saying there's certain guys in the area that, you know what I mean, you've gotta be careful, so he can't just go, 'Yeah, I'm going to Nanny's'. He's gotta watch himself. And Kyle's 12, coming up to that now. But the way Kyle talks and the way he talks about his friends (pause) I wouldn't say he's in a gang, I think he's just friends with everybody… He is just 12."

Linda, Kari and his sisters lived on an estate where drug dealing was rife. She had attended a tenants' meeting with the police to try and get the problem addressed but found they just stopped children playing football and began harassing and photographing boys playing out (including Kari). As Tracey Reynolds (2005) argues, a central part of being a black mother involves developing strategies to enable children to cope with racism. Linda was acutely aware of Kari's vulnerability in any dealings with the police.

> "Every time Kari comes out, I said, 'Keep out of trouble. Don't get into nothing with no one', you know what I mean? Because his record is not gonna look good anyway, in' it – problems at schools, had to be suspended from school, and had to be in a, mentor and them kind of things – it's not gonna look good, he's really gonna look like a, this is a bad child."

While Linda was attempting to equip her 12-year-old son with the skills to survive racism, Dawn (Marcus's mother) was resorting to more direct action in the context of escalating risk.

> "I get a phone call, 'Dawn, Marcus is down the road. He with a group of boys' and I'll be there in two minutes. I'll get in my car and go. Two minutes, I'm there. He doesn't like that because he thinks 'Oh what you doing here mum? I can look after myself'. 'I don't want to bury you'. And

the kids today do not understand, and they don't care. And I don't want him to go to jail 'because your friend has given you a knife, and without you thinking you've stabbed somebody or something'... Even now, there's a little gang up the road that he finds his self up hanging around with them sometimes. I hear he's up there, I walk up there and I drag him away. That's what he doesn't like about me. If I hear he's on a street somewhere he's not meant to, I go, 'get your backside home NOW. And he doesn't like that... I just don't want to see my son on the streets ... it would kill me, and that's why I'm on his back."

Dawn participated in an interview for the research just days before Marcus was stabbed. While she described her worry about Marcus hanging around on the street, she had expressed shock and concern that he had suddenly started staying in a lot. She wondered, somewhat prophetically, whether there were people out to get him. Her distress after the attack on Marcus was compounded by the silence from the school. She was furious and hurt that no one bothered to contact her after the incident even to find out how he was.

Parenting, police and criminalisation

As I have outlined, the line between indiscipline and criminality was frequently blurred, with the police regularly called out for minor incidents occurring within the school. And as was detailed in the previous chapter, teachers could also aid the persecution of particular pupils by police on the streets. Pursued ostensibly to address the problem of violent crime, (and teenage stabbings in particular) the close relationships between the police and schools ensured parents were often having to manage hostile encounters with the police as well as with teachers. For example, Dawn had to deal with the fallout when Marcus was falsely accused of murder.

"The head teacher heard him, Marcus, and another boy talking about it and the next thing I know I had the murder squad at my house, which was bang out of order. Right? For like three days in a row they were contacting me, wanting to know where Marcus was. We were all, because it was my nephew's birthday. He left to walk his girlfriend home, he'd just seen her into the, not when it happened, but when it was all taped up, the head teacher put two and two and got 20! And when it all came out the police even said to me, 'Look, we've got it from the school. The school's got the wrong end of the stick. We know he had nothing to do with it.' I was fuming because why wasn't I notified that you know, 'You heard my son saying whatever'. I would have brought him to the police station myself. My son's got nothing to do with this but because you heard them two talking you assume he knows something. And they didn't send them to the other boy's house."

Dawn's experience highlights not only the capacity for teachers to trigger a potentially catastrophic miscarriage of justice, but also the crucial role that parents play in fighting to keep their children out of trouble and out of jail. Linda and Dawn were wary of involvement with police, having had first-hand experience of the racism directed at their sons. This could be contrasted with the largely positive relationship Louise (Peter's mother) described having with the local police. Louise and Peter were both white and lived on a notorious estate. Louise worried a lot about Peter's safety when he played outside because he often provoked older boys and did not seem to feel much fear. Louise was on first name terms with the police and dealt with them often, both in relation to Peter and more general crime on the estate. For example, she described how Peter and his 14-year-old brother became the target of violent threats.

> Louise: Halloween, the kids had all been out trick or treating, six of them, Peter and his best mate. Well, one of his friends that he was with got jacked. They got their stuff took off them... So the police turned up, and I'm going to the police, "Well, it wasn't him, he wasn't there"... I knew who two of the boys were. But, you know, I didn't want other kids getting into trouble that wasn't there, because to me, I mean, that's going to make it worse for the boys... But there was a rumour went round that him and all were going to get shanked, stabbed, stabbed.

> Peter: My mum likes to pick up all the words that they say now.

> Louise: You need to know. You need to... I was down the bottom, talking to their dad, and there was nine kids walked past me, and I heard them saying about "Paul's

younger brother",… I turned round and went, "Excuse me", I says, "but did you want to know something about Paul's younger brother?" I says, "because he happens to be my son". But they ignored me, and just looked at me and walked off. Next thing, the police have gone past, and I told them, because the police got involved the night before, and the police just said to me, "How's things going since last night?" I told her what had just happened, she said to me, "Go and pick the boys up early, then". She says, "Go and get them out of school early".

The threats issued were remarkably similar to those faced by Marcus, except Paul and Peter were quickly identified as potential victims. Louise was able to approach the police to seek their advice and support, thereby averting the risk to her sons' lives. In contrast, Marcus was firmly marked out as a perpetrator, despite the absence of any evidence. Had Dawn relayed concerns that her son was staying in more frequently to the police she would have merely risked placing him under renewed suspicion. Black mothers quickly came to realise that involvement with the police revolved around a criminalisation of their sons. As a white mother, Louise could afford considerably more confidence. For example, she described how she involved the police when Peter took retribution on a boy who had been publicly insulting Louise, by throwing stones at his window.

> "Peter has come up to me and said to me. He sat there for an hour and I kept saying, 'What's the matter babe?' 'Nothing.' 'What's the matter?' 'Nothing.' About an hour later he said to me, he says, 'Mum' he says, 'we broke erm a window'. The police were looking for a kid called Peter and the police said to me 'it wasn't your Peter'. As, as he was talking I went, 'My Peter' I said, 'It's my Peter'. 'No, no, no, the kid we're looking for, we've got a tall description'. I said, 'My Peter told me, it's my Peter'. I done that because I wanted the police to go to Peter and say, 'Peter you've done this that and the other, you do it again and you're gonna…' And do you know it really worked. It really worked with him. Grassed him up – done him the world of good."

Again, it is noticeable that the police started with a presumption of innocence that was not extended to Linda or Dawn. Using the police as a discipline strategy would have been unthinkably risky for them.

This well-founded fear of the police was not confined to black parents. BM (14) and his family were Spanish migrants who become involved with the youth justice services after BM's older brother, Cedro, was sent to a secure unit for GBH and knifepoint robbery. BM's mother, June, emphasised the huge impact this had on the whole family. Before he was arrested, June existed in a state of constant anxiety, wondering what Cedro was going to do next. BM was particularly close to Cedro and missed his brother desperately when he was sent away. Cedro had wanted to spare his two younger brothers from seeing him in such a grim setting and denied them visiting orders, but this had merely added to BM's confusion and hurt. As June explained, the family mourned the loss of Cedro and worried a great deal about him.

> "I have my ups and downs. When it was Cedro's 18th birthday, the run up to it, for about a week, I was pretty damn low. Had it been any other birthday, I don't think it would have bothered me as much, but his 18th, and it did, it killed me… And when he got first sent down it was hard because it was like two, er a week and a half before Christmas. That was a killer. That was a killer for all of us. I mean, I didn't even put the Christmas decorations up until late Christmas Eve, and the kids, I did feel bad for them, because it's their Christmas as well, but even they weren't, 'Oh, Mum, when are you going to put the Christmas decorations?'"

June's account reveals the trauma the whole family suffered as a result of Cedro's offending behaviour. She described how her house was regularly raided by police, leaving her unable to sleep at night, constantly listening out for sirens. Her marriage was close to collapse because of the strain, and she worried about the impact on her younger sons. As Rachel Condry (2007) demonstrates so effectively, behind serious crime headlines there are devastated and shamed relatives trying to make sense of events and piece their lives back together.

Cedro had also attended Hailingbrooke where his behaviour had been the cause of much concern. When BM was due for secondary transfer, June desperately tried to get him accepted into another school. She was deeply dissatisfied with Hailingbrooke and had worried that he would be identified and pathologised because he was Cedro's brother. June's fears were not unfounded. Teachers very commonly pointed to the behaviour of siblings to make generalisations and interpret behaviour. June had been so worried about the 'stigma' of Cedro attaching to

BM that she mounted an unsuccessful appeal when she did not get the school of her choice. She had decided to try and home-school BM while they waited for a place, but quickly realising that was not a workable option she reluctantly folded and sent him to Hailingbrooke. June was particularly dismissive of Miss O'Conner, the deputy head and described being 'petrified' of her.

> "It was like, 'Oh, please, Mum, come this way', and really nice, but I was sitting in her office, 'Yes, Mum. No, Mum'. And I was like I daren't not take any notice of her! She scared the living ... and she still does to this day!... Even though I'm not even going to see her, sometimes I'll see her around the school, and she's like, 'Oh, hello, hiya, are you all right?' And I think, 'Please go away. I'm not coming to see you. I don't like the feelings I have when I see you!' It's like being back at school, I feel like I'm in detention."

BM had been rapidly transferred to the BSU for a string of misbehaviour (running out of class, setting fire alarms off, fighting). He was loud, spirited and ultra-enthusiastic in our research sessions, but could be over dominant. He mercilessly mocked the other boys and was rabidly and theatrically homophobic, scathingly labelling those he did not like as 'gays'. But he was also surprisingly sensitive. Fights and arguments often made him cry and he complained of being bullied when he was sent to the school's off-site provision. He had developed a close relationship with the staff in the BSU and Dave Stirling had begun to give him particular responsibilities. For example, BM was allowed to carry the keys and lock up at the end of the day, something he took great pride in. He was also in charge of cleaning out the fish in the school pond. BM was particularly passionate about animals and Dave had arranged for him to work on a farm one day a week, something BM and June were very pleased about.

But June continued to worry that BM would repeat Cedro's mistakes. He was bitter and antagonistic towards the police, having witnessed the distress and damage resulting from the raids.

> "I mean, BM has come home from school, and I've had 20-odd officers in my house, tipping my house upside down, so he's not very police-friendly, and I've tried to get it through to him that, if they stop and search you, 'Yes sir, no sir, three bags full, sir.'"

When Cedro had started to get in trouble with the police June was made subject to a parenting order, forcing her to attend parenting classes. She was told that she should have been monitoring Cedro's whereabouts '24/7', even though he was 17 at the time. June explained that while she was at first furious and resistant to the idea, attending the classes was a comforting experience. She was urged not to blame herself by the coordinator and was reassured that she had done all she could. And listening to the stories of the other mothers in the class made her feel grateful that Cedro's behaviour was not worse.

Gendering parenting

In the vast majority of cases we spoke to mothers, even when fathers were resident and closely involved in their children's lives. This reflects the heavily gendered allocation of parental responsibility, more generally, as well as the particular requirements of parenting a behaviourally challenging child. Carefully worded references to 'parenting' in policy and professional literature belies the fact that responsibility for the day-to-day care of children still falls predominantly to mothers. This gender-neutral language also obscures the differential impact of initiatives on mothers and fathers. As Amanda Holt (2009) demonstrates, specific additional duties are associated with parenting an 'at risk' child, including managing all the frequent interactions with teachers and other professionals and waiting 'on standby' for police and schools. As Holt notes these hidden responsibilities are invariably taken on by mothers. And mothers were often very proactive in attempting to manage risks. They went through pockets, rang round other mothers and recruited friends and relatives in an attempt to keep their sons safe and out of trouble. Armani's mother was so worried about gang activity on their estate that she invited her son's friends over every weekend, plying them with popcorn and films to try and keep them off the streets. Ultimately though, like June, parents often found they had limited control particularly as their children got older.

A high proportion of pupils participating in the research came from lone mother households. This over representation almost certainly reflects the greater propensity for lone parent families to face the challenges of disadvantage so commonly associated with a BSU referral. Lone parent families are considerably more likely to be poor, and as such may be over represented in the catchment areas to start with. Yet as I've described, such material and social struggles are very commonly reduced down to issues of parenting practice. In particular, the relatively high proportion of black lone mother families has been implicated in conduct issues and used to explain the disproportionate exclusion rates of African-Caribbean boys. Both the co-ed schools deliberately employed black male mentors in an effort to provide role models and to address the impact of perceived father absence. Tony Sewell (2010) has been a prominent advocate of this approach, claiming that black boys are 'over feminised' in lone mother households and become resentful and defiant towards male authority figures as a result.

However, as Tracey Reynolds (2010) contends, such claims perpetuate a misunderstanding of black British family life. Drawing on her extensive work in the area she points to the way fathers are often involved but non-resident, the strong Caribbean tradition of female-headed households and the role step-fathers, uncles, grandfathers, brothers, and male cousins tend to play in caring for and raising black boys (Reynolds, 2005; Reynolds, 2009; Goulbourne et al, 2009). Certainly, the vast majority of boys in the study had contact with their fathers and other male figures in their lives, although this was not always unproblematic. In several cases boys articulated strong feelings of rejection and anger towards fathers they saw rarely. Positive relationships were considerably more common though. As I discuss in the next chapter, fathers and other male family members often played a significant role in forming boys' plans for the future.

Note

[1] See Nick Triggle (2014) 'Children "being failed in early years"', *BBC News Online*, http://www.bbc.co.uk/news/health-29317098

SEVEN

"Ain't doing tramp's work": educational marginalisation and imagined futures

In this chapter I turn attention to how the young people attending the BSUs envisaged the future. Significantly, the fieldwork for the research coincided with the onset of a global financial crisis, widely referred to in the UK at the time as the 'credit crunch'. This was a period where banks appeared to be teetering on the edge. There was much talk of fiscal meltdown and near apocalyptic coverage in the media. As a well-educated adult I struggled to make sense of events and listened with alarm to a predicted future of recession, job losses, welfare cuts and austerity. It was amidst the confusing terminology and violent metaphors of 'crunches', 'cuts', slashes and squeezes that the young people in this study looked to the future. The focus in this chapter is on their anticipated trajectories and on the ways in which educational marginalisation shaped their understandings of opportunities and prospects. I begin with a consideration of the political and policy context through which the future was framed as troubling at this time. While these discussions did not directly touch the pupils in the units, they infused a sense of insecurity and compounded articulations of risk management as the core function of 'inclusion'.

Highlighting the significance accorded to educational credentials as a pathway to the good life, I draw out the meaning attached to contemporary school failure, contrasting this with the agentic resistance identified in Paul Willis's classic 1970s study *Learning to Labour*. I show how, to all intents and purposes, today's young people have had the tables turned on them and are now often struggling to remain in education rather than to escape to a workplace. In fact, for many, dislocation from educational achievement left them struggling to imagine how they would construct liveable futures (at least outside of highly risky criminal endeavours). I examine the particular strategies the young people devised for future survival and conclude with a focus on hopes and dreams as opposed to 'aspirations' to offer a different insight into the values and ethics that gave meaning to their lives.

Uncertain futures

The talk of financial crisis and instability was an unavoidable cultural backdrop to the young people's reflections on their futures in this research. TV coverage of what became known as the 'Global Recession' included copious references to an impending army of jobless youths whose dire employment prospects will render them a 'lost generation'. High rates of unemployment, it was claimed, will trap the young in a spiral of poverty and social exclusion, sapping them of motivation and skills[1]. Aside from the catastrophising tenor, this claim encapsulates an ideologically ingrained perspective that positions young people as collateral damage in the fight to save capitalism. Originally used in the context of the First World War to describe the young men who had been killed or physically or mentally maimed, the phrase 'lost generation' does considerable contemporary rhetorical work. As Ann Nilson and Julia Brannen (2014) point out, it promotes an individualistic emphasis on supporting the capacities of young people to find work rather than on the responsibility of governments to provide opportunities. The fatalist nature of the phrase also overplays the irreversible impact of marginalisation on the young, suggesting their generation is 'scarred' for life. While there is clear evidence of the negative effects of early unemployment (Bell and Blanchflower, 2011; MacDonald, 2011) the concept of a lost generation writes off a whole cohort of economically disadvantaged youth, depicting their sustained marginalisation as somehow inevitable (Nilsen and Brannen, 2014)

The lost generation discourse also plays into the preoccupation with identifying and neutralising future threats. It is notable how much of the handwringing associated with the plight of the young unemployed centred on the capacity for social unrest, most commonly conveyed through the metaphor of a ticking time bomb for society[2]. As was identified in Chapter 4, a double-pronged articulation of risk deftly conflates vulnerability to harm with potential to cause harm, foregrounding the characteristics of the 'at risk' while obscuring the social conditions that produce the actual harm. The future orientated logic of risk emphasises dangerous trajectories while normalising unjust presents. This tendency to define the young in relation to their futurity is not new (Lee, 2002; Mayall, 2002), but the contemporary emphasis on developing and maximising human capital has dramatically intensified the conceptual dislocation of children and young people from their existent material lives (Gillies, 2014).

Since the turn of the current century a specific category of NEET (young people not in education, employment or training) has emerged as a key signifier of a risk trajectory. NEETs are anathema to neoliberal sensibilities, branded as unproductive and valueless. Portrayed as teenage dropouts, their status has been linked to crime, antisocial behaviour, teenage pregnancy and a range of poor life outcomes. Again, NEETs appear to matter more for what they will become, as opposed to what they are facing in the here and now. In many ways they personify the ticking time bomb. Local authorities up and down the country produced 'action plans' to reduce their numbers, with strategies predictably focusing on remedying perceived personal deficits rather than any social structural solutions. But the NEET taxonomy and promotion of quick fix targets belies the heterogeneous mix of young people categorised by the term and the variety of circumstances and challenges characterising their lives (Yates and Payne, 2007, Furlong, 2006). The term also focuses policy concern on long-term youth unemployment at the expense of a more prevalent 'churning' between jobless periods and low status, insecure and badly paid work (Shildrick et al, 2012).

Aside from the politics of representation, there is no doubt that young people did (and continue to) suffer the economic effects of the global recession disproportionately (Bell and Blanchflower, 2011). Less easily measured is the psychic impact of uncertainty, insecurity and anticipation that marked the run up to what would become a period of great hardship. As well as bleak prospects for the future, many of the most vulnerable young people in this study and their families went on to face the onslaught of austerity-driven welfare reforms. While the financial crisis was never discussed in any real depth in the group sessions it was hard to ignore and often cropped up in passing. I was asked what 'credit crunch' meant several times and had some abstract conversations about what the country could or could not afford in the circumstances (the queen for instance).

Significantly, the ominous predictions of deep, sustained recession and fiscal pain rumbled on alongside the preparations to host the 2012 Olympics in London. There was great excitement from pupils at the prospect of such a major sporting event taking place on their doorstep, but also some confusion over how it would ever be paid for. Few thought the Olympics would be called off and no one thought it should be, but the juxtaposition of dire warnings of financial insolvency with the estimated costs was the focus of some discussion. At Hailingbrooke it was raised by Buggs (14), a black African boy with a passion for all things to do with sports. Buggs was also very interested in politics and current affairs and clearly did a great deal of reading about it in his own time. He had orchestrated some fascinating discussions with the other boys about the election of Barack Obama, the significance of a black US president and the likelihood (or not) of it happening in the UK. Buggs was a highly entertaining debater, exercising a sharp wit and a dry, if sometimes quirky, sense of humour. But Buggs had a history of conflict with Mr Phillips, which had caused him to truant regularly. His prolonged absences meant he had fallen behind the others in his mainstream class, despite his intellect and enthusiasm for knowledge. His referral to the BSU exacerbated that disadvantage.

Encouraged by Buggs' enthusiasm we brought in a very talented performance poet to work with us across several of the research sessions. This was initially approached as a wildcard experiment, given that literacy was such a sensitive issue for so many of the boys. We encouraged the use of a tape recorder or pen and paper and it soon became apparent that poetry and rap was a potent medium for the boys to express their thoughts and feelings. Echoing cultural preoccupations at the time, money was a particularly common theme for the spoken word and written poems. For instance, Buggs produced a lyrical stream of consciousness that reflected the predominant sense of insecurity.

> 2012, 2012 the world won't end
> The Olympics is coming and it won't end then
> The cost is 9.6 billion
> My parents ain't got that not even a gillion
>
> The earth is going into another recession
> If this keeps on happening I will lose my possessions
> Money, money it ain't all that
> All you need is your family that is that
> Losing a member of you family is very hard
> God will help you through this terrible part
>
> Food, food, food
> I love them as much as you
> But don't waste them because there's people that need it
> more than you

Themes of precariousness, loss and scarcity are presented in almost biblical terms here through references to the world potentially ending and recession depicted as a kind of natural disaster. This fatalistic approach highlights Buggs' lack of agency in determining world events and his awareness of their major impact on his and his family's lives. In the austerity years that followed, many in London and beyond did lose their possessions, and came to rely on food banks (Shildrick et al, 2012; O'Hara, 2013). And some also quite literally lost their lives to ill health, malnutrition, and suicide following draconian welfare benefits sanctions (Stuckler and Basu, 2013; Moore, 2015;).

But after Buggs' noble pronouncement about not wasting food the poem then trailed off rather incongruously as his attention wandered and he returned to teasing a boy who had earlier listed Rihanna as a favourite singer.

> There are subliminal messages in our songs

> like Umbrella Rhianna is as dark as fog

This bizarre ending partly reflects Buggs' indulgence in surreal humour but also his fascination with conspiracy theories. He regaled the boys in the group with tales of George Bush's connections to Osama Bin Laden's family in Saudi Arabia and talked about the Bilderburg Group. He also claimed, with his tongue firmly in his cheek, that Tony Blair, George Bush and Gordon Brown were lizards from another planet. While the other boys laughed, assuming it was another of Buggs' surreal jokes, I recognised the claim as originating from some of the more florid teachings of David Ike. But Buggs' knowledge extended far beyond the murky corners of the internet. He retained facts and figures (like the estimated cost of the Olympics, historical dates and obscure capital cities) and I often found myself asking, "How do you know that?"

While the other boys in the BSU recognised Buggs as clever, he seemed to have little self-confidence in his own academic abilities. He claimed his poor literacy would prevent him from getting into university, even though I watched him write the poem himself quickly, by hand, and with no spelling mistakes. Instead, he talked often about self-made men and expressed admiration for those who succeed against the odds through hard work. He named Alan Sugar as a role model alongside an uncle who had set up his own business, made his fortune and moved to Dubai. Alongside the many facts Buggs retained were the names of any famous people who had become successful despite being born in his deprived neighbourhood. He also drew comfort from listing famous people who had been kicked out of school, citing this as evidence that second chances were possible.

Valuing education: learning and labour

"I wanna learn, and I don't wanna be one of them kids who don't go to school and just stay at home." (Alfie, 13)

Alongside most of the boys and many of the girls in this study, Buggs was positioned by a discourse of 'disaffection'. His truanting and disruptive behaviour in the classroom were seen as evidence that he simply did not want to learn or be at school. He had become viewed as one of Mr Phillips' unteachable '10 percenters', unable and unwilling to engage. This discourse of disaffection is in part drawn from a long and established body of educational and sociological research dating back to the 1970s. Among the most acclaimed ethnographies of this genre is the classic study *Learning to Labour* by Paul Willis (1977), which challenged previous prevailing accounts of pupil failure or victimhood and emphasised instead agentic rejection of schooling. In this detailed analysis Willis documented how young working-class men in the Midlands developed and deployed a counter school culture, describing the 'lads' antagonism to formal knowledge and their sense that it would be of little use to them in the long run. He also recounted how their opposition to the school was played out through 'a struggle for symbolic and physical space from the institution and its rules and to defeat its main perceived purpose: to make you 'work' (Willis, 1977: 26). This deliberate self-managed school failure was orchestrated in preparation for the working-class manual occupations awaiting the lads.

While Willis' account of young people's alienation and purposeful disengagement has been formative in shaping understandings of school dynamics, contemporary interpretations have shifted far from original sociologically grounded perspectives. As I have outlined, the concept of disaffection is now abstracted almost entirely from crucial social contexts, approached instead as a potentially curable condition afflicting particular individuals. The notion that young people are choosing to reject school remains a powerful explanation but is now more often regarded as symptomatic of a personal pathology. My research methodology was informed by a critical perspective on this personalised approach but at no point did I think to question the concept of disaffection as a premise. I had instinctively expected the young people in the study to express antipathy to school and possibly to reject education entirely as a valid endeavour. This assumption was very quickly challenged once the fieldwork began.

We often used brainstorming techniques in the group sessions to stimulate debates around particular issues. We would state a word and ask pupils to say the first thing that came into their heads. We used the word 'school' with most groups and found that this tended to elicit just as many and sometimes more positive than negative responses. Pupils shouted out things like 'too long', 'too early', 'boring' but also 'fun', 'opportunity', 'future', 'money' and even on one occasion 'shows you the meaning of life'. At first I wondered whether the pupils were telling us what they thought we wanted to hear. But it soon became clear that there was no straightforward antipathy towards school. In the interviews with pupils we asked what advice they would want to pass on to a son or daughter. To our surprise, almost all wanted to convey the importance of learning and achieving at school. Even in the context of serious academic under attainment, pupils tended to emphasise the worth of education, with most identifying curriculum-based subjects as enjoyable. As the quotes below illustrate, school subjects were often discussed with enthusiasm.

> "[My favourite subject is] English. And science most of the times. And erm… And maths, maths, like I'm not really good at maths, but, like, with the teacher like, he's funny like busses [cracks] jokes and he talks to us and stuff, like he's funny." (Marcus 15)

> "I do like English. It's fun, like, when you can write stories, because I've got kind of a good imagination, I can think of quite a lot of stories and everything, so I like doing stories and everything." (Luke 14)

> "In primary school they just teach A-B-C-D-E and 1-2-3-4 and all that but in secondary school they teach you physics and everything. Good stuff like maths." (Angelina 12)

As I have documented, there was plenty of resentment directed towards the schools and particular teachers (like Mr Phillips) were absolutely detested. But significantly, pupils often justified their provocative and defiant behaviour on the grounds that they were being prevented from learning. For example, Chireal (15) was angry that her good science teacher was replaced by a supply teacher.

> "I can't do science, I hate it! And I need science, science GCSE to be what I wanna be, but I can't do it… We had a supply so obviously we don't do nothing with supply teachers, no one ever has done anything with supply

teachers. So we just sat there, so we forgot all our work, you know, what we did for the past couple of years... If a supply teacher comes, we class it as a free lesson. Most of the time they sit there and do nothing. Most come in, they don't (pause) or they'll try and kick us out the class and we'll just give them hassle, and they'll just give up on us and just sit down."

Chireal's assessment of supply teachers reflected a more common complaint about their ineffectiveness. Chanelle (13) also recounted negative experiences of supply teachers.

"Basically they don't really care, because they're still getting paid, in'it. They just, they're just here to watch you really. They don't teach you. They'll just like, say, 'Read page two' or something. That's it. That's how the lesson starts and finishes."

There was, then, was very little sign from boys or girls of the kind of gleeful antagonism towards school expressed in *Learning to Labour* and certainly no sense of any superiority to those who conformed academically and progressed (pejoratively labelled 'ear'oles' by those in Willis's study). To state the obvious, times have changed quite considerably since the 1970s. Just 20 years later Martin Mac an Ghaill's ethnography of a comprehensive school, also in the Midlands, documented the effects of deindustrialisation and school reforms on boys. He identified the 'Macho Lads', a group of young men sharing similarities to the Lads in Willis's study but in a context of economic restructuring and the decline of the manufacturing sector. In the absence of the job opportunities awaiting the 1970s lads, these boys channelled their resistance to school through a consolidation and celebration of their gender power, creating a 'hypermasculinity' that prioritised 'fighting, football and fucking' (Mac an Ghaill, 1994).

Twenty years on again, in London, the three F's remain key to boys' performance of hypermasculinity in schools, but attitudes towards education appear to have shifted quite significantly. The pupils (boys and girls) in my study are just as marginalised from experiences of academic achievement as the 'lads' before them but are very differently invested in school as a social field. More specifically, education is accorded a high value, despite low prospects of ever capitalising on it. So rather than rejecting the game, the pupils challenged the rules and railed against the unfairness of their enforcement. More significantly, in the context of contemporary segregationist approaches to behaviour support, the struggle for symbolic and physical space characterising Willis's study has been replaced with a much more basic struggle to maintain entitlement to any educational space in the first place.

It might be argued that the findings of this study reflect the specificity of London, and more particularly the high number of pupils from migrant backgrounds (traditionally viewed as more aspirant). But white working-class pupils were equally as likely to express a positive account of school and education in the context of very negative experiences. In fact, only one boy articulated anything like the contempt for school I had initially expected to encounter. Steve (14) explicitly stated that he hated school and all the teachers. Steve had been excluded from his first secondary school for setting a fire and had spent a year in a pupil referral unit. He was then accepted into Hailingbrooke but soon found himself in the BSU after throwing a bin at a teacher. When he first joined our research sessions he was rude and aggressive. He sat away from the group at the other end of the drama studio, repeatedly switching the lights on and off and throwing chairs over. He said he wanted to play football so we set up a penalty shoot-out game. He joined in enthusiastically and by the end of the session he was transformed.

Steve became chatty and personable. He was very comedic in his expressions and enjoyed making people laugh. He also had strong opinions, particularly about the importance of loyalty and family. He loved art and spent considerable time in the sessions sketching life drawings and caricatures. However, Steve was in a great deal of trouble outside of school. He had been arrested and charged with criminal damage, and then subsequently for stealing a motorbike. He had been warned he was one misdemeanour away from a secure unit placement. His behaviour was often reckless and impulsive when he was bored or threatened, and he described feeling very bored in the BSU. But Steve's clear antipathy toward Hailingbrooke was contextualised by his previous positive experience of the pupil referral unit. He had enjoyed doing science there and felt the teachers had understood him. As Martin Mills and Glenda McGregor (2014) argue, mainstream schools could learn much from the practices of alternative education provision.

Given that Steve directed so much anger and resentment towards Hailingbrooke, I was surprised to hear him express a desire in his interview to get qualifications in the future. He wanted to join the army and had been told he needed GCSEs. This sense that education is a vital stepping stone to a viable future was shared by most of the young people in the study, reflecting the extent to which labour market entry is assumed to be determined by academic credentials. Since the 1990s, the emergence of human capital as a value system has imposed an ideological hegemony of educational conformity leaving young people struggling to see beyond it. Yet as Patrick Ainley and Martin Allen (2010) argue, emphasis on qualifications and learning merely masks the shrinkage of employment opportunities, ensuring the main purpose of contemporary education becomes social control over youth.

The controlling pull exerted over the young people participating in this research was, in a practical sense, limited. However, at a broader ideological level there was little questioning of the meritocratic ideal of education. Pupils quite uncritically bought into a work harder and move forward mentality as an ethic and a pathway to a better life, but saw themselves as limited by personal flaws, lack of ability and external barriers to achievement (for example, bad or vindictive teachers). This meant that beneath the bravado, school failure was painfully significant; it mattered and couldn't easily be laughed off or dismissed. For some of the younger pupils this understanding was managed through a sense that they would be able to recover their stride and start learning again in the future. Similar sentiments were expressed by some older pupils, for whom FE college was a beacon of hope in the context of an irredeemable school career.

But for others, mainly boys, the very concept of education symbolised a missed opportunity and something they already were and would remain excluded from. For example, the advice Curtis wanted to pass on to a son or daughter was to avoid failing at school as he had done.

> "Take in their education in school, because I never took it in that much… Because if you go school and you get a good, you do your GCSEs, and if you get all your GCSEs, right, you go college, and then you study for what you wanna be."

Curtis was 13 when he took part in this interview. By this time he had spent nearly two years in the BSU alongside his older brother, Jamal. Curtis and Jamal had arrived in the UK from Jamaica with their mother who was very sick at the time, and father who was subsequently deported. They lived in temporary accommodation in various parts of the country, attending multiple primary schools before they ended up at Hailingbrooke. Curtis's conclusion that he had already missed out on education was a bleak but realistic assessment. His behaviour was often very difficult to manage and there was no talk of him returning to the mainstream classroom. He was loud, defiant and could barely read or write. Nevertheless, Curtis desperately wanted to stay at school and hated the frequent temporary exclusions he received. This was his response when he was asked what he liked most about school.

> "Everything. Seriously, I would be at school at home. When I'm at home, I look at the time all the time I'll be there… Yeah. I'll be like, 'That's period four now'. 'I'd be doing lunch now', like,… 'It's lunch time', 'It'll be break time'."

Curtis described how he often tried to sneak back into the school at lunchtime when he had been excluded. He felt bored at home and missed the sense of belonging. He would also likely have missed the opportunity for a good meal. He emphasised how much he appreciated the teachers and mentors and listed ITC, English and art as his favourite subjects. He had few illusions about any ability to transform his interest into qualifications. Instead his hopes for the future centred on just getting a decent job. This is an excerpt from an interview Yvonne conducted with him towards the end of his participation in the research.

> Yvonne: So what do you want to most achieve in life, Curtis?
>
> Curtis: Get a job. That's it. Help my mum.
>
> Yvonne: And what sort of job do you want to get? What do you wanna do?
>
> Curtis: Any job, actually. I don't really care, but as long as it's no fucking street job or shit. Fuck that.
>
> Yvonne: What do you mean by 'street job'?
>
> Curtis: Like fucking sweeping the streets. Fuck that!
>
> Yvonne: Okay. What's wrong with that?
>
> Curtis: That ain't right, blood.
>
> Yvonne: What's not right about it?
>
> Curtis: I mean, that's tramp's work, blood. That's tramp's work, and I ain't fucking doing that. That's fucking tramp's blood. I ain't fucking (pause) I ain't.

This quote very powerfully illustrates the complex and volatile emotions that discussions of the future could provoke in some young people. Behind Curtis' bluster there is a keenly felt fear and anxiety that a 'street job' will be all that's open to him. In his imagination cleaning the streets would be a public humiliation. It would constitute a visible demonstration of his inability to attach value to himself through education, representing a shameful symbol of stigma (Goffman, 1963). As Andrew Sayer (2005) notes, those who believe society is basically meritocratic are most vulnerable to shame. Trapping young people in an education system massively weighted against them compels them to accept dominant constructions that ultimately justify and naturalise their disadvantage. This symbolic power also encourages aspiration as a form of social fragmentation, inviting the heaping of contempt upon those positioned at the bottom of society. Pupils at Gravensdale made similar comments about 'dustbin workers'; those who didn't get any qualifications and aren't able to do anything else. This distancing expression of disgust directed at those working with rubbish perhaps reflects their conscious awareness of their 'disposable status' (Giroux, 2014) and vulnerability to becoming in Wacquant's (2007) words 'the refuge of society'.

In contrast to the visceral emotions expressed by Curtis, Daniel's reflections were considerably more subdued and dejected. Daniel was 13 when he was interviewed by Yvonne. He struggled to see any future at all when asked what he might be doing in five years' time.

Daniel: Er ... God knows!

Yvonne: What would you like to be doing?

Daniel: I'll probably be dead.

Yvonne: Oh no! Why do you say that?

Daniel: I don't know.

Yvonne: I, I'm sure you won't be. Why did you say that?

Daniel: I don't know. I (pause) like, never know (pause) I don't know. I don't know. If I say something, yeah, and tell you lies, that's not gonna come true, but I'll never know. I don't know. I don't know.

Daniel was another long-term BSU attendee at Hailingbrooke. His mother was Turkish and his father was African-Caribbean. He lived in a small and very overcrowded flat with his mother, sisters and brothers. His mother struggled to make ends meet on benefits and she looked tired and stressed. Daniel had a large family network including three adult half-brothers but only saw his dad intermittently. He was particularly angry about this and the lack of financial support the family received from his father.

> "The last time I seen him was last week. I say, 'I need money', yeah, like, 'to get stuff', yeah, 'Look at me, I look like a tramp!' Not like a tramp, 'Look at me, like a little rough. Look at my trainers. Look, they're messed up'. 'Don't worry, I'm trying to sort you out. I'm going to work'. I'm doing this, I'm doing that. My brother, yeah, he's been asking my dad for a jacket for how long?… The only time he did call us, yeah, was to say, yeah, like my granddad died. It's the only time he called, yeah, then after that, yeah, we went to the funeral a couple of days after … like we were all sitting there, yeah in the church, yeah, and he was all the way back there with his family. But it's our dad, like, he's meant to be with us, in'it. Yeah, but he's there with his other family and shit."

Like Curtis, Daniel was boisterous, unruly and at times belligerent. He missed numerous research sessions because of temporary exclusions (usually for fighting) and had spent a period at the off-site provision. He was also very excitable and enthusiastic. He threw himself into the research activities with abandon. As the previous quote demonstrates, Daniel struggled to imagine leaving school and could see little future for himself outside of hustling. He found it difficult to sit still for any length of time, ensuring he was very detached from academic skills. All the same he still valued school highly and expressed resentment about being segregated in the BSU.

> "Stuffed up in this, like, a cage. Look at it! Look, look, they've got all them bars and shut the window. I don't like being, like, all in one room, yeah, with kids that's all being bad and that. I just wanna go back and have normal schooling."

'Normal schooling' may have been Daniel's ambition, but his volatility continually sabotaged his progress. He was loud and overfamiliar with teachers and they often complained that he was rude. He also rose to any provocation and overreacted towards minor perceived slights or insults. Daniel always seemed like he was on borrowed time in the unit, yet he still drew on school as a measure of self-worth. When Yvonne asked what made him most proud about himself he replied, "That I'm at school. That I'm at school and I'm trying to work".

He never did make it back into mainstream though. At Hailingbrooke there was a white working-class caretaker who proudly identified himself as a disciplinarian. He made no secret of the fact he disapproved of the BSU and he kept a close eye on attendees as they made their way into and out of the unit. He could be very provocative. I had watched him chase a BSU pupil who had been quite innocently waiting at the school gates for a friend, pursuing him down the road and barking threats. The caretaker goaded Daniel in front of a group of other pupils. Predictably, Daniel threw a punch, despite being half the size of the caretaker, and was permanently excluded as a result. Yvonne visited Daniel at home several months later. He was dishevelled, very down and had put on a lot of weight. Close to tears, he begged for us to persuade the head to reconsider and allow him back to the school. But the decision had already been taken and there was very little we could do.

Dirty money: weighing up the options

The bleak employment prospects facing the boys in particular led many to consider more nefarious ways to make a living in the future. Many were already involved in minor criminal deals, making bits of money here and there, but most saw this as a temporary way to supplement income. Running the occasional 'errand' for older boys or fencing stolen goods within the school was a useful way to access funds. Pupils were often acutely aware of their family's financial struggles and could feel unable to ask for money from parents for things they needed, especially if they had younger siblings. The temptation to make easy money through illegal means was difficult for some to resist. As Marcus commented:

> "It's dirty money but it's helping you. I'd rather hustle than make my mum hustle."

There was a large and thriving black market running in both of the co-ed schools. Trading took place across a large selection of commodities, ranging from sweets to cigarettes to fireworks. As Fletcher et al (2013) report, state regulation of school meals has driven a large number of pupils into clandestine buying and selling of junk food, drinks and confectionary. The selling of crisps and chocolate appeared to be particularly profitable, with many pupils eating little else during the school day. These supplies were generally cheaper and considered more appetising than school lunch options, which were often dismissed as inedible. At Hailingbrooke many of the BSU attendees sold stuff, but it was a sensitive subject to probe around and I never properly got to grips with the exact workings of the market.

Among the most prolific of sellers was Peter (the tiny 12-year-old boy with ADHD) whose entrepreneurial activities were apparently supported by his mother's supply of wholesale chocolate bars, which he sold on at a handsome profit. Peter and his mother were planning to use the money to buy a computer. Peter was very assertive and adept at haggling. He kept a mental slate for his customers and pursued them for their debts. At first, I worried that his tiny stature would make him vulnerable to being ripped off or robbed, but everyone eventually seemed to pay up and no one ever crossed him. Having an older brother and cousin in the school probably helped to bolster his status. Notably, BSU staff turned a blind eye to Peter's very visible dealing and secretly expressed some admiration. But most other trading took place under the radar, perhaps reflecting the less legitimate nature of much of the goods on sale. At Gravensdale there were repeated efforts to stamp out black markets in the school, with 'show expulsions' of those caught in the act regularly occurring.

But this kind of dodgy trading alongside 'errands' or 'shotting' was viewed as a provisional measure. Crime was generally acknowledged to be a poor option for the future, replete with risks and insecurity. Daniel's jokey reply to the question of what advice he would want to pass on to a son or daughter conveys the absurdity of criminality as an aspiration.

> "To the boy I'll say, 'Stay on the street, sell drugs' – I'm joking! I don't know! Be good in school. That's the only thing I can say. Because if you're good in school, you're not going to mess up your whole future… Yeah, I would say it to both of them. I'd say, 'Yeah, because my life, yeah, is messed up, yeah. Obviously yours ain't gonna be, like so I'll tell you this'."

Daniel's sarcastic suggestion that he would want his son to 'stay' on the streets highlights the acceptance of minor crime as a temporary measure. Even Kieran, the boy who had become heavily involved with a criminal street gang (discussed in Chapter 3), was striving to get GCSEs and find a legitimate job. For the older boys, the question of how to make ends meet was more pressing with stark options considered. For example, Marcus's hopes revolved around passing a GCSE in PE and studying on a vocational course at college, but he was aware his poor literacy skills might hold him back.

> "If I pass some of my exams, yeah. If I pass PE, 'cos half of it is doing things rather than writing. 'Cos my writing is a bit behind. If I pass it then I'll get into college and do sports psychology and then just get a little job like make children play football and like make them pay like £40 pound a week like [laughs]. If people keep me behind I'll probably be on road. I swear I'll be on road teefing [stealing] or something. I'm telling the truth ain't it. Or selling drugs, boy."

His mother was set on encouraging him to apply to train as an electrician and had provided the appropriate college forms, but he struggled to fill them out. He dismissed those without qualifications as 'dustbin people', emptying the bins or working in McDonalds, while being fully cognisant of his own poor prospects. The consequences of economic restructuring, in terms of the replacement of more traditional, secure working-class employment with low skilled, low paid insecure work, has been well documented (Wacquant, 2007; Standing, 2011; Shildrick et al, 2012). As Shildrick et al (2012) have so powerfully demonstrated, such 'flexible' jobs are physically and mentally demanding, poorly valued and highly precarious, trapping young people in a 'low pay, no pay cycle'. This was a vision of the future few of the pupils could countenance. As a result, many continued to place their faith in the transformative power of education, even in the absence of any practical connection with, or experience of success.

For some young men, particularly the older ones, discussions about the future focused on risks and survival mechanisms. For example, considerable time was spent imagining what life in jail might be like and how it could be managed.

> Mica: Say if you go to jail when you're young but you're intelligent and that you might find a way to get a job using your brains.

Marcus: Say if you're a hustler but you know how to make good money. I mean I'm not saying it's not wrong but they have good reason for doing what they do. Do you get me? Like some people will go and rob yeah, then they'll get caught and they'll be in the bin. Some of them will come out like, "Yeah, I was in the bin man, loves it". Some of them will be like, "I don't like it". But once you've been in it can be like home for you, 'cos all your boys have been in. Some people like to be in jail.

Mica: Bullshit!

Will: It's the five-year stretches I don't like.

Mica: Yeah if I get caught right, six months, seven months, yeah. No longer than a year.

Will: That's what I'm saying man, no longer than a year.

Marcus: It would be hard yeah. But then I wouldn't want my son to go through that. When he's born I would tell him right from wrong. I will say straight up life is hard do you get me. But say to him don't go there or I'll slap you up. I'll beat your bum black. Scare them from young and he won't... My dad used to say, "I'm going to Jamaica for a couple of years". That's what he used to say and he'd give me bare presents before he goes and then I won't see him for the next five or six years.

Like Marcus, large numbers of the pupils had fathers or brothers that were or had been in jail. There was talk of how to endure it by keeping your head down, taking up opportunities to study, or even converting to Islam. Many of the boys were convinced that becoming a Muslim would entitle them to privileges in prison like a personal shower and extra time to pray. Some even claimed that Muslims would be given their own TV and phone. More realistic assessments of the benefits of conversion stressed the experience of a brotherhood and the protection this provided. A Muslim brotherhood was viewed as stretching across creed and colour, offering a framework of support and security in a harsh environment. As Shane [not yet a Muslim] explained:

"[in prison] If you need help then you go to your Muslim friends for help. Because you're a Muslim you have more power."

Marcus (whose father had converted to Islam in prison) remained unconvinced. He valued his identity as a Christian and vowed not to change his faith for anyone.

But risks extended far beyond going to prison, as the boys knew only too well. Most had personally experienced the brutality of street crime, having been victimised, attacked and robbed on the street, while others had seen members of their family targeted. For example, Curtis's stepbrother was shot and nearly lost his life and Daniel's sister's boyfriend had been killed in a street attack. These events must have been traumatic but they were narrated with angry insouciance and a declared indifference to personal fate as this quote from Curtis demonstrates.

> "I don't really care if I get stabbed … shot, I don't care. That's me! I (pause) I just don't care. I get shot, if I die, I die. If I don't, I just go to hospital, in'it? That's it. I'm telling you straight up… It's just like my brother, he don't care. I'm not talking about [Jamal]. My other brother … he got shot once, he never cared. Got admitted at hospital. Bare blood. Couldn't stop bleeding… Like 50/50 chance, like. Like … no, actually it was 30/80 … 30/70 chance, 70% chance of him dying, and 30% chance of him living. He was lucky."

Fatalism appeared to be a common defensive response to discussing the hazards on the streets and the risks that may need to be navigated. Resignation was also to the fore of Marcus's account when I attempted to probe around the risks of turning to crime.

> Val: What you were saying about money troubles and if you have to rob, but there are high risks aren't there?
>
> Marcus: There are high risks.
>
> Val: Getting involved with high-risk people.
>
> Marcus: That's just something you have to go through.

At a later date, in his interview, Marcus, like Curtis, emphasised his aggressive fearlessness in the face of death.

> "I mean, if I get stabbed, I think it will just make me madder, and I think, 'You stab me, so I'm coming back to get you'... if you get shot, and you know that you're gonna die, you're not gonna be scared until, like, you proper think of stuff you're gonna leave behind and 'Tell my mum I said bye' and all that. Like your last words. Like what you have to remember for when you die and stuff."

The exposure to danger associated with clique (or gang) membership had to be weighed up against the protection it could provide. Buggs had found himself moving with a clique that were committing street robberies. Uncomfortable with this, he told his mum and she grounded him, warning the boys to stay away when they knocked for him. While this 'clique' was a far cry from the more organised criminal gang Kieran had become involved with, retreating from it left Buggs vulnerable. The first time Buggs was robbed he got his phone back by drawing on his clique connections. The second time he was unprotected.

> Buggs: Two weeks ago, Friday, in the same area, I've got robbed for my phone. And there's a couple of boys, they said to me, "Come down this alleyway", they said, "Give me your phone right now, or I will stab you", they said, "I'll stab you". And then yeah ... and then I just gave my phone, and they told me, they asked me, "Has it got a PIN number?" And I said, "No". Then they asked my SIM card, I gave them my SIM card, and they set some dog, they set some dog on me.
>
> Val: God, Buggs, that's horrible!
>
> Buggs: So I had to run away.
>
> Val: Was it one of them like pit bull things?
>
> Buggs: Yeah. No, it wasn't a pit bull, a staff. I jumped over some wall, quickly enough. My friend was going to come down the corner, so I ran to his house, told my mum to pick me up from there.

Val: And did you report it to the police or anything?

Buggs: No. There's no point.

Buggs had been arrested once and was repeatedly stopped and searched, compounding his fear and mistrust of the police. In fact, Buggs had not even told his mother about the incident because he did not want to worry her.

Aspirational girls

Relatively few of the boys considered going to university. Echoing the findings of previous research, they professed to 'know their limits' with most identifying a low capacity to focus and poor potential to improve (Archer and Yamashita, 2002). In contrast, almost all the girls at Meedham discussed higher education as a viable option and tended to express quite ambitious hopes for the future. Angel (14) wanted to study to be a paediatrician, Makida (14) was confident she would be starting university in five years time although she was unsure whether to become a teacher, doctor or lawyer. Charpane wanted to study business but was caught between pursuing the option of running her own beauty salon or becoming an investment banker. If university was not discussed as a foregone conclusion it was seen as an active choice.

> "'Cos when I turn 14, which is February I'll probably be looking for a Saturday job to get some money and then when I get my national insurance card I will probably be looking for a part-time job because I'll probably be starting college, so I'll need bus fare... Yeah, I'll be doing college. I'll make a decision to go to university. If I do not choose to go to university I would be looking for a job that gets me money, like lots." (Choima)

Notably, very few of the girls spoke of wanting children, and there was no consideration that they would face gender or class-based obstacles in realising their ambitions. At Meedham, this self-belief was actively cultivated though a valorisation of aspirational subjecthood. As Kim Allen (2014) notes, a socio-political rhetoric of aspiration becomes institutionalised within school practices and cultures. Meritocratic values were conveyed through an emphasis on aiming high and remaining focused on objectives. Determination and hard work were repeatedly stressed through an almost spiritual account of the power of the individual to achieve personal goals. In the context of Meedham BSU these exhortations became narratives of redemption. Attendees were encouraged to steel their convictions and steer themselves back on to the virtuous road to success, self-propelled by aspiration. This fostered much inward focused reflection and a virtual fetishisation of self-discipline as this quote from Melody (14) highlights.

> "My sister, she studies and studies until she achieves her goal. I think I said that in the poem. She will just work hard and hard and hard until she finally gets what she wants. That's what I learnt through her. In other words, she does not give up. She keeps strong. She believes in herself. And when you believe, you can achieve anything. That's what I believe."

For many of the girls at Meedham, a BSU referral was viewed almost as a retreat; an opportunity to develop a more self-focused approach as Natasha explained.

> "The teachers in the [BSU] just thought that I should come to [BSU] just to like settle down a little bit and try to not get influenced by other students so that I could just make something good of myself at school and make sure that I stay focused as well."

Meedham BSU was a relentlessly positive space, particularly in comparison to the volatility and grim realism characterising the co-ed BSUs. The aspirational mindset among the Meedham girls may also reflect the culturally situated meanings accorded to career achievement by black girls (Mirza, 2009). For example, Tracey Reynolds (2005) has suggested that black girls' determination to succeed despite the odds is contextualised by the poor prospects facing black men and an anticipation of needing to be a provider in the future.

The white girls at Gravensdale were considerably less confident about their abilities and while some discussed going to university, their ambitions tended to focus around working with children in some capacity. Keely (13) wanted to work in a nursery and Tiffany (13) was keen to teach young children to dance, although, as she explained, she was unsure she would be able to tolerate secondary school pupils.

> "We was talking about it the other day, me and my dance teacher outside school, because she's pregnant, so I have to

help her teach the little kids. Like she sits there and does the music, and I, like, teach them and that. And, like, she was talking to me, and she says, 'You could either do, like, a job in a secondary school', but then I was thinking, if I do a job in a secondary school, I'd most probably like (pause) I don't think I'd be able to do it, because, like, I know the way some people's kids treat a dance teacher and that, and if I was a dance teacher I wouldn't take it."

Chireal (15) talked at first about wanting to become a child psychologist but as the following exchange during a group discussion at Gravensdale made clear her aspiration was fragile and vulnerable to real life demands.

Chireal: Do you have to pay for university?

[Boys] Yeah.

Chireal: How much?

Val: If, if your parents are on a low income...

Will: If you're broke yeah then you don't have to.

Yvonne: You can get student loans.

Chireal: I'm not going then. I'll go to college then that's it.

Val: Chireal would you go if it wasn't for the money?

Chireal: No the money ain't the problem. It's just a bit of paper in'it and it's another extra year. It all school then. It's all school. I'll just do college. That's all I need. What you do in college you do in university anyway. You don't need it.

Several weeks later, when Chireal took part in her interview, she discussed wanting to become a primary school teacher although she was clearly very uncertain she would get the necessary GCSE grades. Her mother had offered her a £50 reward if she raised her grades but Chireal continued to struggle. Her mother was worried she would end up taking a course in childcare instead as an easy option, sensing it would be a dead end leading to poorly paid, insecure care work. Yet for Keely and Charmaine, a childcare course was articulated as a viable future aspiration, offering a practical route into meaningful, if low paid employment.

Strikingly, motherhood were barely mentioned by the girls in their reflections on anticipated futures. The boys were more likely to talk about having children (albeit with a 'wifey'), while the girls tended to focus solely their career options. This highlights another key shift from 1970s economic, social and cultural expectations that girls would eventually become homemakers. Contemporary young women foreground their anticipated labour market trajectory drawing on a post-feminist lexicon of choice and independence (Allen and Osgood, 2009). But such neoliberal sensibilities precariously position working-class girls like Chireal, Keely and Charmaine for whom career aspiration is limited by practical and financial barriers. And in the context of sustained pathologisation of young working-class mothers as irresponsible, vulgar and a drain on society, motherhood as a desire becomes literally unspeakable for some young women. As Kim Allen and Jayne Osgood (2009) suggest, motherhood has been problematised as non-ambition, ensuring discussion of it particularly among working-class girls is considered risky.

Keeping it in the family

Some of the young people in the BSU articulated a relatively clear sense of what they would be doing employment-wise in the future and how they would get there. In this case, family or family friends were identified as a bridge into the world of work, revealing some remaining continuities with Willis's *Learning to Labour* study from the 1970s. More specifically, careers advice, work experience and useful contacts were accessed through family networks. Some boys were relying on fathers, brothers or uncles who were in trades to employ them or help them secure future employment. For example, Peter wanted to be a gardener like his dad, and Kari and James were hoping electricians in their family network would help them join the trade. Luke described being spoilt for choice with his uncle working as an electrician, his father as a floor layer and his cousin as a plumber.

> "My uncle said he'll take me on as an electrician. But my dad, my dad would like to take me on, but he said, 'I want you to do something else first' … because he doesn't want me just to go to school, like muck around in school, and go, 'Oh well, I'll go and work with my dad'. He wants me to learn something else … because he thinks that I'm just

gonna go, 'I can go with my dad', like. He went, 'I ain't doing that'. He went, 'No, you go and learn something for, like, a couple of months or a year and then I'll teach you the trade'. I don't mind. But if I do really like being an electrician, then I'll stick to it, I won't be bothered to learn floor laying, because it's sort of like the same money anyway. I think electrician's a bit more, but, like, it's all around the same money... My mum said, 'You need people around like that'. All the young kids think they're going do lawyers, the big jobs, but when they fail all that ... she went, 'Look, it's not really easy to get into, but it's easy enough. So once you learn the trade, you know what you're doing'. Plumbing would be all right, for me. It would be all right, but I would like to do the flooring and electrician. Big, probably bigger money, I know that sounds greedy but (pause) that would be easier wouldn't it."

Family members also often acted as careers advisors and motivational coaches. For example, Alfie described how his parents instilled aspirational values and the need for hard work.

"If you just sit down and do your work, you're going to be the one with the company car and the job that pays a hundred grand a year. That's what I get from my mum and my dad... I wanna be like ... I don't know, a bank accountant, or a property developer... My nan's friend is one. And I think I'm doing that for work experience as well.

My dad's more like a role model. He's sort of like ... he's sort of like the stricter one of the two, because he likes to put me on track, and he's like, 'Don't muck about all your life, or you're going to end up doing stupid things that you shouldn't be doing, when you could have a decent job'. And he just wants to make me a better person, and, like, end up with a nice desk job, instead of working on a building site – earning half a wage."

It is difficult to read this quote though, without remembering how hard Alfie struggled to 'just sit down and do his work'. He described the BSU as his last chance to 'redeem' himself and prove he can work well, but his attention often wandered and he found it difficult to keep up in class. His desire to achieve educationally clashed with his mounting frustration creating an unbearable tension. He would sometimes explode: "It gets to the stage where I just don't care, I just wanna get out the lesson and get away from the teacher". In Alfie's case it was strong personal investment in education rather than any classic disaffection that triggered his BSU referral.

In the absence of family contacts in trades, mothers might take on a key role in negotiating vocational routes, evidenced in Tracey's efforts to secure Armani's placement in a garage and Dawn's research around appropriate college places for Marcus. But family members also offered an insight into the possible and achievable for young people. Those who had succeeded against the odds were particularly admired. For example, Makidah cited her aunt as a role model, while Luke named his uncle.

> "I like people like my auntie. She came back from America, like three years ago, and, like, she couldn't get a house or anything, she couldn't do anything really, so she was staying with us, and then all of a sudden, when she got jobs, there was, like, workplaces calling her up and then she finally got a very good job, and in that space of time, she's done good. So I look up to my auntie as well." (Makidah)

> "He was, he was struggling with money and everything, and he pulled himself together, and, just amazing, he's got the biggest house, Porsche, swimming pool. I think that was that was like what he done, he said, because he just split up with his wife, like his girlfriend basically, and he was depressed, and he said, 'Do you know what?' He said, 'I'm gonna go [to] university.' He learned, done law and all that. Does law… But he was, like, it was upsetting, because he was really struggling for money, because. like, my dad's side of the family, was, like, a bit involved with drugs and everything, so, like, and then he pulled himself together." (Luke)

Transcending aspiration: hopes and dreams

While I have described and evidenced the strong instrumental attachment to education that the young people in this study demonstrated, it is important to highlight the alternative values articulated beyond dominant conceptualisations of human capital. The strategic benefits of educational qualifications were acknowledged and coveted, but discussions of hopes and dreams as opposed to imagined futures generated very different conversations. As Darren Webb (2013) outlines, hope as a concept has many dimensions and spans very different standpoints. Emphasis placed on aspirational hope to achieve personal goals can obscure a less easily defined but more powerful yearning for life to be different. This was often expressed in group sessions through fantasies of escape. There was much talk of finding a better place to live and breaking away from the stress and degradation characterising their neighbourhoods. Significantly, such fantasies almost always involved moving as a family or reuniting with family members, rather than a personal quest for a better life. Disconnection from local networks without the support of family was distinctly less conceivable reflecting the importance of social connectedness in rooting young people in an area (Johnston et al, 2000). Consequently, those from transnational families had a much broader and more cosmopolitan take on geographical possibilities. For example, a particularly popular discussion topic revolved around winning the lottery. At Hailingbrooke money was seen as offering a way out.

Daniel: If I had £1,000 yeah I'd go to Turkey where it's nice and hot. I'd have a beach across the road from where I live.

Yvonne: Have you been to Turkey on holiday?

Daniel: Yeah for six weeks.

Val: You've got family there?

Daniel: Yeah aunties, uncles, loads. I'd give money to my Mum get a new phone. Get me straight.

BM: I'd go to Spain or Portugal 'cos Portugal that's where I'm half from yeah and in Spain my Dad's. Dad lives there and he's got a massive house over there.

Jake: I'd go to America.

Daniel: This country's SHIT.

Jake: Too much gun violence, stabbings, muggers, rubbish and paedophiles and prostitutes and druggies in this country.

In contrast, the white working-class pupils at Gravensdale imagined staying in London but moving to a more upmarket part of their own neighbourhood. They simply could not imagine belonging anywhere else. Dreams related to winning lots of money were often very simple, revolving around buying new clothes and giving money to family members. There was also a general consensus that some of the money should be given to charity. More broadly, being freed up from financial worries was seen as enabling pursuit of more fulfilling careers in sport, art or performance. While money could provide status it was very much seen as a means to particular ends. It could facilitate escape, secure the future and help others but making it was less often articulated as an aspiration in its own right. More specifically, discussions about wanting money were often morally qualified by disclaimers and justifications. Buggs described wanting to be a billionaire, but emphasised how he would 'work his socks off' for it. Makida was keen to contextualise her ambitions "[I want to] have a very good career, and have a big house … so my mum, my gran and all my family can live with me". The absence of a moral justification appeared to provoke mild embarrassment, as was evident from Luke's admission that prioritising a better paid option sounded 'greedy'.

Yet disadvantaged young people are very commonly positioned by a discourse of consumer greed articulated as part of a 'something for nothing' culture. Shortly after the research was complete an outbreak of rioting and looting spread across English towns and cities, sparked by police shooting dead a 29-year-old Tottenham resident, Mark Duggan. For four days in August 2011 there was the worst bout of civil unrest in a generation (Rusbridger and Rees, 2011). I found myself compulsively staring at the TV coverage, scanning the chaotic scenes for any familiar faces from the research. Amidst hysterical public condemnation from all quarters, a dominant narrative of out-of-control consumerism and poor parenting emerged, to demonise the marginalised young people who took to the streets. Efforts were made to firmly and quickly set these riots apart from previous politically motivated disorder and cast them instead as animalistic criminality, driven by a mindless desire for consumer goods[3]. As the dust settled, research emerged to highlight a very different picture of the resentment and frustration experienced by those who took part. Relations with the police were cited as a particularly strong precipitating factor, alongside social and economic injustices including increases in university tuition fees and the scrapping of a grant supporting participation in further education.

As I've outlined in this chapter, attachment to education as a principle, was an unexpectedly powerful finding in the context of educational exclusion and marginalisation. While most commonly articulated as a strategic path to a better job, the young people participating in the research also related to education in terms of a much broader desire to learn and know about things. Somewhat incongruously given their unhappy experiences, education was often identified as a potential path to self-fulfilment. This was poignantly conveyed in my field notes documenting our first session with the performance poet.

> "Keishawn turned up just as we were about to start. According to him and Buggs, Shak has been excluded – they weren't sure exactly why, but Keishawn said Lloyd had also been excluded for carrying a shank and, as Buggs emphasised getting caught. [The poet] started by asking what they wanted to get out of the session. Keishawn said he really wanted to come away having learnt something. The others agreed. I felt slightly guilty because he doesn't usually learn much from our sessions."

Angelina's visible joy at learning about physics and to play chess and the guitar, Jamal's interest in black history and Malcom X in particular, Peter's fascination with numbers, Buggs' engagement with politics, and so on, highlight a capacity to engage with and prioritise knowledge in way that radically challenges the educational status quo. This enthusiasm for learning was most powerfully illustrated for me through a quite accidental follow-up encounter with one of the pupils we had worked closely with. Manny, the boy who had fled civil war in West Africa (discussed in Chapter 3) had been 12 when he participated in the research. By 13 he had been permanently excluded from Hailingbrooke. Quite by chance I came across his details several years later while researching family support initiatives for a completely different project.

By 15 he had been arrested, charged with robbery and sent to a secure unit. The family support service were involved partly because of this but also because of the severe domestic abuse Manny's father had subjected his mother to, up until he seriously injured her and was convicted of battery. Home must have been a dangerous as well as an overcrowded place for Manny, and without the haven of school to escape to it is unsurprising that he took his chances on the streets. But by all accounts, Manny's time in the secure unit was lightened by the opportunities he accessed to improve his learning. His enthusiasm and achievements are noted throughout the case file, including the fact he was 'student of the week' 26 times during his sentence. When

I read this I remembered back to the earnest proclamations Manny made when he was 12 about the importance of education. At the time I had gently probed around why he got into so much trouble in the classroom. He described feeling frustrated because he could not follow what the teachers were saying. His subsequent academic success in prison highlights how badly he was let down within the school system.

But the trouble Manny was in extended further than the criminal justice services. Before he was convicted he had been caught between two feuding criminal gangs. Both operated from local estates that Manny had lived on previously and it seems his loyalties may have been questioned. Manny maintained that he had never belonged to either gang and this was backed up by the police intelligence on his file. Nevertheless, he had been attacked, chased and threatened with a gun by a high-ranking member of one of the gangs. Police were so concerned for his safety on his release that Manny, his mother and younger brother and sister were rehoused in a completely different area, albeit one with a criminal gang problem of its own. This brought some relief for Manny and his family, but also new anxieties and challenges associated with adapting to a different neighbourhood. Manny was disorientated and did not feel able to move freely on the street for fear of attack from the local gangs he had no practical knowledge of. He was offered a place on a mechanics course at a further education college but this would have required extensive travel through dangerous areas. I do not know whether he decided to take the risk and complete the course. As this example demonstrates, formal engagement with education, for vocation or enrichment, was invariably achieved against the odds for young men like Manny.

Notes

[1] See for example Anthony Spota (2014) 'The EU Youth Guarantee: A "Lost Generation"?', *Fair Observer*, http://www.fairobserver.com/region/europe/eu-youth-guarantee-lost-generation-69584/

[2] See for example John Podesta (2013) 'Relentlessly high youth unemployment is a global time bomb', *The Guardian*, http://www.theguardian.com/commentisfree/2013/jul/09/youth-unemployment-long-term-effects, or Tim Weber (2012) 'Davos 2012: Youth unemployment "disaster"', *BBC News Online*, http://www.bbc.co.uk/news/business-16774301

[3] For example see 'Riots are not a genuine outlet of political angst', *Evening Standard*, http://www.standard.co.uk/news/riots-are-not-a-genuine-outlet-of-political-angst-6431047.html

EIGHT

The politics of exclusion

> So, what about those who do not have access to the dominant symbolic circuits of personhood legitimation from where they can attach dominant symbolic value to themselves; those not just denied access but positioned as the constitutive limit to proper personhood: the abject, the use-less subject who only consists of lacks and gaps, voids and deficiencies, sentimental repositories, sources of labour, negative value that cannot be attached or accrued and may deplete the value of others through social contagion. How do people inhabit personhood when they are positioned as the constitutive limit to it? (Beverley Skeggs, 2011: 503)

This book has explored how contemporary governance regimes operate through British schools to identify and marginalise those deemed valueless to economic-centric models of education. In this concluding chapter I review the major issues raised by the research and outline how the lives and experiences of the young people featured in this book challenge many accepted orthodoxies about disaffection. 'Inclusion' as it was practised in the BSUs amounts to what Kathryn Ecclestone and Kristiina Brunila (2015) have termed a 'therapisation of social justice'. Thus, in the context of increasing polarisation of wealth and poverty, disadvantaged children and young people are depicted as too primitive to engage with education as a project of self-development. They are removed to the periphery of school ostensibly to undergo rehabilitative interventions to address fundamental personal deficits. The effect is to surreptitiously remove entitlement to mainstream education while reapportioning blame for attainment gaps, away from schools and onto parents and young people themselves. Troublesome difference and learning difficulties are identified, diagnosed and isolated from the important business of curriculum learning. Meanwhile, the risk lens applied to those contained within the units extends the purview of criminal justice services, compounding risky trajectories.

At its most basic level this book has revealed how the now commonplace segregation of pupils categorised as 'at risk' actually works in practice in three London schools. It has shown how BSUs could be experienced by pupils as a haven or a hell. For some, a BSU referral was an opportunity to escape the persecution and invalidation encountered in the mainstream school. They were able to build strong relationships and alliances with fellow attendees and sympathetic BSU staff. At Meedham Girls the model was one of a therapeutic retreat. For others the experience was akin to a prison sentence: locked away from the rest of the school for an indefinite stretch and further distanced from the educational tools required to build a liveable future. In the case of girls placed in units dominated by boys, a referral was brutal and punishing. It is also worth noting that some pupils transferring straight into a BSU from primary school knew no other form of secondary schooling.

While the good intentions and sincerity of most staff working in the units was evident, the 'inclusion' agenda framing their work was limiting, stigmatising and very often self-defeating. The model of developmental, psychological and emotional deficit driving core BSU activities barely connected with the very real everyday challenges and hurdles characterising the lives of attendees. In many cases 'inclusion' merely exacerbated existing problems, ensuring pupils fell further behind their classmates. This marked them out for close surveillance and increased harassment in the mainstream school. The more relational focus of the units and the strong, supportive bonds built between staff members and pupils (particularly mentors) were undoubtedly experienced as highly valuable, but they operated at the bounds of legitimacy (Gillies and Robinson, 2013). Such relationships could be highly subversive to the therapeutic philosophy framing inclusion, as well as the interests of the mainstream school. Intimate knowledge of pupils' lives sensitised BSU staff to the injustices and discrimination pupils were encountering inside and outside of the schools, encouraging many to take on more of an advocate role. The high turnover of BSU staff members points to the career risks this more politicised practice engendered.

Dave Stirling was issued with a redundancy notice by Hailingbrooke shortly after we had finished the fieldwork. He opted instead for early retirement, ensuring his years of experience and specialist skills were lost to the education sector. Jocelyn left Meedham Girls after expressing disillusionment with the low status accorded to the unit. Only Anita, the intransigent and well defended manager at Gravensdale, remained in place to oversee restructuring of the BSU (which included the redundancies of the mentors who had participated in our research). A similar churn of mentors occurred at Hailingbrooke. Most notably a Jamaican man, particularly well liked by pupils, was suspended and subsequently dismissed for developing unprofessionally close relationships with unit attendees.

We need to talk about race

A more specific focus of this book has been the detachment of 'inclusion' from an agenda of equality and social justice. The term 'inclusion' is now more often used as a verb to describe the expulsion of troublesome or troubling difference to the margins of school life. In tracing how 'inclusion' is practised I have exposed the raw dynamics of class, race, and gender running under the surface of school policies, procedures, judgements and decisions. More specifically, I have demonstrated how discourses of 'inclusion' are inextricably linked to a depoliticised appropriation of 'diversity' as a virtue. More often than not the term is explicitly yoked to inclusion to convey a general commitment to equal opportunities, as in the phrase 'diversity and inclusion policy'. Drawing on this rhetoric the schools actively produced and marketed themselves as diverse, inclusive institutions in the hope that this display of goodwill would overwrite the disconcerting and stubbornly enduring issue of racism.

But while cultural differences were recognised and celebrated within the schools, institutional practices and unconscious assumptions continued to position minority ethnic pupils as most in need of 'inclusion'. Our inability to access demographic data on BSU referrals in any of the schools is telling in its own right. While such figures were claimed to be collected by the schools, none of them was prepared to share this information. From visual observation, there appeared to be a clear disproportionality and Dave Stirling unofficially confirmed that non-white students were more likely to end up in his unit. More bluntly, the protective stance assumed by the schools points to a policy of silence and denial around the issue. The 'screen and intervene paradigm' structuring the practice of 'inclusion' very effectively conceals the social, cultural and political dimensions lying beneath the apparently colour blind objectivity of risk factor analysis. Yet as I have shown, the consequences of becoming subject to 'inclusion' could be profoundly disadvantaging.

The reluctance of the schools to share internal ethnic monitoring data reflects a more general discomfort around the topic of race. The schools worked hard to construct an inclusive environment, attaching different national flags to the walls, showcasing ethnic foods and festivals, black history month and drawing on culturally diverse examples to teach the curriculum, but this celebratory approach stopped far short of examining the power hierarchies shaping such cultural differences. This is not to suggest that the visible inclusion of different ethnic identities within school agendas was not important. The deeply marginalising effects associated with lack of recognition are well documented in studies of children from Gypsy/Traveller communities (Bhopal, 2004; Cudworth, 2008). However, the routine reification and celebration of approved minority ethnic culture concealed the more troubled dynamics of difference characterising everyday school life (Gillies and Robinson, 2012). As such, the positive rhetoric comprising multicultural education initiatives acts as a protective veneer shielding the unexamined workings of institutional racism, legitimating rather than challenging social and political orders (Goski, 2008).

Race and racism as opposed to notions of inclusion and diversity provoked defensiveness among school staff, and there was very little reflection on how institutional practices might position pupils differently (Gillies and Robinson, 2012). As Sara Ahmed (2012) notes, to talk about racism is 'to occupy a space saturated with tension' (p 162). The very acknowledgement of race and racism generates a moral imperative to action, powering discussions that are often hostile and accusatory. The teachers participating in the research were generally very well aware of racialised patterns of academic underperformance and school exclusion, but most instinctively externalised the problem, attributing it to forces beyond their control and existing outside of their schools. Meanwhile, efforts to promote inclusion and diversity were pursued through a socially disembedded appropriation of culture as a particular component of personal identity. Culture and ethnicity are conflated, essentialised and attributed to minority ethnic experience. Distinct characteristics (skin tone, religious practices, nationality etc.) then come to be recognised and valued as sources of self-esteem, with little consideration of the social and political context through which these characteristics are actually lived as differences (Gillies and Robinson, 2012).

As Paul Goski (2008) argues, the good intentions framing the actions of individual educators are not enough.

> Do we advocate and practice intercultural education so long as it does not disturb the existing socio-political order?; so long as it does not require us to problematize our own privilege?; so long as we can celebrate diversity, meanwhile excusing ourselves from the messy work of social reconstruction? ... Such questions cannot be answered through a simple review of teaching and learning theory or

an assessment of educational programs. Instead, they oblige all of us who would call ourselves intercultural educators to re-examine the philosophies, motivations, and world views that underlie our consciousnesses and work because the most destructive thing we can do is to disenfranchise people in the name of intercultural education. (p 516)

Goski calls for a different way of seeing and reacting to the socio-political contexts that shape education policy and practice. In particular, he proposes a prioritisation of justice, a firm rejection of deficit theory and a reflexive recognition of hierarchies of power and their political institutionalisation. He also notes the importance of embracing (as Dave Stirling and others did) the risks associated with speaking truth to power, and of accepting the negative attention such an antagonistic position may bring.

Post-feminism and gendered power relations

While racism in schools was downplayed and denied, the effects in terms of disproportionate exclusion rates (if nothing else) are clearly captured in statistical form. The pernicious gender oppression evident in the co-educational schools remains largely invisible, amidst broader anxiety that girls are outperforming boys and gaining the upper hand. As I've shown, boys' and girls' behaviour was perceived very differently and attracted very different responses. Boys were considerably more likely to be viewed as potentially dangerous and to endure harsher sanctions, but girls were subject to subtle but intense disciplinary control to reinforce appropriate gendered behaviour and appearance. For boys, exclusion was the ultimate penalty for challenging authority. For girls, 'inclusion' in male-dominated groups was a more daunting and more probable prospect.

The relationships between boys and girls within the schools was complex and shaped by a power imbalance that pupils and staff alike accepted and attributed to natural gender differences. The boys were highly judgemental and often explicitly cruel about the girls, commandeering authority to comment on their appearance, morality and general weakness. Even girls rated highly attractive could be dismissed as manipulative, conniving gold diggers (including girlfriends). And as I have shown, physical restraint and violence was used to enforce this gender hierarchy. In the context of fear and vulnerability on the streets, boys for the most part felt safe in school. This was not the case for girls in the co-ed schools who were routinely subject to threats, coercion and in some cases sexual assault. Girls were even at risk of violence from adult male teachers, as the incident described in Chapter 3 illustrates.

The extent of sexual bullying, intimidation and violence was clearly recognised by the schools but their responses were tied to dominant representations of girls as vulnerable and needy. The aggressive, sexualised behaviour boys directed at girls was normalised, while challenging (but not too challenging) girls were isolated for their own good. The necessity of separating boys from girls was articulated through a post-feminist discourse of empowerment with groups provided to help girls make better choices and curb 'bitchy' tendencies. The lack of attention given to boys' aggressive behaviour towards girls was striking. More specifically, the desire to cover up sexual assault while at the same time calling out police to deal with trivial playground incidents reveals a disturbing (but very telling) order of priorities.

The aggressive and often abusive dynamic characterising gender relations in the schools could be viewed as part of a much broader hypermasculinisation of the education system. As Haywood and Mac An Ghaill (2001) have suggested, schools now preside over a neoliberal macho ethos that stresses performance, competition and testing. In this context, displays of physical strength and gender superiority may mediate boys' experiences of low status and under attainment. Certainly girls were central to the affirmation of boys' identities (and vice versa) sustaining a shifting but heavily imbalanced power dynamic.

It is also worth noting the grounded and situated nature of gender dynamics. The boys expressing hostility and disrespect towards girls were the same boys that described such strong and loving relationships with their mothers. In the interviews, the mothers themselves conveyed similar sentiments and often painted a considerably softer picture of their sons as vulnerable and sensitive. At times, boys' expression of familial devotion could be attached to a macho proprietary discourse of ownership (particularly when insults to mothers were vanquished in physical fights). But there was no doubting the genuinely close relationships so many of the boys enjoyed with their mothers and other female family members (sisters, aunts, grandmothers). Misogyny was clearly not an integral feature of their lives, but was instead learned through the process of growing up and performed within the public arena of schooling and beyond.

Beyond critical pedagogy

This book has detailed the process through which young people are problematised, defined as uneducable and pushed to the edge to undergo 'inclusion'. While the muted public discussion of this practice revolves around progressive alternatives and developmental support, a more stark reality has been revealed in these pages. Despite the best intentions of BSU staff, the units (particularly in the co-ed schools) largely acted as holding pens marking out and segregating pupils regarded as surplus to the broader educational project of the nation. At a more abstract level the proliferation of BSUs marks a dangerous acceptance of contingency, undermining principles of universal entitlement to education. State education for all becomes state education for the 'school ready' with alternative provision for others who have failed to reach a requisite standard. As I have shown, those unable to produce a convincing enough performance of white, middle-class neoliberal-infused subjectivity were set on a very differently regulated trajectory. For all the rhetoric of 'inclusion' a BSU referral effectively places young people outside of the remit of educational entitlement for the period of their confinement.

The emergence of BSUs can be viewed as a strategic weapon in the armoury of symbolic violence, working to embed an all-encompassing framework of human capital. The significance accorded to educational recognition in determining personal worth and future prospects in schools is almost totalising in its effect, leaving little space for the articulation of alternative values and motivations. Even those pupils detached from any reality of educational progress expressed a longing to achieve, move forward and avoid the precarious low life of a 'dustbin worker'. The strength of this finding was a disorientating contrast to the insouciant defiance expressed by Willis's 'lads' in the 1970s. The bleak reflections of Daniel and Curtis, alongside the poignantly modest but improbable hopes of Marcus and Chireal, reflect the extent to which a moralising discourse of meritocracy holds sway, even in the context of ever diminishing opportunity.

Amid experiences of discrimination, stigma and failure, school remained a crucial anchor for the young people in this research, with many pinning hopes for a legitimate, liveable future on qualifications or college courses. I am acutely aware that this shared perception of education as a ladder to the good life could be spun as a positive story. The accounts explored in this book highlight the potential for educationally marginalised young people to be re-engaged in training. But this would require a deliberate disengagement from the broader truth that late capitalist, post-industrial landscapes depend on forcing the poor, vulnerable and disadvantaged into low status, insecure, badly paid 'dustbin jobs'. The BSU pupils were commonly aspirational in their thinking, drawing on educational blueprints to ground their hopes and ambitions. Many had strong academic capacity but had found themselves left behind and locked out of a system not designed for them. The human capital model of education conceals its competitive zero sum logic behind rhetoric of narrowing attainment gaps and raising standards for all, ignoring the strategic purpose of academic failure.

Pupils' understandings and discussions of academic achievement were clearly shaped by an economic-centric model prioritising vocational profit. But, as I began to outline in the previous chapter, the value accorded to education more generally extended beyond the logic of capital to embrace a much broader and potentially more subversive project. Education as a principle was cherished both as an instrumental strategy and as a source of personal enrichment. While it lay out of their reach, most of the young people in this study retained the notion that education could be transformative. In effect, this buying into a narrative of self-betterment accorded a power to knowledge that extended beyond narrow exclusionary models of fact 'banking' (Freire, 1996) to embrace an idealistic emancipatory model. From this perspective learning could be elusive but powerful, characterised by creativity and critical engagement. Many pupils pursued this form of learning on their own terms outside of school. Buggs searched the internet to try and make sense of the structural and political forces determining his life. Keishawn read and wrote poems. Chanelle and Natasha enthusiastically pursued the art of singing and acting. Others clung on to brief experiences in the classroom when they felt engaged and enthused. Peter recalled his enjoyment of maths, Angelina described excitement at learning physics, while for Daniel it was exploring how equipment worked in a music studio.

This elevation of learning among disadvantaged groups and the desire to reclaim education for self-betterment has a long and distinguished history. As many historians have documented, working-class intellectualism and efforts towards self-improvement stretch back over centuries. Jonathan Rose (2010) for example, details how working-class people joined and established libraries, read and engaged with classical literature and wrote books themselves. As Rose notes, autobiographies were produced in every stratum of the British working classes, including tramps and petty criminals. Those at the bottom of society listened to classical music, visited the theatre and learnt to play instruments. Mutual improvement societies were founded, such as the miners institutes in South Wales, which in some cases acted as cultural centres offering evening classes, lectures, photography studios and theatres and gymnasiums (Rose, 2010).

This historical perspective also exposes the enduring efforts made by the dominant classes to marginalise the working classes from the tools of education for fear of the consequences. Reading and intellectual pursuits were regarded as encouraging a dangerous propensity towards critical thought and political questioning. Attempts to discourage popular engagement with literature extend as far back as the mid-16th-century ban on heretical texts and bible reading (Rose, 2010). Library records indicating that the Welsh miners were engaging with Das Capital and the poetry of Shelley suggest such fears are well founded. It has also been argued that self-driven engagement with high culture by the working classes triggered the modernist movement in the late 19th and early 20th centuries to consciously and unconsciously craft a mechanism of exclusion. John Carey (2001) has claimed that the intellectual elites turned to inaccessible works of literature and art in an attempt to reassert their superiority to the unwashed masses.

While transversing a rich history of critical theory, the depiction of modernism as an exclusory project connects to more contemporary debates over the role and function of education for the oppressed and marginalised. With the emergence of critical pedagogies in the 1970s and '80s came a focus on liberating the working classes from the dominant cultural frameworks imposed upon them at school. Alternative, empowering forms of learning were encouraged to legitimise working-class culture and equip them with the tools to deconstruct and critique their oppression. These more radical approaches to education largely articulated a recognition focused account of social injustice, centring the psychic and emotional costs of inequality and the need to raise consciousness and self-esteem. From this model came a populist emphasis on psychological damage and vulnerability as disadvantages to be overcome though a therapeutic focus on personal development, which as this book has shown, currently operates as a subtle and highly effective method of marginalising the working classes from education. In short, we have seen the mainstreaming of individualistic, economic-centric values through the strategic and opportunistic appropriation of emancipatory discourses (Boltanski and Chiapello, 2005; Fraser, 2009).

For school staff, the apparently progressive ethos driving therapeutically inflected 'inclusion' is deeply appealing. This interventionist approach ameliorates guilt felt by education professionals at their relative privilege and affirms that their practice can make a difference in the context of enduring and ingrained structural inequality

(Ecclestone and Brunila, 2015). As Seehwo Cho (2006) points out, critical pedagogy has merely modernised rather than challenged the system, with the oppressed becoming further marginalised from the educational tools that would allow them to understand, evaluate and dismantle structures of domination.

> I do not see culturized and self-orientated identity politics as counterhegemonic but rather as a reflection of the defeated consciousness of the Western postmodern society that believes neither in revolution nor any other structural changes. This is indicative of what Margaret Thatcher coined the TINA (there is no alternative) syndrome. (p 132)

This observation speaks to the all-encompassing hegemonic force of neoliberal ideology and the extent to which its logic is internalised as apparently unassailable. It also highlights the seditious potential of young people cut adrift from the competitive hierarchy of mainstream education. As Lawrence Grossberg (2001) suggests, young people are by their very nature dangerously subversive, not only because they highlight the importance of investing in the future as something that is and should be different from the present, but also because they are the vessels of agency and possibility that allow alternative futures to be imagined. The extent to which a repressive and often brutal neoliberal state apparatus is dedicated to the surveillance, subjectification and policing of children and young people in 21st-century society attests to the fear they instil in the powerful.

Values beyond value

Beverley Skeggs (2011) answers the questions posed in the quote at the beginning of this chapter by exploring the way those marked out by their deficiencies and 'negative capital' generate alternative 'circuits of value'. Those who are excluded from dominant frameworks of worth are able to see beyond a logic of capital to produce a different kind of ontology (Skeggs, 2014). The BSU attendees featured in this book are similarly rendered abject through the problematisation of their minds and bodies, and as unincludible and lacking in value. Marginalised from an economic-centred rationale of contemporary education they mobilised very different ways of relating to the world and prioritised values above value.

Their alternative 'circuits of value' centred family, friendship, loyalty and an emotional connectedness to the vicissitudes of day-to-day survival, cutting across dominant ideals of calculated self-promotion. In many cases it was this very capacity to find 'values beyond value' (Skeggs, 2014) that compounded their educational marginalisation. They valorised their families and the sacrifices that had been made for them, rather than embracing an ideology of instrumental personal development. They refused to blame their mothers for their educational disadvantage and instead expressed passionate gratitude. They commonly ordered friendship over self-interest, keeping secrets (refusing to snitch), taking the blame for others' misdemeanours and regularly stepping up to fight for friends, particularly in the context of injustice. And many looked beyond a narrow credentialist model of education, expressing a longing to learn just for the sake of learning.

This is not to romanticise the lives of the BSU attendees, which as I have shown were shaped by anxiety, fear, violence and hardship. It does, however, highlight the ill-fitting model of inclusion structuring the BSU interventions. The heavily individualised conceptions of self and other framing the activities misrecognised BSU attendees as socially corroded, disconnected individuals who must learn to communicate appropriately with each other (Gillies, 2011). This prescription for emotional and social training required a systematic overlooking of the quality, depth and sophistication of the relationships sustained within the units. There was no space to acknowledge that within the schools conflict was more often associated with social connectedness rather than its absence. Breached social codes, moral frameworks, personal loyalty and misplaced humour drove confrontations, and where bullying occurred it was usually perpetrated by more than one individual. The deeply felt allegiances pupils expressed toward family, friends, ethnic groups, neighbourhoods, and even the schools themselves were not spoken of by staff except through the language of gang membership and risk.

A vocabulary of disaffection and risk is routinely drawn on to position marginalised children and young people. This book reveals the troubling reality behind such conceptualisations and highlights an urgent need for more critical analysis of exactly who or what is really 'at risk' in the education system.

References

Ahmed, S. (2012) *On Being Included. Racism and Diversity in Institutional Life,* Durham: Duke University Press

Ainley, P. and Allen, M. (2010) *Lost Generation? New strategies for youth and education,* London: Continuum.

Aldridge, J. and Medina, J. (2008) *Youth Gangs in an English City: Social exclusion, drugs and violence*, ESRC End of Award Report.

Alexander, C. (2004) Imagining the Asian gang: ethnicity, masculinity and youth after 'the riots', *Critical Social Policy* 24 (4): 526–549

Allen, K. (2014) 'Blair's children': young women as 'aspirational subjects' in the psychic landscape of class, *Sociological Review*, 62 (4) 760–779.

Allen, K. and Osgood, J. (2009) Young women negotiating maternal subjectivities: the significance of social class, *Studies in the Maternal*, 1 (2), www.mamsie.bbk.ac.uk

Archer, L. and Yamashita, H (2002) 'Knowing their limits'? Identities, inequalities and inner city school leavers' post-16 aspirations Journal of Education Policy, 18 (1) 53-69.

Archer, L., Holingworth, S. and Mendick, H. (2010) *Urban Youth and Education: Education in an urbanised society*, Buckinghamshire: Open University.

Ball, S. (2008) *The Education Debate*, Bristol: Policy Press.

Barrie, C. (2013) From welfare to workfare: how the helping hand became a contract, OurKingdom, https://www.opendemocracy.net/ourkingdom/christopher-barrie/from-welfare-to-workfare-how-helping-hand-became-contract

Bauman, Z. (2003) *Wasted Lives: Modernity and its outcasts*, Cambridge: Polity Press.

Bell D. and Blanchflower, D. (2011) Young people and the Great Recession, *Oxford Review of Economic Policy*, 27 (2) 241–267.

Berkley, R. (2011) Foreword to *Gangs Revisited: What's a Gang and What's Race Got to Do With It?,* London: Runnymede Trust.

Bhopal, K, (2004), Gypsies/Travellers and education: changing needs and changing perceptions, *British Journal of Educational Studies*, 52 (1) 47-64.

Blackman, S. (2007) Hidden ethnography, *Sociology*, 41 (4) 699–716.

Boltanski, L. and Chiapello, E. (2005) *The New Spirit of Capitalism*, London: Verso.

Bourdieu, P. (1979) *Distinction: A social critique of the judgement of taste*. London: Routledge.

Bourdieu, P. (1986) The forms of capital, in J. Richardson (ed) *Handbook of Theory and Research for the Sociology of Education*, New York: Greenwood, 241-258.

Bourdieu, P (1993) *The Field of Cultural Production*, Cambridge, UK: Polity Press

Bourdieu, P. (1999) 'The abdication of the state', in P Bourdieu et al, *The Weight of the World: Social suffering in contemporary society*, Cambridge: Polity Press, 181–88.

Bourdieu, P. and Passeron J. (1977) *Reproduction in Education, Society and Culture*, London: Sage.

Bowling, B. and Phillips, C. (2007) 'Disproportionate and discriminatory: Reviewing the evidence on police stop and search', *The Modern Law Review* 70(6): 936-961.

Brown, L. (2003) *Girlfighting: Betrayal and rejection among girls*. New York: New York University Press.

Brown, P. (1990) The 'Third Wave': education and the ideology of parentocracy, *British Journal of Sociology of Education*, 11 (1) 65-86.

Burman, E. (2014) Manifesting resilience, Paper given at ESRC Seminar Series on Psychological Governance, Birmingham University, 23 June.

Butler, J. (1990) *Gender Trouble: Feminism and the subversion of identity*, New York: Routledge.

Cain, P (2007) Empire and the languages of character and virtue in later Victorian and Edwardian Britain, *Modern Intellectual History*, 4 (2) 249-273.

Carey, J. (2001) *The Intellectuals and the Masses: Pride and prejudice among the literary intelligentsia, 1880-1939*, London: Faber and Faber.

Castel, R. (1991) From dangerousness to risk, in G. Burchell, C. Gordon and P. Miller (eds) *The Foucault Effect: Studies in governmentality*. London: Harvester Wheatsheaf, 281–298.

Chase, E. and Walker R. (2013) The co-construction of shame in the context of poverty: Beyond a threat to the social bond", *Sociology* 47 (4) 739-754.

Children's Commissioner (2013) *"Always Someone Else's Problem": Office of the Children's Commissioner's Report on Illegal Rxclusions*, http://www.childrenscommissioner.gov.uk/content/publications/content_662

Cho, S. (2006) On language of possibility: Revisiting critical pedagogy in C.A. Rossatto, R.L. Allen and M. Pruyn (eds) *Reinventing Critical Pedagogy: Widening the circle of anti oppression education*, Maryland: Rowman and Littlefield.

Claxton, G. (2005) *An Intelligent Look at Emotional Intelligence*, London: Association of Teachers and Lecturers.

Condry, R. (2007) *Families Shamed: The consequences of crime for relatives of serious offenders*. Abingdon: Routledge.

Connolly, P. (1998) *Racism, Gender Identities and Young Children: Social Relations in a multi-ethnic inner-city primary school*, London: Routledge

Cooke, B. and Kothari, U. (2001) 'The case for participation as tyranny', in B Cooke and U Kothari (eds) *Participation: The new tyranny?*, London: Zed Books, 1-15.

Crossley, S. and Slater, T. (2014) Benefits Street: territorial stigmatisation and the realization of a '(tele)vision of divisions', Values and Value Blog, https://values.doc.gold.ac.uk/blog/18/

Cudworth, D. (2008) 'There is a little bit more than just delivering the stuff': Policy, pedagogy and the education of Gypsy/Traveller children, *Critical Social Policy*, 28 (3) 361-377.

Department for Education and Skills (2002) *Good Practice Guidelines for Learning Support Units*, London: DFES.

Department for Education and Skills (2005) *Excellence and Enjoyment: Social and emotional aspects of learning: guidance*, London: DfES

Dickerson, A. and Popli, G. (2012) Persistent poverty and children's cognitive development: Evidence from the UK Millennium Cohort Study, CLS Cohort Studies Working Paper, Centre for Longitudinal Studies.

Dorey, P (2010) A poverty of imagination: Blaming the poor for inequality, *The Political Quarterly*, 81 (3) 333-343.

Ecclestone, K (2012) From emotional and psychological well-being to character education: challenging policy discourses of behavioural science and 'vulnerability', *Research Papers in Education*, 27(4) 463–480.

Ecclestone, K. and Brunila, K. (2015) Governing emotionally vulnerable subjects and 'therapisation' of social justice*, Pedagogy, Culture and Society*, 23 (4) 1-22.

Ecclestone, K and Hayes, D. (2008) *The Dangerous Rise of Therapeutic Education*, Abingdon: Routledge.

Edwards, R., Gillies, V. and Horsley, N. (2015) Brain science and early years policy: Hopeful ethos or 'cruel optimism'? *Critical Social Policy* 35 (2) 167-187.

Edwards, R. and Gillies, V. (2011) Clients or consumers, commonplace or pioneers? Navigating the contemporary class politics of family, parenting skills and education, *Ethics and Education*. 6 (2):141-154.

Fairclough, N. (2000) *New Labour, New Language*, Abingdon: Routledge.

Featherstone, B., White, S. and Morris, K. (2014) *Re-imagining child protection: Towards humane social work with families*, Bristol: Policy Press

Fletcher, A., Jamal, F., Fitzgerald-Yau, N. and Bonell, C. (2013) 'We've got some underground business selling junk food': qualitative evidence of the unintended effects of English school food policies, *Sociology*, 48 (4) 500-517.

Foucault, M. (2008) *The birth of biopolitics: Lectures at the College de France 1978-1979*, Palgrave Macmillan.

Fraser, N. (2009) 'Feminism, capitalism and the cunning of history', *New Left Review*, 56: 97-117.

Freire, P. (1996) *Pedagogy of the Oppressed*, Penguin (2nd edition).

Furedi, F. (2004) *Therapy culture*, Abingdon: Routledge.

Furlong, A (2006) Not a very NEET solution. Representing problematic labour market transitions among early school leavers, *Work Employment and Society* 20 (3) 553-569.

George, R (2007) *Girls in a Goldfish Bowl: Moral regulation, ritual and the use of power amongst inner city girls*, Sense Publications.

Giddens, A. (1998) *The Third Way*, Cambridge: Polity Press.

Gill, R. (2008) 'Empowerment/Sexism: Figuring female sexual agency in contemporary advertising', *Feminism and Psychology*, 18(1): 35–60.

Gillborn, D. (2008) *Racism and Education: Coincidence or conspiracy?* Abingdon: Routledge.

Gillborn, D. (2010) The white working class, racism and respectability: victims, degenerates and victim convergence, *British Journal of Educational Studies*, 58 (1) 3–25.

Gillies, V. (2005) Meeting parents needs? Discourses of 'support' and 'inclusion' in family policy, *Critical Social Policy*, 25 (1) 70-90.

Gillies, V. (2011) Social and emotional pedagogies: critiquing the new orthodoxy of emotion in classroom behaviour management. *British Journal of Sociology of Education*, 32 (2) 185-201.

Gillies, V. (2014) Troubling families: parenting and the politics of early intervention, in: S. Wagg and J. Pilcher (eds) *Thatcher's Grandchildren*, Palgrave Macmillan.

Gillies, V. and Robinson, Y. (2010) Shifting the goalposts: researching pupils at risk of school exclusion, in M. Robb and R. Thomson (eds) *Critical Practice with Children and Young People*, Bristol: Policy Press.

Gillies, V. and Robinson, Y. (2012) 'Including' while excluding: race, class and behaviour support units, *Race, Ethnicity and Education*, 15 (2) 157-174.

Gillies, V. and Robinson, Y. (2013) At risk pupils and the 'caring' curriculum, in C. Rogers and S. Weller (eds) *Critical Approaches to Care: Understanding caring relations, identities and cultures*, Abingdon: Routledge.

Giroux, H. (2014) Neoliberalism and the machinery of disposability, *Truthout*, http://www.informationclearinghouse.info/article38209. htm

Glassett Farrelly, S. (2013) *Understanding Alternative Education: A mixed methods examination of student experiences*, California: California State University.

Goffman, A. (2014) *On the Run: Fugitive life in an American city*, Chicago: University of Chicago Press.

Goffman, E. (1959): *The Presentation of Self in Everyday Life*. Garden City, NY: Doubleday/Anchor Books.

Goffman, E. (1963) *Stigma: Notes on the Management of Spoiled Identity*. New York, NY: Simon and Schuster.

Goski, P. (2008) Good intentions are not enough: a decolonizing intercultural education, *Intercultural Education*, 19 (6) 515-525

Goulbourne, H., Reynolds T. Solomos, J. and Zontini, E. (2009) *Transnational Families. Relationships and resources*, Abingdon: Routledge.

Grossberg, L (2001) Why does neoliberalism hate kids? The war on youth and the culture of politics, *Review of Education* 23 (2) 111-136.

Harding, S. (2014) *The Street Casino: Survival in violent street gangs*, Bristol: Policy Press.

Hartas, D. (2011) Families' social bagrounds matter: socio-economic factors, home learning and young children's language, literacty and social outcomes, *British Educational Research Journal* 37 (6)

Hartas, D. (2012) Inequality and the home learning environment: predictions about seven-year olds' language and literacy, *British Educational Research Journal* 38 (5) 859-879

Hartas, D. (2014*) Parenting, Family Policy and Children's Well-being in an Unequal Society: A new culture war for parents*, London: Palgrave Macmillan.

Hayward, A (2006) *Making Inclusion Happen: A practical guide*, London: Paul Chapman Publishing.

Haywood, C. and Mac An Ghaill, M (2001) The significance of teaching English boys: exploring social change, modern schooling and the making of masculinities in W. Martino and B. Meyenn (eds) *What about the Boys?*, Buckinghamshire: Open University Press.

Haywood, C. and Mac An Ghaill, M. (2003) *Men and Masculinities: Theory, Research and Social Practice*, Buckingham: Open University.

Hey, V. (1997) *The company she Keeps: An ethnography of girls' friendships*. Buckingham: Open University Press.

Hillian, D. and Reitsma-Street M. (2003) Parents and youth justice, *Canadian Journal of Criminology and Criminal Justice*, 45 (1).

Holt, A (2009) (En)gendering responsibilities: Experiences of parenting a 'young offender', *The Howard Journal of Criminal Justice*, 48 (4), 344-356.

Illouz, E (2008) *Saving the Modern Soul: Therapy, emotions and the culture of self-help,* Berkeley: California Press.

Jackson, C. (2006) *'Lads' and 'ladettes' in school: Gender and a fear of failure,* Maidenhead: Open University Press.

Jay, A. (2014) *Independent Inquiry into Child Sexual Exploitation in Rotherham (1997–2013),* http://www.rotherham.gov.uk/downloads/file/1407/independent_inquiry_cse_in_rotherham

Johnston, L., MacDonald, R., Mason, P., Ridley, L. and Webster, C. (2000) *Snakes & Ladders. Young people, transitions and social exclusion.* Bristol: Policy Press.

Jones, O. (2010) *Chavs: The Demonisation of the Working Class,* London: Verso.

Jordan, B. (1974) *Poor Parents: Social policy and the cycle of deprivation,* London: Routledge.

Joseph, I. and Gunter, A. (2011) *Gangs Revisited. What's a gang and what's race got to do with it?,* London: Runnymede Trust

Kehily, M.J. and Nayak, A. (1997) 'Lads and Laughter': humour and the production of heterosexual hierarchies, *Gender and Education,* 9 (1) 69-88.

Kintrea K, Bannister J, Pickering J, Reid, M. and Suzuki N (2008) *Young People and Territoriality in British Cities,* York: The Joseph Rowntree Foundation.

Krueger, K. (2014) #FergusonNext: Here's how to end the school-to-prison pipeline, starting now, *The Guardian,* http://www.theguardian.com/commentisfree/2014/dec/10/end-school-to-prison-pipeline

Kultz, K. (2015) *Mapping the Exclusion Process: Inequality, Justice and the Business of Education,* London: Communities Empowerment Network.

Kultz, K (forthcoming) *Factories for Learning: Mapping news forms of raced and classed inequality in a London secondary academy,* London: Routledge.

Kupchik, A. (2009) *Homeland Security: School discipline in an age of fear,* New York: New York Press.

Kupchik, A., Green, D.A. and Mowen, T.J. (2014) School punishment in the US and England: divergent frames and responses, *Youth Justice* 1-20.

Lawler, S. (2005) Disgusted subjects: the making of middle-class identities, *Sociological Review,* 53 (3) 429–446.

Lee, N. (2002) *Childhood and Society: Growing up in an age of uncertainty.* Open University Press: Buckingham.

Levitas, R. (1998) *The Inclusive Society: Social exclusion and New Labour*, Macmillan: Hampshire

Lubet, S. (2015). "Did this acclaimed sociologist drive the getaway car in a murder plot?". *The New Republic*, http://www.newrepublic.com/article/121909/did-sociologist-alice-goffman-drive-getaway-car-murder-plot

Lupton, D. (2013) *Risk*, Abingdon: Routledge.

McAra, L and McVie, S (2012) Negotiated order: Towards a theory of pathways into and out of offending, *Criminology and Criminal Justice*, 12(4): 347-376.

MacBeath, J., Galton, M., Steward, S., MacBeath, A. and Page, C. (2006) *The Costs of Inclusion*, London, National Union of Teachers, https://www.teachers.org.uk/node/2269

Mac an Ghaill, M. (1994) *The Making of Men: Masculinities, sexualities and schooling*, Buckingham: Open University.

MacDonald, R. (2011) Youth transitions, unemployment and underemployment: Plus ça change, plus c'est la même chose?, *Journal of Sociology*, 47 (4) 427-444.

McRobbie, A. (2008) *The Aftermath of Feminism: Gender, culture and social change*. London: SAGE.

Maddern, K. (2010) Greater freedom, but twice as likely to exclude, *Times Educational Supplement*, https://www.tes.com/article.aspx?storycode=6053491

Marmot, M. (2014) *Fair Society, Healthy Lives: The Marmot Review*, http://www.instituteofhealthequity.org/projects/marmot-indicators-2014

Mayall B. (2002) *Towards a Sociology for Childhood: Thinking from Children's Lives*, Buckingham: Open University Press.

Mellor, J. and Epstein, D. (2006) Appropriate behaviour? Sexualities, schooling and hetro-gender, in C. Skelton, B. Francis and L. Smulyan (eds) *Sage Handbook of Gender and Education*, London: Sage.

Mirza, H. (1997) *Black British Feminism: A reader*, Abingdon: Routledge.

Mirza, H. (2009) *Race, Gender and Educational Desire: Why black women succeed and fail*, London and New York: Routledge.

Mills, M. and McGregor, G. (2014) *Re-engaging young people in education: Learning from alternative schools*, London: Routledge.

Moore, D. (2015) Further evidence of deaths due to UK welfare benefits sanctions, World Socialist Website, http://www.wsws.org/en/articles/2015/02/05/welf-f05.html

Morris, E. (2008) 'Tuck in that shirt'. Race, class, gender and discipline in an urban school, in J. Ballantine and J Spade (eds) *Schools and Society. A sociological approach to education*. California: Sage.

Murphy E. and Dingwall, R. (2001) The ethics of ethnography, in Atkinson, P., Coffey, A., Delamont, S., Lofland, J. and Lofland, L. (eds) *Handbook of Ethnography*, London: Sage.

Nilsen, A. and Brannen, J. (2014) An intergenerational approach to transitions to adulthood: the importance of history and biography, *Sociological Research Online*, 19 (2).

Nixon, J. and Parr, S. (2006) Anti-social behaviour: Voices from the front line, in J. Flint (ed) *Housing, Urban Governance and Anti-social Behaviour*, Bristol: Policy Press.

Ofsted (2003) *Learning Support Unit Strand Study*, London: Ofsted

O'Hara, M. (2013) *Austerity Bites: A journey to the sharp end of cuts in the UK*, Bristol: Policy Press.

Osler, A. (2006) Excluded girls: interpersonal, institutional and structural violence in schooling, *Gender and Education* 18 (6) 571-589.

Osler, A. and Vincent, K. (2003) *Girls and Exclusion: Rethinking the agenda*, London: Routledge.

Osler, A., Street, C., Lall, M. and Vincent, K. (2002) *Reasons for Exclusion from School*, London: Department for Education and Employment.

Parton, N (2006) *Safeguarding Childhood: Early Intervention and Surveillance in a Late Modern Society*, London: Palgrave Macmillan.

Pica-Smith, C. and Veloria, C. (2012) "At risk means a minority kid": Deconstructing deficit discourses in the study of risk in education and human services, *Pedagogy and the Human Sciences* 1 (2) 33-48.

Pitts, J. (2008) *Reluctant Gangsters: The changing face of youth crime*, Devon: Willan Publishing.

Rafferty F. and Barnard N. (1998) 'School "sin bins" to combat exclusions', *Times Educational Supplement*, 2 October. Available at https://www.tes.com/article.aspx?storycode=79122

Ralphs, R., Aldridge, J. and Medina, J. (2009) Who needs enemies with friends like these? The importance of place for young people living in known gang areas, *Journal of Youth Studies* 12 (5) 483-500.

Reay, D. (2001) 'Spice Girls', 'Nice Girls', 'Girlies', and 'Tomboys': Gender discourses, girls' cultures and femininities in the primary classroom, *Gender and Education*, 13 (2) 153-166.

Reay, D. (2004) It's all becoming a habitus: beyond the habitual use of habitus in educational research, *British Journal of the Sociology of Education*, 25 (4), 431-444.

Reay, D. (2007) 'Unruly places': inner-city comprehensives, middle-class imaginaries and working class children, *Urban Studies* 44 (7) 1191-1201.

Reay, D (2013) Social mobility, a panacea for austere times: tales of emperors, frogs, and tadpoles, *British Journal of Sociology of Education* 34 (5) 660.

Reay, D., Crozier, G. and James D. (2011) *White Middle-Class Identities and Urban Schooling*, London: Palgrave Macmillan.

Reynolds, T (2005) *Caribbean Mothers: Identity and Experience in the UK,* London: Tufnell Press.

Reynolds, T. (2009) Exploring the absent/present dilemma: Black fathers, family relationships, and social capital in Britain, *American Annuls,* 624 (1) 12-28.

Reynolds, T. (2010) *Single mothers not the cause of Black boys' underachievement,* Runnymede Trust eConference, http://www.runnymedetrust.org/events-conferences/econferences/econference/alias-3.html

Ringrose, J. (2008) 'Just be friends': exposing the limits of educational bully discourses for understanding teen girls' heterosexualized friendships and conflicts, *British Journal of Sociology of Education,* 29 (5) 509–22.

Ringrose, J. (2013) *Postfeminist Education?: Girls and the sexual politics of schooling,* London: Routledge.

Rollock, N. (2008) Why Black girls don't matter: exploring how race and gender shape academic success in an inner city school, *Support for Learning,* 22 (4) 197-202.

Rollock, N (2007) Legitimizing Black academic failure: deconstructing staff discourses on academic success, appearance and behaviour, *International Studies in Sociology of Education,* 17 (3) 275-287.

Rollock, N., Gillborn, D., Vincent, C. and Ball, S. (2011) Public identities of the black middle classes: managing race in public spaces, *Sociology,* 45, (6) 1078-1093.

Robb, M. (2011) Mothers, sons and masculinities, http://martinrobb.wordpress.com/2011/03/31/mothers-sons-and-masculinities/

Rose, J. (2010) *The Intellectual Life of the British Working Classes,* Yale University Press.

Rose, N. (2010) 'Screen and intervene': governing risky brains, *History of the human sciences,* 23 (1).

Rusbridger, A. and Rees, J. (2011) A Foreword, in D. Roberts (ed) *Reading the Riots: Investigating England's summer of disorder.* London: Guardian Shorts.

Sayer, A. (2005) *The Moral Significance of Class,* Cambridge: Cambridge University Press.

Sewell, T. (1997) *Black Masculinities and Schooling: How Black boys survive modern schooling,* Staffordshire: Trentham.

Sharp, D. and Atherton, S.(2007) 'To serve and protect: the experiences of policing in the community of young people from Black and other ethnic minority groups', *British Journal of Criminology* 47: 746-763.

Shildrick, T. and MacDonald R. (2013) Poverty talk: how people experiencing poverty deny their poverty and why they blame 'the poor', *Sociological Review* 61(2) 285–303.

Shildrick, T., MacDonald, R. Webster, C. and Garthwaite, K (2012) *Poverty and insecurity. Life in low-pay, no-pay Britain*, Bristol: Policy Press.

Skeggs, B. (1997) *Formations of Class and Gender: Becoming respectable*, London: Sage.

Skeggs, B. (2011) Imagining personhood differently: person value and autonomist working-class value practices, *Sociological Review* 59 (3) 496-513.

Skeggs, B. (2014) Values beyond value? Is anything beyond the logic of capital?, *British Journal of Sociology*, 65 (1) 1-20.

Skeggs, B. and Loveday, V. (2012) Struggles for value: value practices, injustice, judgment, affect and the idea of class. *British Journal of Sociology*, 63 (3) 472-490.

Squires, P. and Stephen, D. (2005) *Rougher Justice: Anti-social behaviour and young people<* Devon: Willan Publishing.

Standing, G. (2011) *The Precariat:The new dangerous class*, London: Bloomsbury.

Stoller, P. (2015) Alice Goffman and the future of ethnography, The Blog, Huffington Post Books, http://www.huffingtonpost.com/paul-stoller/alice-goffman-and-the-future-of-ethnography-_b_7585614.html

Stuckler, D. and Basu, S. (2013) *The Body Economic: Why austerity kills*, New York: Basic Books.

Swan, S. (2013) *Pupil Disaffection in Schools: Bad Boys Hard Girls*, Ashgate.

Thorne, B. (2008) The Chinese Girls and the 'Pokémon Kids': Children Constructing Difference in Urban California, in J. Cole and D. Durham (eds*) Figuring the Future: Children, youth, and globalization.* Santa Fe, NM.

Tomlinson, S. (2012) *A Sociology of Special Education* (2nd edn), Abingdon: Routledge.

Townsend, P (1979) *Poverty in the United Kingdom: A survey of household resources and standards*, Penguin.

Tsai (2013) *Black Students more likely to be Disciplined at School than Whites*, Population Reference Bureau, http://www.prb.org/Publications/Articles/2013/race-school-discipline.aspx

Tyler, I. (2013) *Revolting Subjects: Social abjection and resistance in neoliberal Britain*, London: Zed Books.

Tyler, I. (2008) 'Chav Mum Chav Scum': class disgust in contemporary Britain' ,*Feminist Media Studies*, 8 (1) 17–34.

Vanderhaar, J.E., Petrosko, J.M. and Muñoz, M.A. (2013) Reconsidering the Alternatives: The relationship between suspension, disciplinary alternative school placement, subsequent juvenile detention, and the salience of race, Civil Rights Project,

Vincent, C., Rollock, N., Ball, S. and Gillborn D. (2012) The educational strategies of the Black middle class, https://www.ioe. ac.uk/Study_Departments/CeCeps_The_Education_Strategies_ Summary.pdf

Wacquant, L. (1993) On the tracks of symbolic power: preparatory notes to Bourdieu's state nobility, *Theory, Culture and Society*, 10, 1-17.

Wacquant, L. (2007) Urban Outcasts: A comparative sociology of advanced marginality, Cambridge: Policy Press.

Wacquant, L. (2009) *Punishing the Poor: The Neoliberal government of social insecurity*, Durham: Duke University Press.

Wacquant, L (2010) Crafting the neoliberal state: Workfare, Prisonfare,and social insecurity, *Sociological Forum*, 25, (2) 197-220.

Webb, D. (2013) Pedagogies of hope, *Studies in Philosophy and Education*, 32, 397-414.

Welshman, J. (2006) *Underclass: A history of the excluded, 1880–2000,* London: Hambledon.

Willis, P. (1977) *Learning to Labour: How working class kids get working class jobs*, Surrey: Ashgate.

Willow, C. (2015) *Children behind Bars: Why the abuse of child imprisonment must end,* Bristol: Policy Press.

Wright (1987) Black students – white teachers, in B Troyna (ed) *Racial Inequality in Education*, London: Hutchinson.

Yates, S. and Payne, M. (2007) Not so NEET? A critique of the use of 'NEET' in setting targets for interventions with young people, *Journal of Youth Studies* 9 (3) 329-344.

Youdell, D. (2003) Identity traps or how black students fail: the interactions between biographical, sub-culture and learner identities, *British Journal of Sociology of Education*, 24 (1) 3-20. Youdell, D. (2006) *Impossible Bodies, Impossible Selves: Exclusions and student subjectivities*, Dordrecht: Springer.

Index